This Is My Body, This Is My Blood
Miracles of the Eucharist
Book II

Bob and Penny Lord

Journeys of Faith
1-800-633-2484

Other Books by Bob and Penny Lord
THIS IS MY BODY, THIS IS MY BLOOD
Miracles of the Eucharist - Book I
THE MANY FACES OF MARY
a Love Story
WE CAME BACK TO JESUS
SAINTS AND OTHER POWERFUL WOMEN
IN THE CHURCH
SAINTS AND OTHER POWERFUL MEN
IN THE CHURCH
HEAVENLY ARMY OF ANGELS
SCANDAL OF THE CROSS AND ITS TRIUMPH
MARTYRS - THEY DIED FOR CHRIST
THE ROSARY - THE LIFE OF JESUS AND MARY
VISIONARIES, MYSTICS AND STIGMATISTS
ESTE ES MI CUERPO, ESTA ES MI SANGRE
Milagros de la Eucaristía
LOS MUCHOS ROSTROS DE MARIA
una historia de amor

ISBN 0-926143-33-6

Cover Art by Denys de Solére

Table of Contents

Dedication

God is so good. He puts so many Heavenly Angels and earthly angels in our path to affirm us, to give us inspiration and courage to continue when everything seems impossible. We know that we say this with each book, we write, but never have we seen such obstacles as in the writing of this book, so many attacks and distractions. Without Our Lord Whose work it is, and the Angels He sent to help us, nothing would have happened. We would like to acknowledge some of the *earthly* angels who made this book possible.

Pope John Paul II - We were blessed to have an audience with His Holiness, where we could actually speak to him. We told him, we were concerned about his trip to Denver in 1993; that we feared for his well-being. His response to our concern was, *"Then let us pray together."* He never belittled our fears. He gave us the only solution. He has complete faith in Jesus, Mary and our Heavenly Family. His faith and love for the Eucharist has given us strength in times of stress. Thank You, Jesus.

Mother Angelica and the Poor Clare Nuns of Perpetual Adoration of Our Lady of the Angels Monastery - Mother has always been a strong supporter of our Ministry, but her consistent love for the Eucharist, and the priority that Jesus in the Eucharist has in her life and the lives of her Community has given us confidence *to keep on going when the going got rough.*

Fr. Antonio Giannini - Siena, Italy - Fr. Giannini has always pushed us beyond ourselves, pressing us to focus on the importance of keeping the Real Presence of Jesus in the Eucharist in the forefront of everything we do, even when we felt, we could better serve the Lord by moving into other areas. Thank You, Jesus, for Fr. Giannini's persistence.

Fr. Michael Fraser - Pearl River, LA - Fr. Michael has been a constant source of support for us. He has nourished us spiritually with his profound and enlightening homilies, helping us to maintain our sanity in what would otherwise seem like an insane world. We can never thank him enough for the invaluable aid he has given us with this book.

A Priest who has asked to remain anonymous - Father has always supported us, fed us with his wisdom and given us hope through his holiness. We thank him, from the bottom of our hearts, for the important editing he did, with particular attention to areas that could have lead to error in Theology.

Brother Joseph and Luz Elena - More and more, they become indispensable to the Ministry and to us personally. They are always there for us and, more importantly, the Lord. The song which says, *"Nothing I desire compares with you,"* most aptly describes them and their Love, the Lord. They have worked by our side to all hours, giving up all personal wants and needs, little luxuries like weekends, and going to bed before midnight, at times. We can honestly say that, as with all parts of our Ministry, we could not have written this book without them. Thank you Marcos and Agustina for Luz Elena, and thank you Willie and Marie for Brother Joseph. But most especially, thank You Jesus.

Rob Ziminsky, our Grandson for loving us and allowing us to love him, for sharing all the important moments of his life. When we think about him and his family to come, he keeps us going, on days when we feel we cannot. We are given added strength and added reason to work more, to fight more for the Roman Catholic Church in the United States, so that his family and yours will have a church to go to.

Lura Daws especially, Brenda Anglero, and all the tireless laborers in the Lord's vineyard, our Ministry, who kept the wheels turning so that the four of us could be free to bring you this book. These are the unsung heroes and heroines of our Ministry. The Lord loves them and so do we.

All the Production Angels who have supported us spiritually with your prayers, physically with your labor at the Ministry, financially with your donations, powerfully with your spreading the Good News to the Church.

Introduction

My brothers and sisters, we are in a time of great sorrow; we are in a time of great joy. Our Church is at its most exciting juncture in its history. We are on the threshold of a new millennium, the third Millennium. We're going into the twenty-first century. That is awesome. We can see great advances for the Church and the world. We have an opportunity, through the gift of communications, to reach out and touch 7 billion people. It can be done; Jesus has given us the means to do it. It's up to us. *That's the Good News.*

The world is in the most depraved state in its history. Never have we known of such wholesale evil being accepted as an alternate life style. All the things we have held sacred, for the thousands of years of our existence, are being taken away from us. We're being told that what has always been right is now wrong; what has been against the laws of our land and our Church are now good and proper and legal, and we have to support them with our money and our lives. *That's the bad news.*

But we, the Body of Christ, have been through this before, or at least the near equivalent of it. Our past is one of the pendulum swinging to the far left, then to the far right, and back to the middle. But sadly, it doesn't stay in the middle that long. It's that narrow road to the Kingdom which Jesus speaks of, just a short rest stop on the way to the next big swing. Over the centuries, the world has been on a suicidal path to destruction, yet we have survived. We've been hit in every century, with every possible type of arms possible, by every monster imaginable, with the surety that *this time,* with *this weapon,* we would be destroyed, and we're still here.

We've got a major job to do, especially now when many whom we had always counted on to be our allies, our friends, are quickly turning out to be our enemies. We've got to save this world; we've got to turn it around, and give Jesus a new world, and a new people; the world He died for, and the people He lived for. How do we do it? What weapons do we have that can compare to the great evil machines that have been created in this century, Satan's last century, his last stand? *We have the Real Presence of Jesus in the Eucharist, the Body and Blood of Jesus Christ, the most powerful Weapon ever given mankind.*

We were appearing on Mother Angelica Live with Fr. Harold Cohen. He made a statement which shocked us to the core. He spoke about a Gallup Poll which had been taken among practicing Catholic people. It was reported in the Wanderer, a Catholic weekly newspaper, to which we all subscribe. The subject of the poll was the Real Presence of Jesus in the Eucharist. *There were multiple choice questions, but they all boiled down to one question, which was, "Do you believe you are receiving the Body, Blood, Soul and Divinity of Our Lord Jesus when you receive Holy Communion?"* I believe 1,500 young Catholics took part in the poll. We're not sure what cross-section of the Catholic population this covered, or their ages. But bottom line, the response was that *only 30% of practicing Catholics believed that Jesus was truly present, Body, Blood, Soul and Divinity, in the Sacred Species.*

We were completely dismayed. We had written the book, *"This Is My Body, This Is My Blood, Miracles of the Eucharist"* in 1986. We made a television series of the same name for EWTN, which has been showing since 1987. EWTN reaches 35 million homes in the United States, Canada and Mexico. We have been going all over the world, the United States, Europe and Mexico, giving talks, Retreats, and Days of Recollection on the Eucharist and Miracles of the Eucharist. We have been leading Pilgrimages to the Shrines of the Miracles of the Eucharist. We could not believe that after all of that, only 30% of our *practicing* Catholic population believed in the Real Presence of Jesus in the Eucharist. This really depressed us. We shared our disappointment and dejection with Father Cohen that evening after the program. We told him we felt like we had accomplished nothing in the years we had been out on the road, proclaiming the Real Presence of Jesus in the Eucharist. He's a saint of a man. He smiled that beautiful New Orleans smile of his, and said, *"Just think what the percentages would have been, had you not been out there, promoting the Real Presence of Jesus in the Eucharist. You've made a real dent. You've put a spotlight on the Real Presence of Jesus in the Eucharist. But your work's not over. It's only just begun."*

When we wrote our first book, we never thought, we were defending the Real Presence of Jesus in the Eucharist. *We never thought the Real Presence of Jesus in the Eucharist had to be defended.* But little by little, we began to receive phone calls and letters from dear people, sharing war stories about how the Eucharist was being disrespected in their Churches, how the importance of the Eucharist was being belittled in some areas, and downright denied in others.

We find ourselves back in the front lines of the battle. Penny has always had a burning desire for us to write a second book on the Miracles of the Eucharist. But the focus of this book would be to emphasize as much as is humanly possible, the Real Presence of Jesus in the Eucharist, through the Miracles. If there was ever any doubt as to the necessity of emphasizing the Real Presence of Jesus in the Eucharist, Fr. Cohen's statement about the Gallup poll has eliminated any of that.

Then, if that wasn't enough incentive, the Lord hit us with a 4x4. We were at the Basilica of St. Francis in Siena, talking to Fr. Antonio Giannini, our mentor, the Franciscan priest who had given us so much information on the Miracles of the Eucharist, and directed us to so many places to visit and write about in our first book. He has been very proud of us, and of the American people, for embracing the Miracles of the Eucharist. On this particular meeting, he looked at us very seriously, and said, *"You know, you haven't written about all the Miracles of the Eucharist. There are still many important Miracles, you haven't covered."* Then he brought us over to his files. This was reminiscent of how we had worked together in 1982 through 1985, gathering material, comparing notes. We knew what we were in for, even before we began. *"But Father,"* we said, in our best Italian, *"we have written about Miracles of the Eucharist. We have to write about other things. We're writing about heresies of the church right now (**Scandal of the Cross and its Triumph**). We want to write about the Martyrs of the Church, and our Popes."*

He gave us that look, he gives us. You really have to be there to experience the look. Then he said those words which cut us to the heart, *"Is anything more important than the Miracles of the Eucharist?"* We were finished and we knew it. There's no way you can come up against a statement like that. And so we began putting together all our research material which we had worked on since we wrote our first book, *"**This Is My Body, This Is My Blood, Miracles of the Eucharist.**"* When we went back to Siena last year, we showed him our progress. He had an urgency that we had never seen before. *"There's not much time. You must get the book written now. Don't let anything distract you."*

We were with Fr. Giannini again this last summer. We told him what we were doing, that our sequel, the book containing all the Miracles of the Eucharist, we had not written about previously, would be out this Fall. He smiled his beautiful smile. He knew that if we said we would do it, we would get the job done. And so here we are.

We really believe the Lord is speaking to us. We can see that the urgency is greater than ever to bring His message, about the Real Presence of Jesus in the Eucharist, to the people. The

Eucharist is many things to us. Our Lord Jesus gives us strength and power in the Eucharist. It's what holds the Church together. A Catholic historian of the early Church made a profound statement. He said the Church would not have lasted 100 years after the death of Jesus, had it not been for the Eucharist. Jesus gives us Himself in the Eucharist, not for Him but for us. " *I will be with you always, until the end of the world.*"[1]

We are so excited about writing another book on the Miracles of the Eucharist. We've learned a lot over the years. We didn't want to write another book about Miracles of the Eucharist just because they were so popular. There had to be a need in the Church; we believe the need is to refocus on the Real Presence of Jesus in the Eucharist.

We have always maintained that if the Lord ever made it clear to us that He wanted another book written on the Miracles of the Eucharist, we would include all the insights the Lord has given us these last eight years to share with His people. We would tie in the occurrences of the Miracles of the Eucharist with what was happening in the world and the Church at the time. We wanted to show how the Lord battles the evil one every step of the way, and one of His most powerful weapons has always been the Eucharist.

Nothing is coincidental. The Lord has a reason for everything. When we share with you all the facets of the Miracles, the time frame, the lack of belief in the Real Presence of Jesus in the Eucharist, problems in the world, problems within the Church, all the elements trying to destroy the Church from within and without, you will understand, as we have come to understand, what the Lord had in mind when He gave us the mandate to write this second book. Our meeting with Fr. Cohen last year, and the very sad results of the polls, regarding the lack of belief of practicing Catholics in the Real Presence of the Eucharist, were

---

[1]Matt 28:20

just one more indicator from the Lord in a very loud and clear Voice, that there is still much work to do with regard to the Real Presence of Our dear Lord Jesus. He is the ultimate weapon; the ultimate ammunition. Jesus in the Eucharist is not a sign; He is not a symbol. So when our non-Catholic brothers and sisters, or those Catholics who don't believe, tell us that the Eucharist is only a symbol, share the Scriptures with them. Tell them about the urgency Jesus had to give us that gift, so much that He made that a priority upon His people. Tell them that gift is for all of us. He lived for us; He died for us. He made a promise for all of us; He has kept that promise. He is your God, letting you know without the shadow of a doubt that He is with you in all things, through His Real Presence in the Eucharist. In the new *Catechism of the Catholic Church,* we are told that the Eucharist is the *"source and summit of Christian life."*[2]

Jesus is gathering an army of believers, and Defenders of the Faith. We pray you gather strength from this book to boldly go forth and put on the armor of God to defend the Church, and possibly the greatest strength the Lord has given us, Our Lord Jesus in the Eucharist. We pray it touches you the way the Miracles of the Eucharist, we have written about, have touched us. Come with us now; live the message of Jesus in the Eucharist. As the Mexican Martyrs of the 1920's and 1930's cried out before they were executed for the Faith, *"Viva Cristo Rey y la Virgen de Guadalupe"*, which translates to *"Long live Christ the King, and Our Lady of Guadalupe. "* **Can we do less?**

---

[2]quote taken from Lumen Gentium 11- Pg. 334 - Section 1324

Trani - 1000 A.D.

A story of Love and hate
The Power of Jesus in the Eucharist

This chapter is about Love and hate. What would make a Man give up His Life for those who mock Him, reject Him, betray Him, choose a murderer over Him, strip Him, scourge Him, spit upon Him, nail Him to the Cross? Love, unconditional Love!

What would make a woman take a consecrated Host, the vulnerable God-man and desecrate Him? Hate! But how does someone acquire that much hate and anger against an innocent, vulnerable Lord Who died for her?

Maybe, we can explain it in this way. Let us tell you a little about Auschwitz, where two Catholics gave up their lives for others, out of love, the same kind of Love, their Savior had for even those who would crucify Him. One of the Catholics was Saint Maxmilian Mary Kolbe, a Catholic priest who took the place of another prisoner in the death camp of Auschwitz.[1] The other was a Carmelite Nun, a convert from Judaism, who willingly died for the Jewish people. She told her sister, as they were being taken to the death camps, *"Come let us go for our people." "One day, this will have to be atoned for."*

"Blessed Edith Stein died as a Jewess and Catholic Nun, for the Jews who were being persecuted because of their belief in the One God, and as a German for the Germans who were persecuting the Jewish people, saying if she did not pray and do retribution for the German who will?"[2] She willingly walked to

---

[1]Maxmilian Kolbe died on the Feast of the Assumption, August 15, 1941, one year before the first Jews were brought to Auschwitz.

[2]from chapter on Bl. Edith Stein, in Bob and Penny Lord's book: *"Martyrs, They died for Christ"*

the Cross, not only for *Jewish* brothers and sisters, but for the Nazi soldiers who were killing them and would kill her and most of her family. So, like Jesus, she died not only for the innocents, but for their persecutors.

The war is over, and now Auschwitz is a stark memorial of man's inhumanity to man, when he stooped below the animals and killed innocent people whose only sin was they believed differently from him. But is the war over? One dark and ugly day, prejudice raised its venomous head again, and brought back all the nightmares that can never be forgotten. An act of hate filled the air, and the shrine to those victims of Auschwitz was soiled. Some Jewish-Americans climbed over the fence of a Carmelite convent outside Auschwitz, and ordered the Nuns off the land, they had purchased from the Polish government. [The convent and chapel had been a run down building where the Nazi guards used to store Cyclon B gas, which was used to exterminate innocent men, women and children, Jews and Catholics, alike; no one was spared from this insane hatred.] And now, these Americans part of a people who had been prejudiced against, were turning their hate against innocent Nuns, whose only crime was the Cross above the convent. They said it offended them, reminding them of those who had killed their fellow Jews. It was futile to say that these Nazis were atheists; and as followers of Christ, they could not have done this infamous act against His creation, His chosen people. And so, these Nuns who turned a house of death into a house of Love, had to leave. *Does Hate ever die?*

Why did the Jewish woman, involved in our Miracle, do what she did? How much anger and hate did it take to go through with this horrible act? Had something happened to her? We don't know. What we do know is that when we allow anger and hate to enter our hearts, then the enemy of God can do all forms of evil through us, as his instruments. But, let us go to our story.

The Miracle where Hate was converted to Love

Our miracle takes place in Trani, a small coastal town located near the boot of Italy in between Foggia and Bari, not far from San Giovanni Rotondo (*Padre Pio*) and Monte St. Angelo (*the Cave of St. Michael*). In 1985, Trani only boasted a population of 45,000 inhabitants. Can you imagine the size of the community at the beginning of the second millenium?

But it doesn't matter to Satan how big or small a town is. If there is *one* soul who can be brought down to the flames of hell, he'll go after him, or send his demons after him. If he has his way, that soul will burn with him for all eternity. So when he saw a prideful Jewish lady, a self-proclaimed sorceress who hated the Church, who was so angry at Jesus, looking for a way to discredit Him, Satan saw a way to sucker one more soul down into the fiery pits of hell.

In around the year 1000, there was quite a sizable number of Jewish people living in Trani. The church of Saint Anna which had originally been a synagogue, was now a church where Jews, who had converted to Christianity, worshiped. But for the purpose of this Miracle, let us go to the Church of Saint Andrew, where there is a plaque which tells of the sacrilege and the Miracle of the Eucharist that came about because of this act of desecration, till today.

There was a Jewish woman who had an overpowering hatred for the Church. We can't be sure what brought about this hostility and loathing; we only know that she felt driven to deal a death blow to Jesus and His Church. But her priority, even more than fulfilling her wrath against Jesus and the Church, was to make herself famous. She wanted to demonstrate her powers of magic. Too many people were turning to prayer and Jesus, instead of to her. She needed to do something which would bring her a great deal of publicity, and at the same time prove to Catholics, their belief in Jesus was unfounded and ridiculous.

It was *Holy Thursday*. There had been so much reverence among the villagers, during the period of Quaresima.[3] The witch was furious! She specially hated this night, when the Christians

---
[3]the forty days of Lent

celebrated the *Last Supper*, the first Mass. They insisted that Jesus gave them the Eucharist, His Body and Blood, this night; and to add salt to her wounds, it had been at a *Seder*, the first night of Passover! She had always heard the age-old question, at the Seder table, *"Why is this night different from other nights?"* Well, she would show these Christians how *she* had the power to change this night into one *no different* from any other night. This night would be the perfect night to humiliate this God Who had such power over them. She would show them what a sham it all was, their belief that Jesus came to them under the appearance of bread and wine.

They had been focused on the Passion and Resurrection of Jesus all through Lent, and had ignored her, turning to their God for help. They thought, they had something to mourn about, on Good Friday? They did not know what sorrow was. Well, she'd show them! She would show them that everything the Church, had taught them was a lie![4] She would shoot them down before they had a chance to rejoice, on Easter Sunday. The day of hope, they celebrated with such joy, she would turn into a day of despair.

The One Who they believed was in their church, was just a piece of bread, and she would prove it to them. The people had dared be filled by the grandeur of God and not the need of her? She had to do something to disprove His existence. It became an obsession with her. She realized the most vulnerable way that Catholics could be attacked, is through their belief that Jesus is truly Present and comes to them, in the Eucharist. That had always been their strength. She would find a way to disprove that He was really in that piece of bread. She would get a Host from the church, and desecrate it. She was apprehensive about going into the church. She was known to be a Jewess. In addition, she had a reputation of being a witch or sorceress or magician, as you wish. Add to that, she had not bothered to hide her hatred for the Church, needless to say, she would not be very welcome at Mass,

---

[4]Doesn't that sound like Lucifer when he, the father of lies, called God a liar, in the Garden of Eden.

that evening. For her to go into the church, unnoticed, would require a major miracle. For her to walk up to the Altar and try to get the priest to give her Communion would be next to impossible. Besides, even though she insisted she did not believe, Jesus was Present in the church, she was afraid the walls would fall down upon her, if she dared to enter, especially with her evil intent.

So, she adopted another plan, which would actually be better than her going up to the Altar, and receiving the Eucharist. Get a Catholic to do her dirty work. In this way, if God was in the church, she would not be zapped, but the poor fool doing her bidding. This way, if what they believed was true, then according to the Catholic Faith, the Catholic would be sharing in the same sacrilege, as the sorceress; so she was helping a believer to sin against her God! She called a woman, a lapsed Catholic, who had come to her many times for potions and answers to questions about the future. She had chosen someone who either had no idea what went on during the Sacrifice of the Mass, or worse yet, knew and didn't care. There are a lot of them out there, you know. The magician was able to find someone who would sell out Jesus for a few pieces of silver. After all, hadn't that happened before? Didn't Judas sell out Jesus for a few pieces of silver?

The lapsed Catholic went to Mass, at the Church of St. Basil, which has since been renamed the Church of St. Andrew. At the time of Communion, she received like everyone else, on her tongue. Only she did not consume the Host; she quickly went into the shadows of the church and removed the Eucharist, placing It in between the folds of a napkin. Then, at the end of the Mass, she left the church and went hurriedly to the sorceress. What were the thoughts running through her mind? Was she nervous? Or was she proud of herself for having gotten away with this blasphemous act? Did she feel important? Would she be famous, along with the witch? This may have been the only thing, she had done of any real importance, and she had done it well. Would she be rewarded?

Our hearts are filled with sadness, as we ask ourselves: Didn't the Catholic care enough about her Lord Jesus, who had suffered and died for her, to protect Him? Or didn't she know that the Eucharist is really Jesus? What could she have been thinking? What did she think, the witch would do with the Host? Did the Catholic know enough, about the Faith, to understand she was about to commit the worst sacrilege? We're always looking out, beyond the borders of our Church, to convert those who don't worship Jesus in the fullest sense, with the gifts of the Sacraments, or those who don't worship Jesus at all. We need to turn to those, possibly who are no farther than in the pews of our own church, or within the folds of our families. Do *we* project the Jesus Whom we receive in Holy Communion? Has the conversion come about in our own hearts? Maybe, just maybe, we all share in the guilt when one of our Church goes astray. We don't know why, but an ignorant or fallen-away Catholic played into the hands of Satan, through his emissary, the sorceress, and was on her way to hell.

The sorceress paced up and down; she couldn't wait for the woman to come to her cottage, with the consecrated Host. When she arrived, the sorceress paid her the agreed-upon sum, and sent her away. The magician held the Body of our Lord Jesus Christ, vulnerable in this Eucharistic Form, in her hands. She could do whatever she wanted. No matter what she did, it would hurt the Christians. *Let's burn the wafer*, she thought. She envisioned herself showing the ashes to Catholics, then to fellow enemies of the Church interested in seeing the people's faith destroyed. *This was a good idea!*

She went to her kitchen, to her stove. She filled a pot with oil, and heated it. She couldn't wait for it to begin smoking and boiling. Then she would throw her prize into the fire. She waited for what seemed like an eternity, until the oil was bubbling. Then with great pomp and ceremony, she threw the white Host into the fire. She watched for the results.

To her shock and astonishment, *the Host turned into Flesh* immediately, upon contact with the oil. The Flesh began to Bleed profusely, bursting from the Host as if it were hemorrhaging,

The Host turned into Flesh and began to Bleed profusely

gushing into the oil, mixing with it, almost consuming it. The contents of the pot began to overflow, Blood cascading down onto the floor, as it continued to gush out of the Host-turned-Flesh like a geyser. The woman panicked! She was terrified. She didn't know what to do. She tried to hide the crime by sopping up the Evidence, but the more she did, the more the Blood flowed. Realizing the evil, she had done and unable to undo it, she began to weep uncontrollably, shedding tears of true remorse. He really was present in the Host, and now through her, He was bleeding, and she could not stop it. She had wounded Him. She cried out in pain, like a woman in labor. People near by, upon hearing her screams, at first were curious but soon became alarmed. The neighbors ran into the house to see what had happened. Her hands and dress full of Blood. She tried to compose herself. She began to share the whole ugly plot. It didn't take long for them to understand what treachery against their God had taken place in this house.

Some Catholic women ran to the Bishop's house to inform him of the sacrilege. Others summoned the Pastor of the church. Upon seeing His Lord's Blood, he immediately prostrated himself on the floor, kissing His Savior's spilled Blood. He returned to the church, vested up, and immediately led a Procession of Penance, with Altar servers carrying lit candles, in the direction of the witch's house. The whole town followed the cortege, even the authorities. Remember, at this time, the Catholic Church was the official religion of the country. Actually, Italy was part of the Holy Roman Empire. All Europe was Catholic. A sacrilege or blasphemy against the Church was the same as a crime against the state, and punishable in the fullest extent of the law.

The Pastor took the remaining bleeding Flesh out of the pot

and brought It, in reverent procession, back to the Cathedral of Trani. The number of villagers kept increasing, as they poured out of their homes to accompany their Lord, miraculously with them, back to safety. A beautifully ornate, silver Monstrance was designed in the shape of a house, with four pillars, and a dome overhead, for their Lord to repose in. In the center of the Reliquary is a crystal lunette containing the two Particles of the fried Host, of unequal size and shape. The color of the larger Portion of the Host is dark brown, and that of the smaller Piece is bright reddish brown. It

The Reliquary of the Miracle of the Eucharist of Trani

has been determined that this was most likely caused by the difference of the intensity of heat, one side of the Host was subjected to, when It was fried versus that which the other half of the Host suffered. The Blood soaked Host is incorrupt, till today, and can be seen and venerated, in the Cathedral. It is a

The Church of St. Andrew in Trani, Italy

most beautiful tribute to the Real Presence of Jesus in the Eucharist.

As this was a crime, punishable by death, the sorceress was executed, but not before confessing her sins, asking for pardon of the Lord, she now believed in. They say, you could see the Heavenly Angels battling the fallen ones for her soul. The witch's house was reserved right from the beginning, for the Faithful as a place of reverence since the miracle occurred there. Then in 1706, it was made into a chapel, with the title of Most Blessed Savior, *SS Salvatore.*

There in the chapel, is a marble plaque which tells the entire story. Was the fault all hers, or was it the ignorance of the people who contributed to the crime? Who was their God, really? Had they not turned to her at times, for help? If they had believed, and been strong and resolute in that belief, maybe she might not have dared to do the horrible thing she did.

The Miracle was probed and poked for centuries with always the same conclusion. It happened, and it was through the Lord's generous Heart that it came about and remains, till today. Pope Urban VI went to Trani in 1384, and declared in his Bull that the Host was miraculously preserved.

Over the years, Bishops have authenticated this Miracle. In 1841, during a Pastoral visit, Archbishop Gaetano da Franci, had the Miracle examined, and he concluded that the Host had not been conserved except by the Will and intervention of God, and placed his seal of approval on the Miracle.

In 1924, The Inter-Diocesan Eucharistic Congress was celebrated in Trani, in which there was an immediate recognition of the Precious Miraculous Host by the mandate of Archbishop Joseph Marie Leo. Before that in 1886, the Eucharistic Miracle was examined and the results were that it occurred through Divine intervention.

Traveling from distant provinces, Kings and Queens, Dukes and Duchesses, Lords and Ladies, the wealthy and the poor came, saw and believed, and upon believing, turned to their Savior Miraculously Present in the Host.

✝

"All power in Heaven and on earth has been given to me."[5] Do you believe in the words in that statement? Do you believe, no, I mean *do you really believe*, that Jesus has the power over everything in Heaven and on earth? Do you project that belief to others inside the church, and non-believers outside the church? Is your belief so strong that no one would dare come up against that belief, for fear of how you would react?

---

[5]Matt 28:28

Ferrara - 1171
The Blood of Christ

On our Journey of Faith to explore more shrines that show us proof of how the Lord shows His love for us through Miracles of the Eucharist, we go to the province of Emiglia Romagna, in the northeastern part of Italy, to Ferrara, a city known for its peace and quiet. There is an ancient section there, called the Borgo Vado near the Po river. They never knew if they would be flooded by a sudden rise in the river, or if their men would be caught in the current, and pulled underwater. The inhabitants have always had strong faith. Here, we found not only the Lord through the Miracle of the Precious Blood, but His Mother, Our Lady of the Precious Blood.

We had been given this Miracle of the Eucharist, to research, by Father Giannini[1] back in 1981, but it took till 1992 for us to go and discover this remarkable way, our Lord and His Mother chose to touch and reach us. This Miracle took place in 1171; Father Giannini told us of it in 1981, 810 years later. And now, 823 years after the Miracle, we are bringing it to you. *Why now?* As so many have asked, when we wrote our first book on the Miracles of the Eucharist.[2] Stay with us, and let us try to discover the answer, together.

---

[1]Father Giannini is our mentor who gave us most of the information we received to research Miracles of the Eucharist.

[2]*This is My Body, This is My Blood, Miracles of the Eucharist - Book I*

It was 1992; we were on pilgrimage, and it was time to investigate the Miracle of Ferrara. I still remember that first time, we went to the church on Borgo Vado. Before leaving on pilgrimage, we telephoned Father Peter Mercurio, the custodian, advising him, we would be bringing pilgrims and wanted to videotape the Miracle. When we arrived, it was obvious that Father and the Altar Society had worked

Bob and Penny Lord
with Fr. Peter Mercurio

extremely hard to prepare the church for us. Everything was cleaned and polished. The lights were brightly lit. The only problem was that Brother Joseph and the camera had to return home before the pilgrimage was over, *as it had jammed up* at another shrine of a Miracle of the Eucharist, in Blanot, France, and was not working.

The Altars were covered with white flowers. The candelabras were shining from the loving rubbing that had been done. The crystal chandeliers sparkled. The priest was ready! The church was ready! We were not ready! I can still feel the deep sadness in my heart. Father never said anything, but this must have been a great disappointment. We vowed, we would return the following year and film the Miracle.

The next year (1993), Father Peter Mercurio, was not there; he was on holiday. The sacristan cordially assisted us in the taping and in preparing the Altar of the Miracle of the Eucharist, for Mass. We taped a lot of great footage, but Father Peter was not there, and we knew we could not complete the program until he was available. We would have to return to interview this holy priest.

Father Jay Voorhies of the Diocese of Lafayette, Louisiana

was our spiritual director. You know, we tape and tape, and we do not know what the Lord has prepared for His children, until we begin editing. As Brother Joseph was preparing our new programs on Miracles of the Eucharist for Eternal Word Television Network, he called us into the editing studio. Some of the most powerful teaching on the true presence of Jesus in the Holy Eucharist was imparted by Father Jay, in his homily at the *Altar of the Miracle of the Eucharist*. Does this surprise us? Only when we forget that the Pope, our Bishops, Archbishop Fulton J. Sheen; all turned to the Blessed Sacrament for inspiration.

Wherever you find the Mother, there you will find the Son. We returned in 1994, and we discovered Mother Mary, once more, involved in Her Son's ministry and in the lives of her children here on earth. In the church of the Miracle, there is a fresco of a ship with Mother Mary in the middle of the boat. Father Mercurio said that through the Miracle, occurring at the Altar of Our Lady of the Precious Blood, we learn, once more, that wherever the Lord is, His Mother is; and through the painting, wherever the Church is, Mary, Mother of the Church is, guiding her Pope and the Church to shore.

Santa Maria in Vado

The church, where the Miracle occurred is called *"Santa Maria in Vado"* (Blessed Mary in the water). Father Mercurio told us that it got its name because the Faithful had to walk through water to get to church. The original church was located along the left bank of the Po river. The Borgo Vado district for many Christians was the center of devotion to the Sacred Image of Our Lady from, as far back as, ancient chronicles tell

Basilica of Santa Maria in Vado

us, the fifth century. The Image of Our Lady, has been reported as having been painted by St. Luke.

[Now, some skeptics say, How many paintings did St. Luke create? Saint John Bosco, in addition to founding a home for hundreds of boys and starting a Religious Order of priests, brothers and nuns, wrote more than 139 books. Why couldn't St. Luke have painted many pictures of the Blessed Mother?]

When Christians from Borgo Vado, wanted to be baptized, they had to cross the river, which was at best unreliable, and could turn on you and become treacherous in a minute. But this was the only way they could get to the Cathedral of St. George, on the other side. This became a problem for the Faithful, to the degree that many waited, *till* a safer time to cross, *till* the water was not so high, *till* it was not so treacherous, *till* almost the point of death, to be baptized.

What did they do? They built a little church in honor of our Lady. No one knows how far back that was, but they do know that since the seventh century, the Faithful have prayed to our Lady there and she has answered them.

Our Lady came to this little district, to a community of Faithful in need. How, no one knows. Since the fifth century, she has been venerated, especially by the devout of the area. In the middle of the seventh century, in around 656, a small chapel was built; now the children of God would be able to attend Mass and be baptized on this side of the river. To give honor and thanksgiving for the church that was built, and for all the favors received through her intercession, the chapel was named after her and the special favor the Faithful had received: *"Santa Maria in Vado,"* Blessed Mary in the water.

The area was also renamed after the miraculous intercession of Mother Mary, "Borgo Vado" - Burgh[3] Way. Many miracles came about through the intercession of our Lady in the Water. The Faithful flocked to the little chapel. They reached out to her,

---

[3]district

asking for her help. And she was there for them. To her, the fishermen entrusted their lives, imploring her intercession that they would return safely from the sea; and bring in a good catch, so that they could feed their families.

But did our Lady want the people to focus on her? Just as she did, when her Son walked the earth, she pointed to Him! But her priest and bishops were being deluded by heretics like the Albigensians and through them, the Faithful had lost belief in the true Presence of Our Lord Jesus in the Eucharist. They still came to pray to the Mother, but they ignored the Son. Something had to be done! How would Mother Mary turn her children back to their Lord?

The Miracle

In 1135, Bishop Landolfo officially turned the custody of the little chapel over to the Canons Portuensi of Ravenna. On **March 28, 1171**, Easter Sunday, the small church was filled with the devout and the twice-a-year Easter/Christmas church-goers.[4] The Prior of the Canon

Fr. Peter of Verona broke the consecrated Host, and Blood sprayed onto the dome

Regulars Portuensi, Father Peter of Verona, ascended the Altar to celebrate Solemn Mass, assisted by three of his Canon Regulars, and several Altar Boys. Before distributing Holy Communion to the Faithful, at the moment he broke the consecrated Host into two, the Host turned into Flesh and from the Flesh, Blood sprayed from the Host and splattered on the vaulted dome behind the

---

[4]Today we call them Easter Lillies and Christmas Poinsettas

Altar.

As we looked upon the blood-splattered dome, which, after 813 years, still graphically evidences the Blood Which burst forth from the Host, our minds and hearts went back to the 8th century and the Miracle of the Eucharist of Lanciano, when the Host turned into a Human Heart and the wine into Blood (which later petrified into five pellets - the five wounds of Christ). On the Cross, when the centurion Longinus pierced Our Lord's Heart with a lance, Blood and water gushed forth from His Side. Longinus became the first Christian, as he beheld the Precious Blood of Jesus being poured out, out of love for him and all mankind. We believe that the Church flowed from the Heart of Christ that day, at that moment, and we were all saved. At the time of the Miracle, when His Blood gushed forth onto the dome, was Our Lord's Heart being pierced, once again, out of love for the people who no longer believed in Him and His Words: *"This is My Body, This is My Blood, the Blood of the New Covenant which will be shed for you."*

The Blood stained dome of the Basilica of St. Maria in Vado

The Miracle that took place before their eyes, both astonished and touched those who were blessed to be eye-witnesses. But, there were those who saw, in addition to the crimson Blood splattering on the wall, *the Figure of a Child.* To those who might find the latter difficult to accept, the indisputable truth, before our very eyes, over 800 years later, is a wall still stained red by the Blood shed by Our Lord in the Eucharist. And if you still have a problem, then come with us on Pilgrimage to Italy (or in your own home[5]) to the Basilica of Santa Maria in Vado where

---

[5]through watching our program on Eternal Word Television Network or on our video: The Miracle of Ferrara.

you, too, will witness how far Our Lord will go, even to putting aside that which He has created, Mother Nature, to glorify His Name, and save His Children.

What had transpired was immediately reported to Bishop Amato of Ferrara and Archbishop Gerard of Ravenna. They came, and ascertained unequivocally that the irrefutable evidence of the Blood on the vaulted wall, was conclusive proof that a Miracle had come to pass. *They came; they saw and Jesus conquered* their minds and hearts. We have seen and witnessed the hearts of our pilgrims when they too have knelt before this Miracle of the Eucharist.

There is a document by Gerald Cambrense, authenticating the Miracle, which dates back to the year 1197. It is conserved in the Library Lamberthiana of Canterbury. It goes as follows:

"In Ferrara, Italy, in these our times, the Host on Easter Day, was transformed into a small piece of meat. The Bishop of Ferrara was called, and having verified the Miracle, the citizens of that city who had been Patarini and had professed heretical ideas on the Eucharist, the Body of Christ, returned to the Truth."

Being able to appraise it with authentic proof from those giving testimony who were alive and had witnessed the Miracle, the Miracle was clearly affirmed. The Miracle came about, to lift the fog of the heretical smoke screen with which *the enemy* had clouded the minds and hearts of the Faithful, as to the True Presence of Jesus in the Eucharist, and to the reality of the Lord's resurrection. A Bull was issued by Cardinal Migliorati on March 6, 1404.

During the middle of the 1500s, a copy of this Bull arrived, and was placed in the Archives of the Canon Regulars of the Lateranensi in Rome (which has ancient writings speaking of the Miracle of Ferrara), *a Bull which granted Plenary Indulgences*, under the proper conditions, to those who render homage to the Precious Blood. This ancient document written in 1197, contains the history of the antiquity of the Chapel, of the vaulted ceiling stained with Blood and the testimonies of those who had witnessed the Miracle.

Even more authoritative is the *Papal Bull* issued by Pope Eugene IV, on March, 1442, which proclaimed that a Miracle had truly occurred. He based his acceptance on the unshakable memories, of believers who had been passing on the tradition of the Miracle, which concurred with the testimonies written by witnesses at the time of the Miracle.

November 12, 1519, the Bishop of Albano, Cardinal Nicholas Fieschi who was also administrator of Ravenna, granted other Indulgences. Many other bishops came and investigated over the centuries and all agreed that the Lord had truly brought about a Miracle to make us aware that He was alive and His Precious Blood is not ancient but is, was and always will be with us.

A new church was begun in 1494, and completed in 1518, still under the Canon Regulars. The vaulted dome was transferred to the new church in 1501. From 1594 to 1595, Alphonse II had a chapel, devoted to the Miracle, built in the new church, which was raised to a Basilica. It stands there, till today, available for the Faithful to see and be reminded, what really happens on the Altar is *the ongoing Sacrifice of the Cross*. Kneeling before its vaulted dome, it calls us to the foot of the Cross with Mother Mary, now and forever, as Her Son Jesus pours out His Blood for the redemption of sin. The Precious Blood still there, for us, brings our minds and hearts to the Tabernacle, and Who it is Who is waiting in what resembles a golden box but is in reality, a palace for a King. It is for Our King - for Our Lord Jesus, alive and waiting - for us!

As our priest Father Harold Cohen began the celebration of the Mass, assisted by our other two priests on pilgrimage, in front of them[6] was the painting showing the Host bursting and

---

[6]Our priests had to celebrate with their backs to us, as the Altar had been turned around in the Chapel.

splattering Blood on the dome. Here we were, over 800 years later, in this small chapel devoted to the Miracle of the Precious Blood, awaiting our Lord in His Body, Blood, Soul and Divinity. Here, once again, a priest would break a Host into two. What would we see? Would we see Our Lord lifted up high on the Cross, crucified? For you see, that's what it's all about.

The Basilica was under the custody of the Canon Regulars until 1797, when the terrorism of Napoleon, with its oppressive and subversive laws against the Church, caused them to be expelled from it. But unofficially, they continued to serve till 1847. Then, the Basilica changed hands from the Canons Regular, to Diocesan priests, to Camilliani priests for a short time, to *Missionaries of the Precious Blood* in 1930 when the custody of the Basilica was placed in their hands. The Missionaries were founded by Saint Gaspar of Bufalo, a Roman priest who Pope John XXIII called *"The true and greatest apostle of the Blood of Jesus in the world."* Years of candles had caused a haze to cover the dome. In 1970, they removed the smoke from burning candles with a drop of alcohol swabbing it carefully. Although the Basilica has been cleaned, and been restored several times, the vaulted dome is as it was 823 years ago; nothing has been done to preserve the Blood stains; They have never been touched.

On Sunday, May 19,1957, on the occasion of the *Feast of the Precious Blood*, the restoration having been completed, the Faithful processed into the Basilica, with the Bishop and clergy of the Basilica following, carrying the miraculous Image of Our Lady which had been over the dome where the Miracle had taken place. The miraculous Image of Our Lady was placed, where she is till today, over the Altar where the Miracle took place March 28, 1171.

The people of God, the Faithful of Ferrara, have always believed in the Miracle of the Precious Blood and have passed on that belief from generation to generation. In 1971, the Archbishop of Ferrara, Bishop Natale Mosconi, came to officiate over the 800th anniversary of the Miracle. He said that it was his wish that this not be an *empty* splendid festival, not that the Miracle was not worthy of such ceremony, after eight centuries of renewed belief in the Miracle, but that it be more for renewed *awareness* and new *faith* in what happens on the Altar during each Mass, and *Who* is alive in the Tabernacle. He said, it called them (and us) to a new calling to live a *Christian life*, being the new creation formed by our union or Communion with Jesus in the Eucharist. God was asking us to share that what happened (with this Miracle), when the Host was broken into two parts, came about to point to the *reality* of the Eucharistic Statement that Jesus made, and his Faithful priests have made for almost 20 centuries, that at the moment that the Host is broken in two, after the Host has been consecrated, it is first *Sacrifice* and then *Communion*.[7]

The Archbishop's words re-echo, reverberate and renew what Pope Paul VI said in his Encyclical: *Misterium Fidei*, in 1967, when he recalled Christians to the certainty of the *"Real Presence"*, to the true reality of the *"transubstantiation"*,[8] to the celestial intangibility of the Eucharistic Dogma, that is to the center of the life of the Church, like a *"sign of unity and bond of charity."*

Pilgrims, till today, 823 years later, come to pray before the *Mother of Christ, Our Lady of Vado*, at her Chapel where her miraculous Image is reserved; she then leads them to the *Body of Christ*, the Eucharist, where they kneel in adoration to Our Lord Who is present in the Tabernacle and no less present in His Blood on the vaulted dome through the Miracle of the Precious Blood.

---

[7]"The cup of blessing which we bless, is it not a participation in the Blood of Christ? The bread which we break, is it not a participation in the Body of Christ? Because there is one Bread, we who are many are one body, for we all partake of the one Bread." (1 Cor 10:16-17)

[8]As defined by the Council of Trent, *transubstantiation* is a singular and wondrous conversion of the total substance of bread into the Body and of the total substance of wine into the Blood of Christ, the external appearances only remaining unchanged. It is by this *transubstantiation* that the Body and Blood of Christ are present in the Holy Eucharist (Mark 14:22-25)

We know that Mother Church teaches us that when we consume from the Chalice, we receive the Body and the Blood of Jesus, and when we consume the Host, we likewise receive the Body and the Blood of Jesus. Therefore when we worship Our Lord Whose Blood is miraculously before us, on the vaulted dome, we are adoring Our total Lord[9] in His Body, Blood, Soul and Divinity.

The Eucharistic Blood, shed on the vaulted dome can be equated to the living memory of the Passion of Jesus Christ, to which we owe our salvation. As St. Augustine cried out:

"Learn, O Man, perceiving how you are and how you should be, and the great heights to which the Redemption raises you, you blush at your faults. You for whom Pity was flagellated instead of heartlessness; Learning was mocked instead of stupidity; Truth was immolated instead of the liar; Justice was condemned instead of corruption; Compassion was tortured instead of cruelty; Purity drank vinegar in place of the defiled one; Sweetness was saddened by bile in place of bitterness; Innocence was punished instead of guilt; He Who was Life died instead of he who is death; All nature is frightened of the wickedness of men, and the earth trembles and the sun hides from sight, attesting that the Master of the world, that King of Heaven, is He Whom the disowned creature rebels against."

Isaiah the prophet, foretelling the price Jesus would pay, said:

"He was wounded for our transgressions, He was bruised for our iniquities, upon Him was the chastisement that made us

---

[9] question arose as to whether the Real Presence of Jesus is present when, by miracle, a consecrated Host turns into Flesh, or a Baby, as in the instance of Zaragoza. We go to the teachings of St. Thomas Aquinas for the answer. He states: "Under these new aspects, the Body of Christ remains really present in sacramental form."- p.113 in Bob and Penny Lord's first book on the Miracles of the Eucharist, *"This is My Body, This is My BLood, Miracles of the Eucharist"*

whole, and with His stripes we are healed."[10]

What did we come away with from this Miracle, this Basilica? Before we left the Basilica to go on to Padua and St. Anthony and the Miracle of the Eucharist, we paused in front of a fresco. When they built the 2nd church, which became a Basilica, they had this fresco painted on one of the walls. In the painting, we see a ship with Mother Mary standing in the center of the craft. On the sail of the ship we observe signs of the Eucharist. Is this painting not affirming the Catholic Catechism which teaches: *"The summit and center of the Church is the Eucharist."* There are two angels; wherever you see Mary, you will see her Heavenly escort accompanying her. Here one is shoring and the other is steering the vessel. Part of the ship which is the Church is the Gospel. The angel and the Gospel are synonymous (the Greek word for Gospel - Evangelicum contains the word angel). Peter is not in the center but Mary, who is helping him guide the ship of the Church to shore. This painting also says that Peter guides the Church, but Mary guides him. And if you do not believe the painting, ask our Peter, Pope John Paul II. What has the Lord been saying to us, at this time, with this Miracle? "I am here, with you till the end of the world, offering Myself, shedding My Blood for you. Be not afraid. I have not left you orphans. I am with you, in the Word. I am with you in My Body, Blood, Soul and Divinity in the Eucharist. I am with you through My Mother." What is Jesus saying? Honor His Mother. For without Mary, there is no Jesus. Without Mary, there is no Church.

On April 26, 1994, thieves broke into the Basilica and stole the miraculous painting[11] of our Lady of the Precious Blood, the Image venerated for over 1500 years. When a new church was built the Image was placed on the wall where the Miracle had originally happened. The police said they found many paintings when they searched the house of the thieves, but not the paintings

---

[10]Isaiah 53:5 Ignatius Revised Standard Version - Catholic Edition
[11]reportedly painted by St. Luke

of the Basilica. They were about to leave, when the police chief felt something, a voice that said, *"Return to the house!"* There was an armoir with a false back. The chief of police decided to open the wall of the armoir; for it was suspiciously of a different color and type of wood as the rest of the armoir. When they lifted the wall, they found the Image of our Lady. And so, Our Lady has returned, just as she has in our Church. In the 60s, there were some who tried to throw her out of the Church, but she has returned more present than ever, with her rightful place beside her Son, just as she was at the foot of the Cross.

What has this Miracle and the miraculous Image of Our Lady said to us? During the ongoing Sacrifice of the Cross which is the Sacrifice of the Mass, remember, it is not only Jesus' Blood which was shed, but the Blood of Mother Mary's Son, and she stood there and she said yes - for you and for us and our salvation. What will it take for Jesus and Mary to get our attention? *If Jesus came for the second time, would we pay attention?*

Alatri - 1228

The Host turned to Flesh

We want to share with you a gift of knowledge we were given by the Lord about *Holy Clusters*.

"There is a concept of God the pilot flying way above the earth. From His vantage point, He can see great distances and occurrences that are about to happen and have already happened. Aboard His plane, we can see a pattern that the Lord has created. We see clusters of holy places and events that seem to have no connection with each other, except that they were all instituted by the Lord. The chronological sequence may be centuries apart. But time is a limitation put on us by man, not by God."[1]

The Lord gives us a series of Holy Clusters in Italy, about 60 miles southeast of Rome, in the province of Frossinone. *Veroli* is the site of one Miracle of the Eucharist, and *Alatri* is the site of another, and they can't be more than twenty miles from each other. If you travel a short distance, perhaps thirty or forty miles, you will see the great home of Western Monasticism, *The Benedictine Abbey of Montecassino*, the corridors of which are illuminated by the presence of one of the most powerful Saints in this history of our Church, *St. Benedict*. Why did the Lord choose this place, this cluster of land, to be a Holy Cluster? Why did He give us two powerful Miracles of the Eucharist, and a great Saint? What does He want us to learn from these shrines? Are they ancient history, or are they for today? Come with us now, as we share Holy Clusters of the Lord.

---

[1] *This Is My Body, This Is My Blood, Miracles of the Eucharist,* Book I -Pg 131

Cathedral of St. Paul in Alatri, Italy

There is a large Basilica-Cathedral of St. Paul the Apostle, in the little town of Alatri, some sixty miles southeast of Rome. In this Church, rests the Real Presence of Our Lord Jesus, in a powerful Miracle of the Eucharist, which has been given the title, *"The Host turned into Flesh"*. It is a very well-documented Miracle, attested to and affirmed by a Papal Bull of Pope Gregory IX. The gift was given to the people of God of the province of Frossinone to give them strength to fight the onslaught of heresies, which ran rampant in Europe in the Twelfth and Thirteen Centuries. It's as if every dissident priest decided to take pot shots at all the things, we hold dear in our Faith, especially, our Lord Jesus in the Eucharist and Mother Mary. The worst part is that these heretics had an audience, groups of people who were willing to listen to them, and even take them seriously.

A deadly heresy floated down from France towards Italy, and found its way into Rome and its environs at this time. This heresy which attacked the Eucharist, so violently, was called *Berengarianism*, named after its founder, Berengarius, a priest from Tours, France.

"Berengarius wrote a dissertation opposing the Church's teaching on the Holy Eucharist and sent it to Rome in care of someone named Lanfranc. Lanfranc brought it to the Pope's attention, and that's when the Popes, one after the other, got involved. Leo IX was the first pope to hear of it in 1050. He called a synod, in 1054, in which he condemned the teaching of Berengarianism which stated that while the bread and wine in the Eucharist become Christ's Body and Blood, they do so

figuratively, remaining substantially or physically what they are. Is this not what our separated brothers and sisters in Christ believe, since the time of Luther, that the Eucharist is only symbolically the Lord?

"Two popes during their Pontificates, called synods, to deal with this heresy. Finally, Pope Gregory VII called two councils in Rome, one in 1078 and then another in 1079. Berengarius was sent for by the first council that convened in Rome, in 1078. They called him in to answer questions about his doctrine. Although he had supposedly relented twenty years before and had sworn to defer to the Church's findings, there were doctrinal errors being taught, which smacked suspiciously of his former philosophy. As with some of our modern theologians who are censored for a time and then return, we judge repentant, but then continue to spread heresies of all kinds, it seemed Berengarius had made an oath with his head and not his heart. The issue of the true presence of Jesus in the Holy Sacrament was still being argued. The Church deemed it prudent to call Berengarius in. After careful deliberation, they required him to make a Profession of Faith and he complied!

"Another council was called in 1079, The Sixth Council of Rome. Although Berengarius would promise to cease teaching his heretical doctrines, he would always turn around, attack the Church, and continue where he left off. When Pope Gregory VII convened this council, he insisted, Berengarius sign another Profession of Faith. After having done so, he was true to form and denied it.

"As is often very deviously presented to us today, in masked terminology, what he said was that since the bread and wine, used for the consecration, remained bread and wine in appearance, They could not be the Body and Blood of our Lord Jesus Christ. Berengarius claimed that since bread and wine remained what they were, bread and wine, the Body of Christ remained in Heaven, and was not truly present in the Holy Eucharist.

"It was common knowledge that Berengarius was not in agreement with the oath he had taken, in 1078, so the following year, the Council required he make an even more explicit pledge of loyalty and obedience to the Church and her teachings. Again, he agreed. And again, with this Profession of Faith, although he fully knew what he was signing, he later reneged.

"We will, once more, see God making a positive out of a negative. Because of Berengarius' heresy, against the true Presence of Jesus in the Holy Eucharist, the Church officially defined the doctrine of Transubstantiation, affirming what the Church has believed and taught from the very beginning.

"In 1562 at the Council of Trent, Mother Church defended the Holy Eucharist one more time, against new heresies, drummed up by new heretics calling themselves reformers. It made this declaration on Transubstantiation:

"'Because Christ our Redeemer said that it was truly His Body that He was offering under the species of bread,[2] it has always been the conviction of the Church, and this holy council now again declares that, by the Consecration of the bread and wine a change takes place in which the whole substance of bread changes into the substance of the Body of Christ our Lord, and the whole substance of the wine into the substance of His Blood. This change the Catholic Church fittingly and properly names Transubstantiation.'

"In other words, the entire host which appears to be bread is changed into the Body of Christ; and the wine although it appears to be wine, is changed into the real Blood of Christ. They are no longer bread and wine; they only appear to be. It is by this Transubstantiation that the Body and Blood of Christ are present in the Holy Eucharist."[3]

While Berengarius repented of his heresies during his lifetime, at least with his mouth, *as much as three hundred years later,* the Church was still fighting to put out the fire he had lit,

---

[2] Matt 26:26; Mk 14:22; Lk 22:19; 1 Cor 11:24
[3] *Scandal of the Cross and its Triumph* - Pgs 205-209

condemning his teachings. And so here we have, in this central part of Italy, as well as other parts of southern and northern Italy, the poison from this heresy, infecting the area, two hundred years after the fact. And yet with all of this, one group of people whom you could not convince of anything but that Jesus was truly present in the Eucharist, and that the Eucharist had great powers, were the *sorcerers and witchcraft advocates*. They knew the great power of the Eucharist. They always wanted consecrated Hosts to *desecrate*, because they knew that it was Jesus they were defiling.

A young woman was willing to accept *bad advice*. How many times have we been guilty of the same offense? We know we shouldn't; yet we pay heed to suggestions which we *know* are going to get us into trouble. She allowed herself to be put into Satan's direct aim. She was a natural for him to use, to try to shame Our Lord Jesus in the Eucharist. She was little more than a teenager. This is not a criticism of teenagers, but to let us know how the Lord allows Himself to be vulnerable to even those beautiful children, He has brought out of their adolescent years. The problem, as we should have known, was that her great love for her *innamorato*,[4] was not being returned. She was not a happy camper.

We're sure, her parents warned her about her ill-fated relationship. And we're sure, she didn't pay them any attention. After all, she was an adult! She was old enough to sin; she had to be an adult. So she did the thing that all adults do,[5] she went to a sorceress, a witch, in Italian, a *Strega*. Didn't she realize, as she entered the lair of the witch, that she was heading for big trouble? Could she not remember all her teachers, the good nuns, and the priests warning her and her friends about witches, sorcerers? But she knew better; after all, she was an adult!

---

[4]love of her life
[5]This is what people (adults) thought could solve their problems

For the witch's part, she saw a chump coming. This was a natural. It was going to be like taking candy from a baby. She knew just how to work this child/woman. First she sympathized with her. *"What a terrible thing to do to a sweet young thing like you." "This isn't fair; it isn't right." "If only I could help you."* Look out; here it comes! The witch has the young girl hooked. *"I know! Go to the church. Be sure you don't arouse any suspicion. When it comes time to receive Communion, have the priest place the Host on your tongue, but don't swallow It. Take It out of your mouth, as soon as you can. Then bring It back to me. I will make you such a potion that you will never have to worry about your lover again. He will be in your clutches."*

We don't know, if the girl was a good girl, who had gotten caught up in her lust for her young man, or a bad girl, who would do anything to get her way. It doesn't really matter. She still had to know, she was doing the wrong thing. She knew that so much, she became very nervous as she entered the Church. Her hands shook, but she was determined in her resolve to do whatever it took to bring her lover back to her.

At Communion time, she went up to the Altar, looking like a little saint. She demurely genuflected, knelt at the Altar, serenely kept her head bowed, her eyes closed, and waited for the priest to come to her. When, at last, she received her Lord, her heart pounded so fiercely, she was sure everyone in the Church could hear it. She looked around. She was safe. No one was paying any attention to her. She left the Altar, and headed towards the back of the Church. She immediately took the consecrated Host out of her mouth, and placed It in a cloth handkerchief, she had brought for the occasion.

Now what? She headed for the sorceress. Sin had taken hold of her heart. She had let the *enemy* in, when she first went to the witch, and once in, he took over, consuming more and more of her, until she no longer had any sense of sin. She had blocked out her God, and she felt all alone. But something strange began to happen. As she was walking toward her home, her package began to get heavy. The farther she walked, the heavier it became.

What could it be? All that was in the folded-up kerchief was the Host. How much could that weigh? *What should I do with it?* she thought. She was supposed to bring it to the sorceress. *Now*, she was hesitant to bring it to her. Memories of her childhood came back to her of Sister and Religious Instructions. She knew she had done something wrong; she knew what she was about to do was even worse. She ran back to her home. There was safety there. She was no longer committed to the great sacrilege, she had consented to, when she went into the church that morning. It was one thing to say it; it was another to do it. She decided to hide the consecrated Host in a bread-trough.[6]

She waited a few days before going back into the trough. As she searched for the cloth which held the Body and Blood of Our Lord Jesus, her hands trembled. She had a great battle going on inside her, as to whether she should go ahead with this sacrilege, whether to bring the Host to the sorceress, or back to the Church, to the priest. All this became very academic when she opened the folded napkin. She gasped! She struggled to breathe! Her heart pounded so furiously, she was afraid it would come out of her mouth. What she beheld was not the Host, she had put inside the folded napkin, but the Host transformed into Living Flesh.

As soon as, she saw the Body and Blood of Our Lord Jesus transformed into actual Flesh, real Flesh, she knew what she had to do. She ran down to the Church, probably to the same priest who had given her Communion. He couldn't believe what she was telling him. But he vested up for Benediction, set out for the girl's house, accompanied by two Altar boys, carrying candelabras with lit candles, in solemn procession to return the Lord to His home.

---

[6]where they would knead the dough for the bread

[Italy is a very beautiful country. Perhaps their greatest
*trait is **inquisitiveness**. One year, when our family traveled alone
to all the shrines of Europe by rented car, Bob left the keys inside
the car, at the Plaza of St. Anthony in Padua. Within a few
moments, our predicament gathered a crowd, including
policemen, waiters, taxi-cab drivers, anybody and everybody who
was inquisitive. That constituted almost the whole town square.
They all watched, as the drama of the keys locked inside the car
took place.]*

The same occurred in this small town of Alatri. Now, just
picture the priest and Altar boys processing down the street, with
the young woman leading them to her house. It doesn't take
much imagination to envision the crowds which gathered,
following close behind them. By the time, they reached the girl's
home, hundreds of local people were with them. Word went out
throughout the entire crowd, speculating on what the priest and
the Altar boys were doing, processing to the young girl's house.
They all crammed the little paths to the house. When the girl
went inside with the priest, they pressed in, gaping through every
door and window.

The priest and the girl went to the place where she had laid
the cloth napkin, with the Host wrapped inside. There It was and
It had turned into Flesh! He picked It up reverently, and placed
the Host in a pyx. Then he carried the pyx reverently, close to
his heart, back through the crowd, down the path, through the
streets, to the church. It was placed in the Tabernacle.

Word spread throughout Italy. People from far and wide
descended on the little church of Alatri, to venerate the Real
Presence of Our Lord Jesus in the Miracle of the Eucharist. It
came immediately to the attention of the local Bishop, John the
Fifth. He investigated the Host turned to Flesh, and officially
recognized It to be a true Miracle, and Gift of Himself from Our
Lord Jesus to the people of the Diocese of Alatri. He sent the
paperwork on the Miracle, to the Pope, Gregory IX. On Easter
Sunday, in March of 1228, the pastor of the Church where the

Miracle was kept, presented and read the Papal Bull, written by His Holiness, Pope Gregory IX, affirming the Miracle of the Eucharist.

A beautiful Reliquary was magnificently forged, to house the Miracle of the Eucharist. It became a strong force, affirming the teaching of the Lateran Council (1215) on the Real

Papal Bull of Pope Gregory IX attesting to the Miracle

Presence of Jesus in the Eucharist, and was extremely instrumental in fighting the heresy of Berengarianism, which had taken a stronghold not only in the secular world, but within the Church, as well. As we said before, although Berengarius renounced his heretical teachings while he was still alive in 1078, his influence on the Church was still strongly felt in 1215, and was not finally dispelled and put down by the Councils of the Church until the 16th Century.

Miracle of the Eucharist of Alatri

Satan could not bear the idea of the Lord being *miraculously present,* to disprove all the lies he and his cohorts had been spreading throughout the Church. He kept pounding and pounding against the Miracle and the Real Presence of Jesus in the Eucharist. Due to his efforts and of those who had said yes to him and no to the Church, the world would go into an anti-Christian spin in the next century, followed by the Renaissance, which, although many claim to be a rebirth of art and intellect, from which the Church flourished from a standpoint of art, it caused such a break in the Church, such a separation that we have never fully recovered from it. Dedication to this Miracle, as well as the Real Presence of Jesus in the Eucharist, went downhill. There is not even a trace of a shrine of the little cottage where the Miracle took place. The Host turned Flesh maintained a fairly secure place in the Cathedral of Alatri. It held a prominent position in the Church. The Reliquary was processed through the town on special Feast Days, such as the Sunday after Easter, the Sunday after Pentecost, and Trinity Sunday. Less than forty years after this Miracle had occurred, the Miracle of the Eucharist of Bolsena/Orvieto took place, and in 1264, the Feast of Corpus Christi was instituted. The Miraculous Host was carried in Procession, for that Feast, from that time on.

A terrible thing happened in 1700. The then Bishop of Alatri, Joseph Guerra, wanted to pay honor to his countryman, Cardinal Camillo Cybo. He thought it would be a noble gesture to give him part of the most precious Treasure he had in his Diocese, the Miraculous Host turned Flesh in the Cathedral of Alatri. He took a Particle of the Host and sent it to the Church of Santa Maria degli Angeli in Terme, where the Cardinal wanted to be buried. Apparently, the Gift was not as important to the Cardinal and the people of Terme as it was to the people of Alatri. The incorrupt piece of Miraculous Flesh given to them, disappeared without a trace.

The remainder of the Miraculous Host is still in the Basilica-Cathedral of Alatri, to this day. It is kept in a sheltered area, so no harm can come to it. Sadly, veneration to the Miracle has been reduced, and the focal point of devotion is generally limited to the feast of Corpus Christi. This does not mean that there is not still a strong devotion among the people of Alatri. Reverence for the Real Presence of Our Lord Jesus in the Eucharist, and pride in the Gift, given to their little town over 700 years ago, is still strong.

Investigations of the Miraculous Host have taken place in 1866, and more recently in June, 1960. The Flesh has been described as follows: " *The relic gives the appearance of a piece of Real Flesh, that has taken a round form, very bright, almost translucent in appearance.* " It's very appropriate to hear that the Miraculous Host almost glows, It is so bright. The love Our Lord Jesus has for us is so strong, so bright, it bursts beyond the limitations put on man and material.

Why *did* He and *does* He do this, give us this ongoing Miracle? We think we've pretty well figured out why the Miracle was given to the people of that time. Berengarianism, Renaissance and everything in between, were designed to destroy the Church of Our Lord Jesus. But, we say to ourselves, what about today? Why is the Miracle still there in the Church, some 750 years later? Well, my brothers and sisters, if it's possible, we're in worse shape *spiritually* than we have ever been. Spirituality, family values, belief in our Faith, or in God at all, are all going through a very serious backslide. The reason, the Lord allows these Miracles to stay with us, is to bring us back to Him, back to Our Church, to strengthen us when everyone around us lacks respect for Our Lord in The Eucharist.

Jesus promised us, and He keeps His promise. He gives us Miracles of the Eucharist as part of that promise; He gives us ongoing Living Signs, so that we can stand up against the non-believers and critics of the Church and our Faith, and be strong and be proud of this Church of ours. He made a promise; "*The Gates of Hell will not prevail against my Church.*"[7] He will keep His promise.

---

[7]Matt 16:18

Florence - 1230 and 1595

Holy Clusters

Again, the Lord gives us a cluster of gifts: two Miracles of the Eucharist, *which came about in the same church, the Church of St. Ambrose in Florence.* The first miracle took place in December, 1230, while the other took place 365 years later, in March, 1595. The first Miracle had to do with the ***Blood of Our Lord Jesus in the Eucharist,*** while the latter Miracle had to do with the ***Body of Christ in the Consecrated Hosts.*** Both Miracles are still venerated in the church dedicated to St. Ambrose in Florence. In this out-of-the-way church, not even mentioned on the maps of Florence, resides two important messages to the people of God, today and always. Do not get discouraged, you will find the church near Piazza S. Ambrogio, in a triangle with the Cathedral and the Church of Santa Croce (Holy Cross).

But now come with us, as we share with you these magnificent Gifts, from a Faithful God to an often unfaithful people, two Miracles of the Eucharist; brought about to let us know how much He loves us, how much He is with us.

December 30, 1230 - The Blood of Christ

It was the end of the year, 1230. The people of God had just completed, with great enthusiasm, the 40 days of anticipation and preparation, Advent. They were filled with joy on the Feast of the Nativity, when Heaven and earth held their breath, and an explosion of hope and joy burst into the world, Our Lord Jesus coming to us in the most vulnerable Form possible, that of an Infant to His Mother Mary. Echoes of the Angels, heralding the

45

Savior of the world, filling the church, the Faithful could still feel the warmth of that special night, at Midnight Mass, and then during the day at all the Christmas Masses. Many had chosen to continue attending the Sacrifice of the Mass every day from Christmas Day through New Year's Day. The Mass which brings us to the Miracle of the Eucharist took place on the day before New Year's Eve, December 30.

The Church of St. Ambrose is blessed with very spiritual parishioners, at least it was in the year 1230. A Benedictine priest, Father Uguccione, who was spiritual director to the Nuns in the monastery, celebrated the Mass that day. After the Faithful had received Communion, during the Purification, the priest unintentionally left some of the Precious Blood in the Chalice. It's not known for sure why the Precious Blood was not consumed, or why the Chalice wasn't purified after the Mass. But, the Precious Blood was left in the crystal Chalice, *that* we do know. We're not sure if the Lord planned it, or just allowed it to happen, so He could use it to reach his children.

Whatever the case, the next morning, when the priest prepared to celebrate Mass, Father discovered the Blood was still in the Chalice, only it had turned into the deep crimson color of Human Blood. A wave of shock went through the Congregation as he shared what had happened. All the women in the Church of St. Ambrose saw the Miracle, as well as the Altar boys, as well as the curious people who ran into the Church, when the news of the Miracle spread like wildfire throughout the town.

As soon as, the Bishop was notified of the Miracle, he ordered the Chalice containing the Miracle, be brought to the Bishop's palace. It remained there for several weeks, under close observation. The Miracle was then returned to the Cloister under the custody of the Church of St. Ambrose. Eventually, all of Florence was privileged to see the wine turned into Blood. Immediately, Miracles took place for all those who looked upon this physical manifestation of the Blood of Jesus.

The Sacred Blood of the Savior was placed in a crystal

ampule, and then placed in a Tabernacle to securely protect It from anyone tampering with It. Responsibility for the safety of the Miracle was given to the republic of Florence by official decree, the College of Judges and Notaries declaring it the most precious Treasure of the Province. The Miracle would be given a position of honor on the Altar of the church, visible so that people visiting the church, could venerate and pray before It. It became a major place of pilgrimage for the people of Florence, and indeed, for all of the Tuscany area of Italy.

An eyewitness immediately wrote the account of the Miracle, Giovanni Villani. He paid particular attention to details, so that nothing would be missed, nor would any of the facts be considered myths or fantasies.

In 1266, Pope Clement IV issued a Papal Bull, declaring the authenticity of the Miracle of the Eucharist of Florence. For five centuries, up to 1779, the Faithful of Florence provided the financing and labor needed to bring about yearly celebrations of the Feast of the Miracle.

Around the end of the 13th century the Miracle was further authenticated. Wishing to bestow additional honor upon the Miracle, Pope Clement IV solemnly requested the Church of St. Ambrose be redesigned and reconstructed in the Roman-Gothic style.

Pope Boniface IX, in 1399 bestowed the same *plenary indulgence of the Portziuncola* to the Faithful, as Clement IV had, before him.

The Chapel of the Miracle was completely restored in 1936, and once again, the Faithful came and celebrated!

In 1980, there was a grand celebration for the 750th anniversary of the Miracle of the Blood. Again, the Faithful all came and joined in, honoring Our Lord in this ongoing Miracle. We are at the close of the 20th century, and at times, we feel the world has gone mad, and there seems to be little hope for the Church, for the world, and then we remember these Miracles and how the Lord cannot be killed, or wiped from the face of the earth, and we have hope, once more. Our Pope John Paul II calls these times, of the 90's, a *Culture of Death*. Well, all we have to do is to pray to Life Himself. We pray that He will send us a sign that will straighten the world out, before it is too late. And this we pray - for ourselves, our children, our grandchildren and those who will follow. Amen!

Miracles, through the intercession of the Miracle

The citizens of Florence continued to have a deep devotion to the Miracle. In 1340, a plague struck Florence, claiming many victims. The people cried out for help. Who did they turn to? They carried the Miracle of the Blood of Christ in solemn procession, petitioning Our Lord for His mercy. The Lord rewarded their faith in Him. The plague ended, as quickly as it had begun.

The Faithful venerate the Miracle of the Eucharist of Florence

Almost 400 years later, in 1729, an earthquake struck the city of Florence. Devastated, now a new generation of Faithful turned to the Miracle, kneeling, as their ancestors had done for centuries, before their Lord in this miraculous Form, begging Him to save them from the rumbling giant (earthquake) who had not stopped venting his angry wrath upon them. The Lord Who is our Shepherd answered the families, of not only the people of that time, but in the name of those who had preceded them, the Faithful of all the centuries. The earthquake ceased its trembling. The giant was dead!

Is it any wonder that the incorrupt Blood of Our Lord Jesus has been kept in a reliquary from that time until this, the Faithful venerating the Miracle, continuing to pray and petition Our Lord in this miraculous Form?

Why did the Lord choose this time to bring us a Miracle of the Eucharist in 1230? What was happening at that time in the Church, in the world in 1230? The heresies of Berengarianism, Albigensianism and Waldensianism[1] had been running rampant. **St. Francis of Assisi** (1181-1226), Founder of the Friars Minor, the Franciscan Order, and **St. Dominic Guzmán** (1171-1221), founder of the Dominicans, *Watchdogs of God*, had been given the mandate by the Lord to reform the Church of the Middle Ages. In addition, the Lord formed these two groups into His *Army against Heresies and Heretics*. Although from Spain, St. Dominic and his followers evangelized southern France and fought the heretics of that area. Our Lady appeared to St. Dominic and gave him the Rosary, which I am sure he prayed, as he fought the enemies of the Church. Is the Lord now telling us to turn to *the Rosary, the Life of Jesus and Mary*[2] as a most powerful prayer weapon against heretics and heresies threatening to destroy our Church and our families, today?

In that time of crisis and controversy, coupled with confusion, the Lord raised up, through these two Religious Orders, such powerful Men in our Church as:

St. Anthony of Padua (1195-1231), **Franciscan** and Doctor of the Church, who earned the title: "*Hammer of Heretics*" fought heresies in Italy and France, as well as taught the Franciscans how to defend the Faith, and

St. Thomas Aquinas (1225-1274), **Dominican** and Doctor of the Church, one of the greatest Defenders of the Faith, especially the Eucharist, one of the greatest minds our Church has ever had. You can see, there was a great urgency for Defenders of the Faith, and in particular, the Eucharist. *St. Anthony* is known for defending the Eucharist against the heretics in Rimini, Italy,

---

[1]Read about these heresies in Bob and Penny Lord's book, *Scandal of the Cross and Its Triumph*

[2]Read more about *the Rosary, the Life of Jesus and Mary* in Bob and Penny Lord's book of the same name.

which brought about the Miracle of the Eucharist of the Donkey,[3] while *St. Thomas Aquinas* was called to write the Liturgy for the Feast of Corpus Christi, and subsequently called to Paris by St. Louis, King of France, to defend the Real Presence of Jesus in the Eucharist convincing the University Students of Paris and the world, that the Lord is *really* present in the Eucharist.

Add to that the Miracle of the Eucharist of Bolsena/Orvieto (1263),[4] which Pope Urban IV attested with his own eyes, the Miracle of the Eucharist of Daroca, Spain (1239),[5] which was brought to Pope Urban IV while he was still in Orvieto, giving him another reason to write the Papal Bull, *Il Transiturus*, which instituted the Feast of Corpus Christi in 1264.

Are we in a time of crisis, controversy and confusion? What is God saying, today? Are you part of the Army, He is forming to defend His Church, today? Are you among the number who will be honored in Heaven as true sons and daughters of the Father? Do we have plagues, famine, earthquakes and devastations of all kinds? Who do *we* turn to?

We have to stop and take a look at the Power of our God, and how He manifests that Power when the Church is in need. These miracles really happened. We're just reporting them. We're taking sections of Church History, which are important enough on their own: St. Francis, St. Dominic, St. Anthony, St. Thomas Aquinas, Miracles of the Eucharist of the early Thirteenth century, and the reason for these Miracles: the heresies that were being spread throughout Europe. Then we're putting them together, to show how the Lord is using His soldiers, how He is setting up His Battlefield, and how He is defeating the enemy with ease. *What a mighty God we have!*

---

[3]Read our first book, *This Is My Body, This Is My Blood, Miracles of the Eucharist - Book I*, Page 165

[4]*This Is My Body, This Is My Blood, Miracles of the Eucharist - Book I*, Page 37

[5]*This Is My Body, This Is My Blood, Miracles of the Eucharist - Book I*, Page 120

In retrospect, we see God and the devil sitting at a huge chess table. Satan is pulling out all his top pieces, his heresies, and heretics. God is using His best weapons, the Miracles of the Eucharist, the Saints, an apparition by Our Lady in Loreto, Italy. Towards the end of the Thirteenth Century, God brought to Loreto, Italy, through His servant Mary, The Holy House of Nazareth, which has continued to be a source of power from that time, till today. Before Second Vatican Council commenced, it was consecrated to Our Lady at Loreto by Pope John XXIII on October 4, 1962. In his pontificate, our Pope John Paul II has visited the Holy House *twice* in his pontiff; he said the following of the Holy House in 1994, the 700th anniversary of the Translation of the Holy House to Loreto:

*"....what the function of the great shrines, **especially Loreto,** should be in today's new religious context; they should not be on the fringe or accessories but, on the contrary, essential places, places where people go to obtain grace even before they obtain favors. Today, to respond to the new challenges of secularization, **shrines must be places of evangelization,** true and proper **citadels of the faith,** in the overall sense which these words had on Jesus' lips when He said, 'Repent, and believe in the Gospel.'"*[6]

We have truly been given Power by our God.

The Second Miracle, March 24, 1595 - The Body of Christ

The Lord brings us to March 24, 1595, Good Friday,[7] bringing to a close the season of Lent. We are still in the Church of Saint Ambrose. Good Friday was a most solemn day; the Passion was read, and Communion was given to the Faithful for the last time until Our Lord would rise from the dead on Easter Sunday. In those days, there was no question of *"in memory of"*. A funeral bier was erected on the Altar. A casket containing an image of the crucified Christ was there. Mounds and mounds of flowers draped the tomb and covered the Altar. The only light in

---

[6]Letter of His Holiness John Paul II on the 7th Centenary of Loreto, 1994
[7]in this particular year

the church were votive candles burning around the casket. Christ died on this day! It was obvious, the priest and the Faithful were remembering what had happened almost 1600 years ago.

[Tears still come to our eyes, as we remember a Good Friday in Padua, quite a few years ago. Mothers and grandmothers, dressed in mourning, filed up to the Crucifix, lying on a velvet pillow, and kneeling, their children beside them, they explained what it all meant and Who it was we were mourning. They, like the people of Florence in 1595, took everything about this day very seriously.]

Back to 1595 and Good Friday in the Church of Saint Ambrose. During the service, before Holy Communion was distributed to the Faithful, a cinder from a candlestick fell onto the Altar Cloth, and a fire broke out. Panic set in! The entire church was screaming, not knowing which way to run, to help or to escape. The priests and many lay people, ran at once, to get something to extinguish the fire, above all to save the Blessed Sacrament. There was a great deal of confusion. One of the priests knocked over a pyx, filled with Consecrated Hosts, ready to be brought to the sick after the Good Friday service. When it hit the floor, the pyx opened, and six Consecrated Hosts fell out. The intense heat did not consume them, but instead caused them to shrink and curl. But an amazing thing also happened. The word that is used in the Italian text is *"re-united"*. More than once, in the account of the miracle, the word *"re-united"* is used. *The Hosts were reunited, became one! The Consecrated Hosts were actually bonded together, like steel!* Although they turned brown from the excessive heat, they were still the Lord in His Body, Blood, Soul and Divinity in their midst, and through His Presence, so assuredly through Divine intervention, a feeling of awe spread through the congregation. After the fire was extinguished, the Hosts were placed on a paten on the Altar, so everyone could adore their Lord in the Eucharist, miraculously saved before their eyes. The climate of the parishioners changed *immediately* from one of panic to one of reverence for their Lord, so Present to them, their God above all other gods.

Word spread throughout Florence, as it had, the first time the Lord had given this church, St. Ambrose, a Miracle of the Eucharist, in 1230. Had there been those in 1595, who had not believed with all their hearts that the Lord had truly manifested Himself in a Miraculous way in 1230? After all, it had been over 350 years ago. Had they thought and possibly verbalized: "Who knows what had really happened?" Maybe! But when

Chapel of the Miracle of the Eucharist of Florence in the Church of St. Ambrose

Miracle of the Eucharist of Florence - 1595

the Faithful, and indeed, everyone in Florence, were told about this *second* Miracle, pilgrims flocked to the church in droves to see the new Gift, the Lord had given them.

A beautiful Tabernacle was created to host the Miracle of the Eucharist. It was placed in a special chapel in the Church of St. Ambrose. Some thirty-odd years later, in 1628, the Bishop of Florence examined the Miraculous Hosts, and declared them incorrupt,[8] and ordered a proper reliquary to be designed which would

---

[8]Free from decay. Usually, in the instance of a Consecrated Host, made of unleavened bread, after a time, the bread will decay, at which point, we believe the Real Presence of Our Lord Jesus leaves the decomposed bread. But in this instance, decay has not set in to this day.

do honor to *both* Miracles of the Eucharist. In 1907, another test was done, and it was determined beyond a shadow of a doubt that the Host were *miraculously* preserved.

Each year, in May, there is a big celebration, in which the Miracle of the Eucharist is exposed for all the Faithful to venerate. People come from all parts of Florence and surrounding areas, to pray before the Miracle of the Two Miracles of the Eucharist that Our Lord Jesus gave them here, in 1230 and again in 1595. Devotion has continued, and the church is kept bright with the candles, lit by the pilgrims who come to the shrine, year round. Our Faith remains alive and strong, through beautiful manifestations of our Lord Jesus in the Miracles of the Eucharist, and His Mother Mary in the many apparitions she makes, and most importantly, through the faith of the people of God.

Why 1595? Why Florence?

The Sixteenth century was one of the most destructive centuries, the Church has had to endure, till now! She got hit from all sides, with *any scandal, every half truth and untruth*, the enemy could fabricate, turning good, holy people into confused heretics. It began with the first really strong attack against the Church, through Martin Luther. German princes wanted to steal Papal lands, originally gifted to the Papacy by grateful Kings and Queens who had had their petitions answered by the Lord and His Mother.

Their schemes were realized, through the disobedience of one of the Church's sons, an Augustinian priest, Martin Luther. One of his own followers, a renowned Protestant professor from Berlin, Professor Seeberg said of Luther, *"Luther strode through his century like a demon, crushing under his feet what a thousand years had venerated."* The century he was talking about was this Sixteenth Century, the same century as the Miracle of the Eucharist. In another instance, the same professor said of Luther, *"In him dwelt 'the Superhuman' or*, in Nietzche's philosophy, the *'Übermensch'*, who dwells *'beyond moral good and evil.'"* That's how we began the century, folks. It went downhill from there. The deception, spread by Luther and his political allies, caused a major split in Germany. By 1555, it became officially a divided country, half Catholic and half Lutheran.

Luther was followed by Calvin, who took up where Luther left off, surpassing him, using hate coupled with violence against the Church. He was the generation after Luther, which would bring him into the last half of the Sixteenth century, the time of the Miracle. What Calvin managed to do was to take the Protestant revolution outside of Germany, and spread it widely and wildly over all of Europe. He was a vicious, violent enforcer of his own brand of *Protest*-ant philosophy. Calvin spread his teaching on predestination (the select few are born predestined to be saved, and the others are born condemned to eternal damnation), using one of the most ruthless blood baths as his means of eliminating his enemies and *persuading* those who rebelled. Calvin, with his stern, unloving teachings never won any popularity contests, but by force, he was able to ram Protestantism across the face of Europe.

About the same time as the enemy was enlisting Martin Luther to do his dirty work against the Church, he was aiming his poison arrow of disobedience at King Henry VIII. There are Protestant scholars who admit that the Protestant revolution, or Reformation (as they prefer to call it), was not successful. I mean, let's face it, when you have to use the worst forms of violence and murder to get your point across, people are not going to embrace your philosophy, openly. Many of the heads of Europe were not embracing Protestantism. The simple faith-filled Catholics didn't even know what they were selling. *The revolution failed!* It wasn't until Henry VIII, who had defended the Church against Heresy, became a heretic himself, going against the very Pope who had awarded him the title: *"Defender of the Faith."* This Faith he had sworn to defend, this title of *Defender*...he so treasured, Henry would give up, for what? A woman, whom he would later have beheaded, so that he can marry another? He would turn against the Pope and the Church, he so dearly loved, because the Pope would not legalize his adultery by allowing him to divorce his first wife, Catherine of Aragon, and remarry at will, as his libido[9] dictated. Henry VIII's crime against the people of God was worse, in our opinion than Luther's, because his only justification was his own self-gratification, his gluttony that did not stop at excessive eating but went on to include all forms of perversion. He murdered his best friends, when they would not swear allegiance to him, as head of the Church, instead of to the rightful descendent of the Chair of Peter, the Pope. When they had to choose between loyalty to him and life or loyalty to their Church and death, they chose death. Some of the first Martyrs of Protestantism who gave their lives during this time, were **St. John Fisher** (1535) and **St. Thomas More** (1535), as well as a group, the Church has labeled: **"The English Martyrs"**, those thousands who went to their death in the Sixteenth Century, rather than turn against their Church. It also heralded the beginning of Martyrdom for the Irish people, which has not seen the end yet, some 400 years later. The ego of one man caused a break in the Church which had perpetuated down through the centuries, until Anglicans and Episcopalians, began to realize that their church, founded on disobedience, has bred a new kind of dissent, one that they, like the English Martyrs before them, cannot be party to; and they are returning to the Church and to the chair of Peter that King Henry VIII once defended, before the enemy took over in his life.

The Council of Trent was begun in 1545 and ended in 1563. It concerned itself with reform of the Church, addressing the unrest which could cause such an attack on the Church from so many areas, and condemned Luther, Calvin, Henry VIII, Elizabeth I, and all their teachings, as well as other enemies of the Church, who decided that the in-thing was to take potshots at the Church. It was a very necessary council, in that it affirmed Pope Leo X's

---

[9]The sexual urge or instinct

condemnation of the teachings of Martin Luther. It was the Church's official answer to the Protestant Reformation. And we wish that that was the end of it; but Jesus is still walking to Calvary, carrying a heavy Cross laden down by men's sins and selfish desires. And His Mother stands beneath the Cross and cries.

A Methodist Minister recently wrote that the *Protest* part of Protestant soon took over what had been termed *The Reformation*, as one group protested over one thing or the other, broke off and formed another denomination; and then a group broke off from that new denomination, protesting against one thing or the other and formed a different denomination; and so, as history sadly reports: one group after another protested and broke off from other groups, forming other denominations, until the precious Cross of Jesus Christ was shattered, splintering into tens of thousands of denominations or differences.

While the Sixteenth century gave us Renaissance, in addition to the above, and with Renaissance, a strong tear in the fabric of the Church, which has never been mended, the Lord gave us **St. Ignatius** of Loyola, and his Jesuits, the Company of Jesus, **St. Angela Merici**, and the Ursuline Sisters, **St. Teresa** of Avila and **St. John of the Cross**, reformers of the Carmelite order, **a powerful apparition** by our Lady in the new World, Guadalupe in Mexico, in 1531, as well as **Miracles of the Eucharist**. The Lord always balances the books.

There is consolation, in knowing what has gone on before us. As we research the Miracles of the Eucharist, as we track the history of the Church and of the world at those times of crisis, when Our Lord deems it wise and good to give us Miracles of the Eucharist, Apparitions by Our Mother Mary, Saints and Other Powerful Men and Women in our Church, we see that the we are never alone. The battle is being fought from both ends. God is not leaving us here, and going off somewhere else. We don't necessarily see it now, but it's happening. Someone or some group of people who *live* the Church, in the next century, or the century after that, will look back at us, at all the terrible things that we've been subjected to. Then they're going to look at all the Saints the Lord has given us, apparitions by Our Lady, and Miracles of the Eucharist in this century. And while we may be bemoaning our outcast state, they'll be marveling at how the Lord has taken such great care of us.

Who will those Saints be, those Powerful Men and Women who will defend our Church, and protect her from her enemies? The other day, we were at daily Mass at a beautiful country church in Picayune, Mississippi. We saw two young people go up to the front of the church to receive Communion. They knelt before they received the Body of Christ. You could just *feel* a great reverence about them. They knew *Who* they were receiving, *Who* was consuming them, and how much He *loved* them. They could not have been more than twelve or thirteen years old. This is the future of our Church. These are the Powerful Men and Women of the next generation. Who are the Saints of this generation? *Will you be among their number, when the Saints go marching in?* We love you.

Valvasone - 1294

Don't you know I'm there?

The Miracle of which we write is credited to the town of Valvasone, Italy, near Venice. However, it didn't actually take place there. It happened in a little village in the province of Venice, called Gruaro, ten kilometers from Portogruaro. The Miracle occurred in the year 1294. There were many Heavenly movements going on in the Holy cluster of the Adriatic Sea in 1294. On December 8, 1294, Our Lady moved the Holy House from Yugoslavia across the Adriatic Sea to Loreto, Italy. The Lord was working powerfully in that area of the world at that time!

The little village of Gruaro had a mission church called San Giusto. It was a very small church, no bigger than a large chapel. A lady of the town volunteered, each week, to wash the Altar linens. She considered it a great privilege, to be allowed to touch the cloths, purificator, corporal, and Altar cloth, as well as the priest's vestments. Washing them was a special honor for her. And so on this one morning, probably Monday, our laundress went over to the church, and stripped it of all its linens, so that she could have them washed, dried and ironed in time for the Mass the next Sunday. She brought everything to the public wash-house in the center of the village. She looked forward to her day of working for the Lord.

She had done this many times, but never, for one minute, took it for granted. She had a proprietary attitude about it, to the point of possessing it! Whenever she was not available, she made sure to get a substitute, to handle her job *temporarily*, to insure, it would not be given away to someone else. She had to fight pride. Most days, she even wished her friends would be at the public wash house, so they could see her washing the linens of the church. She would never brag about doing this important job, but if anyone saw her, well, she couldn't *deny* it.

On this one day, she began her *delightful* chore of washing the church linens. We're not sure what sequence she used in doing her task, whether she did the smaller items first, like the corporal and purificator, or the larger, like the Altar cloth and alb. Whatever the case, at a given point, she began to wash the Altar cloth. She was rubbing it between her hands, to build up enough lather to make the cloth sparkling white. Remember, we're talking about the thirteenth century now. She didn't have the benefit of detergents, like we have in our modern laundry rooms.

She rubbed the cloth as she had done many times before. Only this time, something strange happened. She could see a red stain appearing, where there had never been a stain. She kept rubbing and rubbing; but the more she rubbed, the more pronounced the stain became. She couldn't understand what was going on. It had never happened before. The strange manifestation began to change. What had begun as a red mark now became *blood gushing* from the Altar cloth.

She inspected the cloth. What could be causing this to happen? She looked and looked, her hands becoming bloody now. She became desperate. People began looking at her. What was going on? Finally, in one of the pleats of the Altar cloth, she found a Host, that had been left in the Altar cloth unknowingly. It was the source of the bleeding. This is where the blood was coming from! She realized what was happening. *Our Lord Jesus was bleeding all over the Altar cloth.* She scooped up the Altar cloth, corporal, and all the church vestments, and ran in great haste to the rectory. She was hysterical, raving, almost like a woman possessed. The priest ran out to meet her. She showed him the Altar cloth, full of fresh blood. She tried to tell him what had happened, but the words wouldn't come out. All he could hear was babble. Finally, she reached into the Altar cloth, and took out the small Particle of the Host, which was still bleeding. The priest made the sign of the Cross, and went down on his knees. He prayed, silently.

He got up, ran to the church, and vested up. He had one of the villagers sound the bells, as if Mass was about to begin. The people came out of their houses curiously. This was not Sunday. Why were the bells ringing? They walked slowly over to the church. When the woman and the priest explained what had happened, the villagers picked up on it. Many went down on their knees. Others cried out confessions, thinking it was the end of the world. Others ran from house to house, telling everyone in the little village of Gruaro what had happened.

Meanwhile, the priest, now vested up, with Altar boys carrying candles, processed into the church with the bloody Altar cloth in his hands. The Host had stopped bleeding by this time, but It clung to the Altar cloth. Everybody in the village came into the church, even those who had not been attending Mass, for years. They wanted to see what was happening, and what it meant. They all knelt, and took part in prayers, in honor of the Blessed Sacrament.

The local parish priest advised the Bishop of Concordia. He had a tribunal called and sent a committee out to the little church in Gruaro, to investigate the *claimed* miracle. Within one visit, they agreed that it was authentic, and the bishop gave it his blessing. However, he wanted the miracle to be transferred to the Cathedral in Valvasone. The people didn't think it was a good idea. They argued, if the Lord had wanted the miracle in Valvasone, He would have had It come there, in the first place. The miracle happened in Gruaro, and while It did not actually take place in the Church of St. Giusto, It came about while the cleaning woman was doing church work, linens *belonging* to the

Church of St. Giusto. That's as good as, It being manifested in the church; it was unimportant that It transpired at the public wash house.

A furor arose, which could not be resolved amicably, between the bishop and the local people. It got so impossible the whole matter had to go before the Apostolic Tribunal in Rome. The villagers of Gruaro didn't think they stood a chance. And they were right. The custodianship of the Miracle of the Eucharist was assigned to the Diocese of Valvasone. But there's a slight catch. In accordance with the Lateran Council of 1215, the following had to be done by the Diocese. A *new church* would have to be built, in which the Miracle of the Eucharist could be safeguarded. But, that's not all. The church had to be big enough to hold the large groups of the Faithful, who would come to the church to venerate the Miracle of the Eucharist. It would have to be a *fairly large church*; because another task of the Diocese, in exchange for the privilege of having custodianship of the Miracle, was that they would have to *encourage veneration of the Miracle* and the devotion of Eucharistic Adoration. We're not sure, if the people in the small village of Gruaro weren't finally satisfied that this was a job for a big diocese, not a little village.

A little over a hundred years later, in 1412, records show that a beautiful gilded Tabernacle was ordered to be the home of the Miraculous Host and Altar cloth which was reserved, not in any new, exquisite church, but in the parish church of Our Lady of Grace in Valvasone. From that, everyone was able to deduce that the new, big church had not yet been built. In 1454, Pope Nicholas V issued the first *Papal Bull*, in favor of the Miracle of the Eucharist of Valvasone. In it, he ordered that *a new church* be built, and that the title and privileges of the Miracle which had been assigned to the small parish church in Gruaro, be transferred to the church of Our Lady of Grace in Valvasone, until such time as the new, magnificent church is built.

In 1584, after the Council of Trent, there was a visit made by the Apostolic Nuncio, Bishop Cesare Nores to the Miracle of

*Reliquary of the Miracle
of the Eucharist of Valvasone*

the Eucharist. In his report, he maintained that there was a reliquary made of gilded copper, in which rested the bloodstained Altar cloth, and a bloodstained consecrated Host. There is no mention of the new church at this time. We know it was finally finished, but there is no date given, as to when it was built. It would seem like the people of Gruaro could have kept the Miracle of the Eucharist until the new church was built, especially if it was going to take over 150 years. But that's our weakness for justice. Had that happened, when the Diocese of Valvasone had been finally ready to put it into a new church, the parishioners of San Giusto in Gruaro probably wouldn't have wanted to give It up. When the new church was finally finished, it was called, *Church of the Most Holy Body of Christ*, and is now the Parochial seat of the region.

In 1755 a proper, beautiful silver reliquary was made in Venice by a well-known silversmith. It was fashioned, in 1755, after an antique monstrance of the Sixteenth Century. It rests on a silver pedestal, and sits majestically in a prominent position in the church.

In 1894, the Bishop of Concordia, who later became the Archbishop of Udine, inspected the Miracle of the Eucharist. At that time, he testified that the Host had decomposed, turning into floury dust, while the Altar cloth still had the blood stains which it had, from the very beginning, in 1294. The reliquary is on display in *Parrocchia del Santissimo Corpo di Cristo* (the parish church of the Most Holy Body of Christ), in Valvasone, near

Venice.

In a Eucharistic Congress held in Udine in 1972, it was reported that in Italy, there are *fifteen* Miracles of the Eucharist that still had something visible, which the Faithful could venerate. The Miracle of the Eucharist of Valvasone was one of them, listed.

As we know, there is a teaching, and a reason for all the Miracles of the Eucharist. We believe that the Miracle of the Eucharist of Valvasone is not only for the time it was given to the Church but for our time, now, to fight the new/old heresies of today.

Church of the Most Holy Body of Christ - Valvasone, Italy

The heresy at the time of the Miracle, *Berengarianism*, began in 1054 and continued up to and including the 13th century,

Interior of the Church of the Most Holy Body of Christ - Valvasone, Italy

spreading its deadly doubts on the Real Presence of Jesus in the Eucharist, heretically contending that *"while the bread and wine in the Eucharist become Christ's Body and*

Blood, they do so figuratively, remaining substantially or physically what they are.[1] Now, this Miracle showed that the Host bled. Bread does not bleed; Flesh, Human Flesh bleeds. Although the Host decomposed, after 600 years, a Miracle in itself,[2] the Lord chose to leave His Precious Blood visible on the cloth, the Altar cloth. Is the Lord not affirming the Sacrifice of the Mass, the ongoing Sacrifice of the Cross[3] for us today, when some priests are removing Crucifixes from our churches, de-emphasizing the Sacrifice, the Victim-Priest and His Presence on the Altar for the Celebration aspect of the Mass? Are they stressing hospitality and fellowship, the horizontal action of the community at the cost of the Vertical relationship of our becoming one in Him, as he is one with the Father, our Lord Jesus, the Son offering Himself to the Father through His priest? The horizontal line is a negative; it is only when we add the vertical that it becomes the full cross.

Is this why we are bringing this Miracle to you? Did Jesus bleed for us on the Cross? Did He bleed once more for us, through this Miracle? How many Miracles are necessary? How many times, does He have to bleed, that we might believe? Is this Miracle for us, for you, for someone you love? Will you stand idly by, and tell Jesus, He bled and died for nothing?

---

[1]a quotation from the synod of 1054 in which Pope Leo IX condemned the heresy and its author, the priest Berengarius.

[2]Bread will decompose or become moldy after days exposed and powdery after maybe at the most weeks or months. This was after 600 years.

[3]Read more about this in the chapters on the Mass in this book

Aniñon - 1300

How Much do I love you?

Spain is a country of Saints and Soldiers, a melting pot with as many different faces of its people as there are landscapes, a land persecuted and occupied only to rise stronger than before, and to give glory to the Lord and His Church. Spain, a land of controversy, a land of holy clusters and holy Saints, is also a land favored by the Lord with Miracles of the Eucharist[1] and an Apparition by the Mother of God while she was still alive.[2] For the purposes of this book, we want to share with you the Miracle of the Eucharist of Aniñon.

Fifteen kilometers to the Northwest of Calatayud we travel to the village of Aniñon and the church of the Miracle which rises high into the sky, almost as if trying to reach up to Heaven. As we have experienced, in our travels in Europe, the church in most villages is at the highest point of the town, looking down over all her children, sometimes weeping as Jesus did when He cried over Jerusalem:

> *"Jerusalem, Jerusalem, you who kill the prophets and stone those sent to you, how many times I yearned to gather your children together, as a hen gathers her young under her wings, but you were unwilling!"[3]*

---

[1] you can learn of other Miracles of the Eucharist, in Spain, in Bob and Penny Lord's first book on Miracles of the Eucharist: *"This is My Body, This is My Blood, Miracles of the Eucharist"* - Book I

[2] Read about our Lady being transported by the Angels to Zaragoza, Spain while she was still alive, in Bob and Penny Lord's book: *"Heavenly Army of Angels"*

[3] Matt 23:37

In our other books we have written about the Saracen occupation of many nations, for hundreds of years. Spain was one of those who suffered the longest by the occupation of Muslims, 700 years, and the greatest, because of their great love for Our Lord Jesus and His Mother Mary. In many churches, we have visited, you can see the influence of the Saracens or that of the Moors in their architecture. When you enter the church of the Miracle, there is evidence that this church may have been formerly a *mosque*,[4] with the base of the bell tower resembling a minaret.[5] Nestled in the Choir, there was a niche with a series of glazed enameled tiles indicating, it once housed the Koran.[6]

Suddenly, your eyes and heart rivet upon a splendid side chapel on the right side of the church. Towering high above it is a spacious dome, as if rising from its walls, causing your mind and heart to soar *upward* to Heaven and our Heavenly Family. But then your attention turns to *the* Treasure among the many treasures in the chapel, the silver reliquary which houses the *"Holy Mystery"*. In 1980, thieves broke into the church and stole most of the treasures in the chapel, but they left the reliquary with the Holy Mystery behind, judging it not of any monetary value, as it was *only* made of silver. Thank You, Lord that you have withheld from these thieves the *Real* Gift *"more precious than silver, more costly than gold, more beautiful than diamonds,"* that of Our Jesus in the Eucharist.

The documentation, attesting to the authenticity of this Miracle, can be found in the church, till today. There is also a book: *"Aragon, realm of Christ and gift of the Most Holy Mary"* written by P. Faci, a foremost historian of his time, which tells

---

[4]a Moslem temple or place of worship

[5]a minaret is where the sounding of the call to prayer comes 5 times a day, resounding throughout an area.

[6]The sacred book of the Moslems, revelations and commands which the followers of Islam believe the Angel Gabriel gave to Mohammed. (for more on the Moslems - read *"Scandal of the Cross and Its Triumph"* by Bob and Penny Lord which speaks of the battles fought and won by Mother Church.

the history of the church. He used Lanuza's book *"History of the church in Aragon"* which was published in 1639, as reference. Lanuza's writings were based on documents dating back to the 14th century, which included testimonies of the Miracle from reliable witnesses who had lived at the time of the Miracle.

The Miracle

Around the year 1300, a raging fire ravished the church of *"Our Lady of Catillo"* of Aniñon, completely destroying it. All that remained of the splendid church were mounds of ashes, and smoking cinders from what had been walls and foundation of the church. Not even the main Altar and Our Lord's home, the Tabernacle, were spared. When we first researched this Miracle and read that the Tabernacle was destroyed, our hearts sank as if they would break. Oh Lord, did You burn in the fire? This time, Our Father in Heaven would not allow His Son to be hurt. Although the Tabernacle was enveloped by scorching flames, reducing it to nothing but smoldering, twisted fragments of what once was, the flames respected the Lord in His Blessed Sacrament. The pall and the corporal which were wrapped around the six consecrated Hosts in the Tabernacle were only scorched in a few places. But the five Hosts within, were found to be *bleeding*, with the sixth Host *stuck* to the pall.

That Host resembled yeast! Jesus tells us in the Gospel: *"I am the Way, the Truth and the Life. No one comes to the Father except through Me."* [7] Is Jesus not telling us, in this passage that He is the Way to the Kingdom? Jesus tells us that *He is the Bread of Life.* [8] He who eats His Body and drinks His Blood will have life in him. The consecrated Host that was miraculously saved from the fire; is Our Lord Who offers Himself at every Sacrifice of the Mass, the ongoing Sacrifice of the Cross. [9] We believe that the Lord, in leaving this Host unharmed but in the

[7]John 14:6
[8]John 6:35
[9]unbloody Sacrifice of the Cross

appearance of yeast was saying once again, *What you are about to receive is Me. I am offering Myself on this Altar to the Father for you and yours. And the fires of hell will not touch you.* A new church was constructed, more magnificent and majestic than the first. The corporal and the pall were placed in a pyx and reserved in the Tabernacle. The Good News that Our Lord had visited His people, and left His Miraculous sign in the church, soon spread over the plains of Spain. Among many of the Faithful who came to pay homage to the Miracle of the Eucharist, was the King of Aragon and Navarre, John II. King John II was the father of King Ferdinand, known as the Catholic King, husband of the Catholic Queen Isabella. King John II not only faithfully venerated the Holy Mystery but was one of the famous, influential people who fostered devotion to the Miracle.

Because of his deep love and ardor for the Miracle, King John II asked the people of Aniñon for the gift of the Pall upon which the Host had adhered and taken on the appearance of yeast. The people agreed and the King brought it to the Cathedral of Valencia. There, the Faithful have paid homage to Jesus Who is present in the Miracle, alongside the Relic of the Holy Grail[10] of the Last Supper.

The Bishops of Tarazona came to the Church in Aniñon on different occasions to visit and adore the Lord in this Miracle. At those times, they could see that the Blood still saturated the corporal. Upon close investigation of the Miracle, they concluded that the Blood that had soaked the corporal was fresh, like freshly shed blood, as blood that had just flowed out of a human body.[11] Another interesting fact is that the pall and the corporal have remained completely intact, although cloth of this type, from this period, should be threadbare, having deteriorated over the centuries. These Miraculous cloths have been known to emit a

---

[10]believed to be the actual Chalice which contained the wine which Our Lord changed into Blood, instituting the Mass at the Last Supper.
[11]Lanuza's account

heavenly fragrance, when the Faithful have come to venerate them.

On November 23rd of the year 1613, the Vicar General of Tarazona approved the Miracle, attesting that it was due to *Divine* intervention that this had come about. He further proclaimed that the anniversary of the Miracle would be celebrated, the third Sunday of September, each year.

"Holy Mystery, help me."

Devotion began immediately. But did the people start to take the Miracle for granted after a few years, not turning to Our Lord in the Eucharist for His help? Had they forgotten so soon, the gift they had been given? Were they looking to man, instead of to their Lord? Did the Lord need to bring about another Miracle to prove to His children that He is still Really with us, *Body, Blood, Soul and Divinity*?

At any rate, on October 2nd, 1618, something was to happen in Aniñon, that would reinforce belief in the power of Jesus in the Eucharist, through this Miracle present among them. At between 11 and 12 in the morning, on this brisk day, a young girl only 17 years old was walking in the plaza of the town, when the wall of a home on the main square, collapsed, burying her under the rubble. She didn't know what had happened, only that a tiny stream of light was streaming through a just as tiny opening in the huge mass, threatening to crush her. It was the sun warming her, assuring her, she was still alive. She prayed:

"Holy Mystery and Holy Corporal of Aniñon, please help me. Send help!"

She kept praying, but it seemed to no avail. A couple of hours passed, when at last, she heard voices. *"Oh,"* she thought, *"my prayers have been answered!"* But, her joy was short-lived, for she overheard the peasants commenting: *"By now, she is dead; it isn't possible that she is still alive."*

They were anxious to leave the plaza, as the other wall of the house, adjacent to the one that had fallen on the girl, was threatening to collapse. The poor girl could hear their voices fading away, as they left the scene of the accident. But, although the situation appeared hopeless, she never gave up hope. She had a thought: Jesus in the Holy Mystery, the Miracle of the Eucharist in the Church. She kept imploring the Lord, in His Holy Mystery, *believing* He would save her. All of a sudden, all fear left her. A peace like she had never known, shrouded her body. She felt like she was going to Heaven.

As if out of nowhere, peasants returned to the plaza, armed with axes, hoes and pickaxes. They all worked together, to rescue the girl, even though they had no knowledge where she was in the rubble, or if she was still alive. Within a miraculous half hour, the young girl was walking away from the huge mound of stones and mortar that had threatened to bury her alive.

After this sign, this second miracle, faith in the Holy Mystery became greater. No more would they turn to man for help. There is no reason, the peasants returned to dig after the girl. As far as they knew, she was long dead, smothered or crushed under the pile of debris. Or was there a reason? Had Our Lord summoned His Heavenly Army of Angels, those who descend upon the Altar, accompanying the Holy Spirit during the Sacrifice of the Mass? Was it the Angels who remain with Jesus, as He suffers alone in the Tabernacle, just as they were with Him in the Garden of Gethsemane and as He hung on the Cross, on His way to His death and resurrection?

Did Jesus in the Eucharist send out His Heavenly Messengers to us, the New Jerusalem, as God the Father had done, in the Old Testament? *It happened!* The people had their faith renewed, veneration to the Miracle of the Eucharist, *the Holy Mystery*, accelerated, and they continued to worship Our Lord, giving Him thanks for all the graces He had poured down upon them.

We have been meditating on why the Lord saved the Hosts from the fire, only to have them bleed profusely on the corporal. Was the Lord, once again pointing to the truth that the Host is not only the *Flesh* of the Lord Jesus, but the complete Lord, in His Body, *Blood*, Soul and Divinity? Was He again reminding us that the Mass is not only a celebration but the reason for celebration - our salvation through the Sacrifice of the Cross? Why did there seem to be a substance that appeared to be yeast or leaven? This brings to mind what Jesus said to the chosen people in regard to the Bread of Life. They questioned Him: *"Then what sign do You give that we may see, and believe?"....."Our fathers ate the manna in the wilderness; as it is written, 'He gave them bread to eat.'"*[12]...Jesus responded: *"I am the true Bread of Life; he who comes to Me shall not hunger; he who believes in Me shall never thirst."*[13] Is Our Lord once again telling us, reinforcing the truth through this Miracle that the Eucharist is the Food of Life, of eternal Life, true Food and true Drink? Do we believe? Is this Miracle for us, today, when the enemy of confusion is trying to take away our hope, our faith, our very life in Jesus? Do we believe? Or are we like those, He spoke to saying: *"...you have seen Me and yet do not believe."*[14] He promised that everyone who believed in Him would have eternal life and He would raise us up on the last day. Is this His way, once more to reach out to us, that we may know Him on that last day?

---

[12]John 6:30-31
[13]John 6:35
[14]John 6:36

Herkenrode - 1317

The Lord brings us back in time to the early Fourteenth Century. There was a dark cloud of unrest hovering over the Church, as well as all of Europe. The great plague, which would devastate most of the continent, would not be long in coming. There was a strong desire to break away from the Dark Ages. Art and Literature were on the horizon. The Printing Press, which would be the doors to a completely new and different way of life, which would never again be the same, was in the wings, just chomping at the bit, waiting to be introduced. But with that hunger for knowledge would also come a strong yearning to break away from the Church. God's people wanted to be free of the loving Father, who had brought them through so much danger, unscathed. They didn't want to know about that anymore. They wanted something new!

It was like the Garden of Eden revisited. Satan was preparing to attack Jesus and His Church, causing a major crack in the armor of the Body of Christ, beginning with *Renaissance* towards the end of the Fourteenth Century, to the *Protestant Revolution* under Martin Luther and *Calvinism* under John Calvin in the Sixteenth Century, to the *Church of England* under Henry VIII in the Seventeenth Century, to the *Age of Reason* and the *French*

Revolution in the Eighteenth Century, to two major heresies: **Modernism** at the beginning and **New Age** at the end of the Twentieth Century.

On the eve of all of this, the Lord takes us to Belgium in the beginning of the Fourteenth Century, to Hasselt, in the Diocese of Liege, a town just to the west of the border of Germany. *[This is also where, through two of its citizens, a little postulant, Bl. Juliana and a priest who became Pope Urban IV, the Lord brought about the Feast of Corpus Christi, through a Miracle of the Eucharist in Italy in 1263.]* We see Holy Clusters, once again. Now, He will give us our next great Miracle of the Eucharist. The major places which the Lord will use for this Miracle are an abbey, called Herkenrode, and a church, the Church of Saint-Quentin, which has since become a Cathedral in this the Twentieth century. But neither of these are the scenes of the Miraculous occurrence. Actually, the Miracle took place in a peasant's house on a *sick call*.[1] In those days, as in the present time, the priest would go to the house of a dying person and minister *Last Rites*: hearing, when possible the person's last confession,[2] absolving him of all his sins and giving him Holy Communion, then called *Viaticum*, meaning last Holy Communion.

On the day of the Miracle, a Parish priest was called to the bedside of a dying parishioner in Viversel. For who knows why, he chose to leave his kit with the oils for Extreme Unction outside the bedroom, while he asked the family to leave, so he could hear the dying person's last confession. For this short period of time, the Blessed Sacrament, which was also in the priest's kit, was left unguarded. A member of the little village, who knew

---

[1] when the priest went to a parishioner's home and ministered to someone on the verge of death, the *Last Rites* of the Church, a Sacrament that used to be called *"Extreme Unction"*. Today it is called the *Blessing of the Sick* and is not only ministered to the dying but to those seriously ill.

[2] the Sacrament of Penance. During the *Sacrament* of The Blessing of the Sick, as it is now called, the dying person receives two other *Sacraments*: of the Eucharist and of Penance.

the priest was in the dying neighbor's house, entered, to find the familiar-looking kit, which the priest had used to minister to the sick for many years, unattended in the outer room. He opened the kit, lifted out the pyx, and began to remove the Hosts which were inside. As soon as the intruder touched the Hosts, they began to bleed. Frightened, that the Lord had caught him, and he would die and go directly to Hell, the perpetrator closed the pyx, returned it to the priest's kit, and left with all haste, trying to put as much distance, as possible, between himself and what he considered an angry God.

Meanwhile, the priest, having completed hearing the confession of the dying person, went outside the room and picked up his kit, planning to bring the man his Last Holy Communion. He carried the kit into the patient's room. When he opened the pyx, inside the kit, and saw the blood over all the Hosts, he was in shock. But because he was in such close proximity to the person to whom they were intended, he covered up his shock. He did not give the blood-soaked Consecrated Hosts to the sick person. Giving the impression that he had forgotten the Hosts, he went immediately back to the Church, and searched out the Pastor of the Parish. When our priest told the Pastor what had happened, he was instructed to go immediately to the Abbey of Herkenrode, put the bleeding Hosts into the custody of the Abbot, a holy priest, named Fr. Simon. The Pastor offered to bring Communion back to the dying person, in whose house the Miracle of the Eucharist had occurred.

On the way to the Abbey, wondrous, unexplainable incidents were recorded. The voices of choirs of singing Angels accompanied the priest as he carried the precious Miraculous Body and Blood of our Lord Jesus to His final destination. The shrieking of demons, forced to depart the souls of possessed creatures, could be heard, as the Angels and Jesus made their way to the Abbey. Also part of the tradition which surrounds the transporting of the bleeding Hosts is that as the cortege passed sheep and rams in the fields, the animals bowed in respect to their Savior and King. These attributes of the Miracle are shown in paintings at the Cathedral of Saint-Quentin in Hasselt.

Another panel in the Church portrays the arrival of the priest and the Angels with the Blessed Sacrament at the Abbey at Herkenrode. When the priest and the abbot, Fr. Simon, brought the Miraculous Hosts to the Monastery Chapel, all the monks were present for the celebration of the Mass. When the Miraculous Hosts were placed on the Altar, the Monks testified having seen the face of Christ, crowned with thorns, the true image of *Ecce Homo*. Each of the monks testified to having seen this *same* vision.

There are testimonies of many physical and spiritual healings, due to the presence of the Miraculous Hosts in the Abbey over the centuries. There were accounts of fires erupting, threatening to destroy the Abbey; and at the last minute, the monks and the Abbey being saved by unmistakable Divine intervention. They attributed their safety, as well as all the miracles and healings, down through the ages, to the Sacred Hosts being in residence in the Monastery. While there is no documentation as to the separate healings and miracles attributed to the Bleeding Hosts, it is a strong part of the tradition of the Abbey of Herkenrode.

There came a time when it was determined not to be wise or safe to keep the Sacred Hosts in the Abbey, any more. This would have been around the year 1796. No reason is given for the transfer, but the time frame was at the heat of the French Revolution, and a great deal of persecution for the Church. While the area, near Liege, is closer to Germany than to France, there were dangers from persecution on both sides. It is common knowledge that most Catholic Shrines, especially those of incorrupt bodies, were destroyed during the heat of persecution against Catholics. The incorrupt bodies of Saints were desecrated and destroyed. Many beautiful churches and cathedrals were either turned into Protestant churches or museums, theaters, warehouses or stables. So, we would not be surprised at any form of persecution, the Church had to endure, either from

Germany or France, at that time.

At any rate, the Miraculous Hosts were taken out of the Abbey at Herkenrode, and transferred to an airtight container, a tin box. They were then placed in a secret compartment in the wall of the kitchen, of a private home. There can be no question but that it was to protect the precious Body and Blood of Our Lord Jesus from desecration and sacrilege. After what seemed like an appropriate period of time, when the French had calmed down somewhat in their attacks on the Church, the Hosts were taken out of the kitchen wall, placed in a proper reliquary, and settled in the church of Saint-Quentin in Hasselt, which was judged a safe haven from danger.

Now, with all of that, the cures and healings, the danger, the hiding, the near misses, you would believe that there would be a great devotion to the Miracle of the Eucharist in the Cathedral of Hasselt. Unfortunately, this is not so. To the contrary, there seems to be little or no knowledge and veneration to the Miracle, which had seemed to be so precious and so important to the Church of Liege, in Belgium, at a time in its history.

This little country, Belgium, and the area of Liege, has been the approach of the corridor for attacks from ungodly enemies twice in this century alone. Our Lord Jesus through His Mother Mary, has tried to warn these people, through apparitions in 1932 and 1933 in Beauraing and Banneux, respectively. Do you think if they had venerated Our Lord Jesus in the Miracle of the Eucharist, He had given them from 1317 to this very day, those attacks might not have come? We'll never know until we're in the Kingdom. But we do know that the people did not take advantage of the gifts the Lord had made available to them; they did not adore their God in the Miraculous Form He gave them; they were not spared from attacks and domination by Germany in the First World War, and in the Second World War.

Why is the Lord bringing this Miracle to us, today? Why is He unfurling this message, like a huge banner. What is He saying to *us*? Will there be a Third World War? Will Belgium be a corridor again between two warring nations? Or will it be much worse than that? Are we at war, and we do not know it? Millions of Americans are being murdered in their mother's wombs. Children are being alienated from their families, just as they were in Nazi Germany. This nation founded under God, is becoming a godless nation being taught to worship self. Where do we turn? Are we like the people in that little parish in Belgium? The Miracle is still there in that Church. We have a Miracle in our Church. He comes to us in the Eucharist, every day, at every Mass. He remains with us in the Tabernacle. Our Lord is there! He's there for us. He died for us. He comes to us. He loves us! He is our hope! Don't let Him go.

Krakow - 1345

A Light in the Darkness

We talk about *holy clusters*. As we have walked through the corridors of the History of our Church, we have discovered, Our Lord works through holy people and holy places to make His Will known and to protect His Church against the gates of Hell. They may have no similarity in time or space, but the Lord works powerfully in these areas.

Krakow - land of our most beloved Pope John Paul II. If ever there was a time when the jaws of Hell were open, ready to devour our Church, it was in the time of the miracle; as it is now! But we know, the Lord made a promise to our first Pope, Saint Peter, as He commissioned him, and all the Popes who would follow him, to head and shepherd His Church: *"Thou art Peter; and upon this rock[1] I will build My Church, and the gates of hell shall not prevail against it."*

The year was 1345. It was time for Our Lord Jesus to save His Church through Miracles, and Saints. It is not by accident or coincidence that this Miracle took place in Krakow, unless it be by *holy coincidence.* Krakow is in Poland, a land that has been a corridor for invading hordes of barbarians for centuries. Germany would march through on their way to Russia, and Russia stormed through on their way to Germany. And always Poland was the victim. You would think they would be a broken people, a melancholy people (as the Russians often depict *themselves*). Instead they are a stubborn people, a *holy stubborn* people.

A graphic example of what makes up the people of Poland is this true story. We spoke to a Pole, while we were shooting documentaries[2] in Poland. He was a classic Pole, with weathered

---

[1]Peter means rock in Greek

[2]we shot programs for our Television Series: *"Many Faces of Mary"* on *"Our Lady of Czestochowa"* and for our *"Martyrs series"* on The Martyrs of Poland and that dry martyr our Pope John Paul II.

leathery face, no teeth, white hair jutting out from a military cap, gnarled fingers holding a clay pipe. He looked off into the distance as he shared his life with us. He had lived through many occupations. He told us that he built a home. The Nazis came and burned it down. He built another home. The Communists came and burned *it* down. He built another home. This is the Poland we have discovered - land of hope and promise - land that has given birth to a powerful Pope, land of Holy Clusters, land of powerful Saints and Martyrs.[3]

As the place is not coincidental, neither is the *time* coincidental. We find ourselves back in time to the reign of Casimir the Great. The year is around 1345. What is happening in the world? What is happening in the Church?

A devastating plague had swept Europe, called the Black Death.[4] In a period of 100 years, some sixty million people were killed by this dread disease, for which there is still no cure. For Europe, this loss of so many people, in such a short period of time, was an enormous problem, in that it represented anywhere from 30% to 50% of the population. The work force was considerably depleted, if not almost totally wiped out. The best minds of the century were lost. There was a great shortage of people to manage countries, operate farms and factories, supervise monasteries, or do any of the things necessary for survival of body and soul. The world needed something to bring them out of that black period.

They had gone through generations of hard times just defending themselves from hordes of barbarians who were trying to take over their countries. The period commonly known as the Dark Ages had been very austere and depressing, from a religious and cultural point of view. Only the monks and nuns in the

---

[3]Read more about the Martyrs from Poland and other countries in *"Martyrs, They died for Christ"* by Bob and Penny Lord.
[4]later called the Bubonic Plague

monasteries and convents were able to take advantage of the great works of literature handed down by their ancestors.

With the Black Death, the Church suffered greatly. The religious orders were the first in line to help the victims of the Plague. Therefore, they were also the first to die. Their replacements, alas, were not of the same caliber intellectually as those they replaced. These new recruits were much younger, and less educated. The rules had to be relaxed to accommodate the new breed of religious; in many instances they were never brought back to their prior standards. Another problem, which was not meant to be a problem, was that too many people were leaving too much money to the religious orders. The combination of the two does not make a good formula for Chastity, Poverty and Obedience. Perhaps the suffering of doing without for so many centuries had been too demanding.

The Church wanted us to center on God and things of Heaven. Man wanted an earthly source of inspiration and entertainment. With the influx of newfound wealth, the upper classes and the intelligentsia had lots of money and nothing to do. Man wanted to focus the world's attention on man and things of the earth. Man wanted to be free! He didn't know when another plague would strike, and all would die, and so, the time was ripe for Renaissance.

The people were told, what they needed was literature and art to enlighten their minds and lives, to lift their spirits out of the darkness of the past, a rebirth from the austere to the sublime. The proponents of Renaissance advocated the human aspect of mankind in art and literature, as expressed by the ancient Greek and Roman civilizations, rather than that of the spiritual, as portrayed by the Church.

Whereas one philosophy's intention was to explore the beauty of the languages, the sculptors, the artists, the philosophers, another stronger philosophy's focus was to delve into the subculture, the perversion of ancient Rome and Greece, with its open sex, permissiveness, radical homosexual activity, materialism, self gratification and personal advancement, a philosophy of, if it pleases you, go for it!

Renaissance was a time of boldness, of challenge, of adventure. Questions demanded answers; nothing was accepted on face value. Any accepted set of values was open to challenge. Renaissance was accepted by the elite of Europe with open arms. They wanted something new, something different, supposedly to challenge and stimulate their intellect. The pendulum swung wide, too wide! When all the experiences had been experienced, when all the challenges had been met and conquered, they found themselves walking around in Roman togas, celebrating pagan Roman holidays, using pagan forms of revelry and debauchery.

Although Renaissance also brought us the beauty and softness of God, as seen in His creation, manifested in the inspired work of such people as Michelangelo, Raphael, Da Vinci and Dante Aligheri, although great heights were reached in the areas of architecture, engineering, literature, art and sculpture, it also brought us Pagan humanism - "Man was everything. Beyond man, there was nothing. There was no God. Man was enough." We must weigh the horrible price civilization paid for the accomplishments of the Renaissance and ask ourselves if it was worth it. Our Lord said "What does it profit a man if he gains the world and loses his soul."[5]

---

[5]*Scandal of the Cross and its Triumph* - Chapter on Renaissance

What had promised to bring light into the dark, only brought about a black death worse than that of the Bubonic Plague which had attacked most of Europe. How the Lord must have been grieving to see so many of His precious lambs succumbing to the devil's handiwork. Did He think: "*They no longer believe in Me! The Judas goat⁶ has led them toward hell*"? Did He allow them to remain lost? Just as He went after the one sheep who had wandered from the fold, He went about proving He was really present to us, in His Body, Blood, Soul and Divinity.

The Miracle

The Church is in crisis? Time for a Miracle of the Eucharist,Time for Krakow. We are in the octave of the Feast of Corpus Domini, or as it is presently known - *The Feast of Corpus Christi*. As we know, this Feast originally came about through the Miracle of Bolsena⁷ which took place in 1264 and was instituted by Pope Urban IV.

There is a small village, not very far from Krakow called Bawol. People began to swarm to a muddy marsh, very like the swamps of Florida and the bayous of Louisiana. They had seen a light emanating from the marsh, amidst blinding flashes of bolting lightning cutting into the sky. The rays of light which shot forth were like beacons springing from a lighthouse, directing ships safely into harbor. It was as if some unknown force was swinging huge spotlights into the dark sky.

The news spread quickly to the far-reaching hamlets throughout the region. People are always seeking God. The loneliness, the sadness, the lack of joy in their lives is because they have shut their Lord out. At best, He is on the outside sorrowfully looking in. He calls out to them and they hear not. But they know that something is missing. Could it be Him? People came and hard as they tried, they could not come up with

---

⁶The Judas Goat is the one used to lure the sheep into pens or trucks to be slaughtered.

⁷Read about this Miracle in Bob and Penny Lord's first book: *"This is My Body, This is My Blood, Miracles of the Eucharist" - Book I.*

They had seen a light emanating from the marsh, amidst blinding flashes of lightning cutting the sky.

any *human* explanation to explain the sight of flashing lights throughout the sky before their eyes.

But the wonder and awe changed to alarm, when the following night the phenomenon did not end. Paralyzing fear cut through the crowd like a cold damp blade. They were scared! The spectacle before their eyes seemed to take on a life, an urgency all its own, persistent in its mission, *what* mission they did not know. They were not certain, if it was the work of God or the devil. One thing they were sure of, this was not man's doing.

While this was going on, word came that in Krakow, someone had broken into *All Saints Roman Catholic Church* and stole the pyx which contained a Consecrated Host. Although the pyx appeared to be made of gold, it was merely plated with thin gold leaf and not of great monetary value. The glitter of fool's gold has always led mankind to do the most outrageous and in this case sacrilegious acts against God and man.

I often wonder, *"What price Hell?"* It seems inconceivable that there could be those who would jeopardize their immortal souls for a metal they cannot take with them. It would be a good joke on them, except that Our Lord was inside the pyx, being carried off. *Being carried off!* - It reminds us of the time that Our Lord Jesus allowed Satan to bring Him to Jerusalem and set him on a pinnacle of the temple. When I get upset with the Lord for allowing heretics and satanic cultists to desecrate His Precious Body in the Holy Eucharist, I remember, how He allowed Satan to tempt Him in the desert. How He must have suffered sickening repulsion, as he permitted the *filthy one* to carry Him to Jerusalem and set Him high on the temple.

Our Lord Who was sinless and God-man allowed a fallen creation of His to tempt Him, to touch Him? And for what? That we might be redeemed! Because every pain and humiliation, Our Lord endured was part of the redeeming passion of Jesus. And so, one more time, Jesus, You allowed a *filthy one* to carry You off.

The Bishop of Krakow was promptly informed of both the theft of the pyx containing the consecrated Host, and of the unexplainable lights coming from the marshes. The Bishop did not commit himself. He was not going to accept or support those who proposed it was the work of the devil nor would he declare that it was due to the intercession of the Angels. He did what he was called to do, as Pastor of his flock. He led those entrusted to him, to the Lord and His church. He called everyone to pray and do penance, so that the sacred pyx containing our precious Lord in His Eucharist would be returned safely and our Lord unharmed and undefiled. He exhorted them to come together in prayer, to fast and do acts of penance, imploring the Lord to reveal an explanation of the mysterious lights which were emanating from the marshes.

Now sadly, in the middle ages, most phenomenon was credited to the devil and his handiwork, rather than to the miraculous intervention of the Lord and His Angels. Today, no less ridiculously, our society has gone topsy-turvy. It works at *rationalizing* all occurrences into scientific or geological explanations. We are as bogged down with our need to understand, as they were with their preoccupation with the devil.

Are we saying that the devil does not exist? No way! He exists. All you have to do is pick up the newspaper or turn on the television - He exists! Although he is slick and fools us for a time, he always slips and gives himself away. To quote a former president of the United States: *"You can fool some of the people some of the time; but you cannot fool all the people all of the time.*" I have never seen it fail. The devil cannot maintain! We believe that the fruits of an apparition and the test of time will affirm its authenticity, if it is of God. God always reveals. Maybe, not as fast as we would impatiently desire Him to, but ultimately He does - through His Church. Because the Church is far more thorough and scrupulous than any investigating body, you can be assured every possibility has been considered before she makes the statement that a Miracle or an Apparition has occurred.

That there was a *holy* connection between the two holy occurrences is affirmed by the fact that they both happened on the same night: The Sacred Species were stolen and lights shot forth from the marshes. Although everyone searched, far and wide, for the pyx and the consecrated Host within, they came back empty-handed. For three days, the thieves remained unknown and the Host appeared hopelessly gone. But the lights continued to shoot up into the sky from the marshes! After three days of fasting and prayer, the Bishop and the Faithful solemnly processed to the area, in the swamp, from which the rays of light were still shining forth. How did the Bishop connect these two happenings? He had been praying and fasting, as we can be sure were the Faithful, as well. Had the Holy Spirit or the Angels of God told him where to go to find the missing Jesus, as possibly they had told Mother Mary and St. Joseph, the time they found Jesus in the Temple when He was lost?

The Faithful dug into the marshes, never mindful of the slime, pushing tall grass aside until they went to the source of the light, and found the pyx which contained the consecrated precious Host, Our Lord Jesus present. The Host was immaculate, undefiled, uncontaminated by the waters of the swamp. No mud, no stains, completely untouched, could It have been protected by the Angels? What do you think? The Bishop carried the pyx, reverently, as he would have done carrying the Blessed Sacrament in solemn procession. The Faithful processed alongside their Bishop, forming an honor guard, accompanying their Lord back to the Church.

Once the pyx was returned to the Tabernacle, the lights, as if turned off by an invisible switch, no longer sent up their signals. As suddenly as they had begun, they ended. The light no longer needed, the marshes fell into a deep darkness. Oh, if only the grass and the swamps could speak! Would they have protested, "Let us have the Lord present among us, one more night?"

The Bishop carried the pyx, reverently, and the Faithful followed in solemn procession back to the Church.

For us believers, the set of holy circumstances are enough to prove that a Miracle occurred. But to those who do not believe, *"neither will they be convinced if someone should rise from the dead."*[8]

If we reflect on the events of the Miracle, we are reminded of another place, the odor must have been as strong and unpleasant as that of the marshes, where Our Lord lay for three days in a pyx. In *Bethlehem*, Our Lord, the Baby Jesus lay in a stable, a stable shared by animals! And there, too, a light emanated from *that* spot, only that time it was a star! And this star led the shepherds and then the three wise men there to worship and adore Him. Once again, we are receiving the Good News that the Lord is with us, and He will move Heaven and Earth if need be, to prevent anyone from taking Him away from us. In this case, He brought about a Miracle!

There have been many texts recounting and affirming this Miracle, over the centuries. One document which adds much credibility in affirming the Miracle and its ongoing tradition is

---

[8]Luke 16:31

that of Father Cornelio Loapide, S.J. Father Loapide was born in Germany in 1567, and was widely respected as a professor of Holy Scripture at Louvain University in Belgium and looked up to, until his death in Rome in 1637. Among his many works is the account of the missing Host and the lights emanating from the swamp.

The Faithful of Krakow and of the surrounding countryside wanted to do reparation for the sacrilege committed by the thieves, who, when they discovered they had stolen a vessel that was not real gold and worthless to them, discarded it disdainfully into the slimy marsh. Thank God that Our Lord never revealed to them the Treasure contained within. We remember the Gospel passage in Holy Scripture when Jesus explains to the Apostles why He did not speak to everyone as He instructed them:

"...when His disciples asked Him what this parable meant, He said, 'To you it has been given to know the secrets of the kingdom of God; but for others they are in parables, so that seeing they may not see, and hearing they may not understand.'"[9]

King Casimir the Great had the swamp drained and on that ground, he built a great church dedicated to the Body and Blood of Christ - Corpus Christi. It was built in the grand gothic style of that period which so glorified the Lord.

Around the year 1392, the Regular Canons, who were highly favored by the Royal Palace, were granted custody of the church. There are documents, dating from 1392, attesting to the origins of the church.

On our last two trips to Poland and the beautiful, medieval city of Krakow, we had the blessed privilege to interview the Pastor, Fr. Stramyck, and videotape the church where the Miracle occurred, the church of Corpus Christi. There are still paintings there, teaching the Faithful that *Our Lord is Really Present*, as He proved in Krakow, in a swamp, overturning a hideous act into a glorious Miracle.

---

[9]Luke 8:9-11

In referring to the light that emanated from the Host, we are reminded of the word that is given to us at Mass: *'Let your light shine'*, and do not our eyes shine when we are united with the Lord in His Holy Eucharistic Self?

King Casimir was the father of Saint Casimir. King Louis the 8th, the father of Saint Louis, built the church in Avignon, in honor of the Miracle of the Eucharist that took place there 1335[10] approximately 100 years later than the miracle of Krakow.

Bob and Penny Lord with Fr. Jusick Stramyck in the Church of Corpus Christi, Krakow - Poland

Had the Lord brought us up to Mount Tabor with this Miracle to strengthen us, in preparation for the devastating plague of rebellion and protest called erroneously the Reformation that was to take 6,000,000 Catholics from our Church?

Lest we take the Lord for granted in His Eucharist, lest the people of Poland take Him for granted and lose their way, the Lord reminds them and us with this Miracle of the Eucharist that will persistently light our way until we recognize Him, Present in our lives and come home to Him in His Church.

His children had lost their way, swallowed up by the lure and decadence of the Renaissance. What did our Lord do? He set up a lighthouse, and sent out guiding lights emanating from Himself to direct them back to safety on the shore - His Church. *Praise Jesus!*

---

[10] Avignon - Read more about this Miracle in, *"This Is My Body, This Is My Blood, Miracles of the Eucharist"*. - *Book I*

Alboraya - 1348

Alboraya is a small town, of no apparent account by the world's standards, nestled in between Sagunto and Valencia, on the southeastern coast of Spain. This whole area had been a fierce battleground; intense fighting had taken place, as Spain valiantly recaptured its country from its deadliest foe, the dreaded Moors, the Moslems, who had conquered this peninsula in the early part of the eighth century.

This Miracle, we're now bringing to you, took place after bloody warfare with the Moors, in the middle of the Thirteenth century. Having been defeated in 1238, the Moors were deported to the Middle East. However, in Valencia, many of the Moors of Spain came from ancestors who had lived in the country for over five hundred years. There had been a great deal of intermarriage. In other areas, such as Granada, the Arab occupation lasted much longer, up to seven hundred years, and only ended with the bravery of the Catholic Kings, Ferdinand and Isabella, towards the end of the fifteenth century.

We bring you this brief history of what was going on, in this section of Spain, Valencia, to let you know what the cultural background of the people were at that time. As we mentioned, Moslems had intermarried with Christians. The values were mixed. Many Spaniards had embraced the Moslem religion.[1]

---

[1] It is rare that a Moslem will convert to Christianity, as they are taught that Jesus is not the Son of God; merely another prophet like Mohammed.

So, in addition to the influence of the Moslems, based on 500 to 700 years occupation, there were the beliefs of those who had been born into the Moslem Religion. The *Catholic* Faith was only now being re-introduced to the people of the south, after having been kept from them for hundreds of years. It was difficult for many Catholics to understand, because their culture had been so intermingled with Moslem culture. The job of the priests of this period was difficult, in that they were constantly fighting old heresies and superstitions which had cropped up and crept into the way of life of the people of Valencia.

While the staunch Catholics of the province were overjoyed to be able to practice their Catholic Faith freely and openly, many of the rank and file, simple people who knew little about the Faith, were confused for many years, as to what was Catholic and what was Moslem, and why the Catholic Faith was the true teaching of Jesus Christ and why that of the Moslems was heretical,[2] contrary to our Judeo-Christian Beliefs. As if that was not enough of a problem for the people of Spain, there were the *Conversos*, converts from Judaism who were converts in name only. These included priests and bishops, as well as lay people who were trying to convince Christians that the only way to salvation was through the Mosaic law.

It didn't matter to them, in doing that, the *Conversos* were denying the prophecies of Jeremiah, one of their own powerful prophets:

"The days are coming, says the Lord, when I will make a new covenant with the house of Israel and the house of Judah. It will not be like the covenant, I made with their fathers, the day I took them by the hand to lead them forth from the land of Egypt;

---

[2]Keep in mind that Islam, or the Moslem religion, was created by Mohammed, taking parts from the Catholic and Jewish Religions in the Sixth Century, using what he could for his purposes and eliminating what did not suit him. Seeing the unity of the Christians and Jews, he thought this one Religion *Islam* would unify all the Arabs of the world. Read more about this in Bob and Penny Lord's book: *"Scandal of the Cross, and its Triumph"*

for they broke My covenant, and I had to show Myself their Master, says the Lord. But this is the covenant which I will make with the house of Israel after those days, says the Lord. I will place My law within them, and write it upon their hearts; I will be their God, and they shall be My people. No longer will they have need to teach their friends and kinsmen how to know the Lord. All, from least to greatest, shall know Me, says the Lord, for I will forgive their evil-doing and remember their sin no more."[3]

The footnote to that Scripture passage of Jeremiah states: *"According to Jeremiah, the qualities of the new covenant that make it different from the old covenant are: (a) It will not be broken, but will last forever; (b) Its law will be written in the heart, not merely on tablets of stone; (c) The knowledge of God will be so generally shown forth in the life of the people that it will no longer be necessary to put it into words of instruction."*[4] In the fullest sense, this prophecy was fulfilled, **only through the work of Jesus Christ.**

These **Conversos,** or **Judaizers,** as they were also called, although they had converted to Christianity with their mouths, in order not to be exiled from Spain, would not accept Jesus as the Messiah, or the new covenant as being valid, even though it was prophesied by one of their own prophets, Jeremiah. And so, they were just one more cause of dissension and confusion for our brothers and sisters in Spain.

There was a great need in Valencia, in 1348, 110 years after the reconquest of the province had been completed, for the Lord to intercede for the Faithful, that they should understand, in a *dramatic* way, how He was working in their lives through their Catholic Faith. The kind of intercession needed could only have been something as *powerful* as a Miracle of the Eucharist, and that's what the Lord gave them.

This Miracle of the Eucharist has been given the name, quite correctly, **The Fish of Alboraya.** At a time, when there was

---

[3]Jeremiah 31:31-34
[4]New American Bible footnote to Jeremiah 31:31-34

confusion as to who was God, The Moslem *Allah* or the Christian *God: The Father, the Son, and the Holy Spirit*, and *confusion* as to whether Jesus was Really Present in the Eucharist, there was no *confusion* in the minds of the fish. This Miracle is considered one of those worthy to be included in what is called *"The Golden Legend,"*[5] and is documented by two paintings, in the local church of Almacera, near where the Miracle took place.

The main characters in this Miracle are a *Priest* from a local village, Alboraya, *his mule*, and some *fish*. The priest, who has no name for the purpose of this account, was riding on his mule, in the direction of the home of a poor sick farmer, who was on the verge of death. The priest's greatest character trait, we have to believe, was his reverence and his undying faith in Our Lord Jesus in the Eucharist.

The priest brought *Viaticum*,[6] the Holy Eucharist, as well as the Holy oils for Extreme Unction,[7] the Last Rites of the Church. Our priest had, no doubt, spent much time in the spiritual vineyards of the province, bringing people back to the true Faith, counteracting the influence of the elements which would have ultimately destroyed the Church in Spain, if the Lord permitted it. But because of Faithful priests like this one, the Church would survive and grow stronger.

The priest and his little mule had to travel between Alboraya and Almacera. They approached the bed of a river, near the beach of Malvarrosa. It was not a big deal to cross it. He'd done it *many times* before, in his ministering to this area. He also used to play in it as a child. He was very familiar with the river. But on this day, he was not prepared for the very strange way, the river would behave, or his mule, for that matter. As they approached the bed of the river, where it flowed into the sea, the

---

[5]Don't confuse legend with myth. Legend means a story handed down by tradition from the Latin Leggere, to read.

[6]was part of the Last Rites, the *Last* Holy Communion, in those days.

[7]Now called the Blessing of the Sick

waters began churning, like a whirlpool.

The mule panicked, and the priest followed suit. He tried holding on to the beast, but the more he tried to control the animal, the more terrified the both of them became. The ground underneath the mule began to sink, as if he were standing in quicksand. The mule desperately tried to get his legs onto solid ground, while the priest helplessly attempted to calm both himself and his animal-companion. Neither did very well, because the mule lost his footing, and the priest lost hold of the reins. They both went flying, the priest in one direction, and the mule in another, and with that, the little kit, in which he kept the three Consecrated Hosts, as well as the oils for Extreme Unction. He looked on, *helplessly*, as he saw his kit soar into the air.

For a brief moment, the priest's instinct forced him to concentrate on saving his life and that of his animal. But in very short order, he realized what had happened, how the Consecrated Hosts had plummeted into the water, and were now floating down the river. Once the priest was safe upon the shore, he began his search for his kit, peering up and down the river. He could see nothing. The water was still raging. He sat on the edge of the river for a time, and then left, despondent.

Downstream, fishermen were in their boats, trying to net enough fish for a good day's catch. They had been out for many hours, and were just about to call it a day, when one of them noticed an unusual sight near the shore of the beach. He motioned to his partners. They all perceived and testified, as one, *to the same vision*: Three fish were together, with their heads out of the water, each one holding up a **Host** with the tip of his mouth. They were not moving; their heads were in the same position, in an attitude of reverence to the Royalty they were carrying in their mouths.

The fishermen ran to find the priest. They found him in the church, praying. Can you imagine the priest's relief, when they recounted what had happened. He immediately reached into the cupboard and removed the best Chalice he had, to carry the Lord back to the church. It had to be a fitting replacement for the pyx, which was lost when it, and the Hosts, plunged into the water. He followed the fishermen to the spot where the fish were waiting. He could not believe his eyes; he could not contain his joy, when he saw them, perched along the shore, their heads out of the water, the Consecrated Hosts still in their mouths. He knelt along the

Mural depicting the Miracle of the Eucharist of the Fish

shore, where the fish were waiting. He placed the Chalice onto the water, being sure to get no water inside the cup of the Chalice. One by one, the fish came over to the Chalice, and each deposited their Host, their Treasure, into the Chalice. After this was done, they dove back, down into the depths of the river, never to be seen again.

Many local people had heard about the Miracle of the Fish at Alboraya. They all followed the priest to the spot where the fish were waiting for him. Word of the miraculous happenings spread like wildfire. By the time, the priest processed back to the Church with the retrieved Hosts, a huge crowd was following him. They stayed in the Church, while the priest continued the procession up to the main Altar. After he ascended the Altar, he raised the Hosts, blessing the Faithful assembled, and placed the Hosts back into the Tabernacle of the Church.

The Chapel built in honor of the Miracle of the Eucharist of the fish at Alboraya, Spain

On the huge, wooden church doors, are carved different segments of the Miracle of the Eucharist of the Fish. As you walk through the church, you will discover a special Tabernacle, inside which is displayed, the Pyx and Chalice from the time of the Miracle. The people of Alboraya erected a small Chapel, a *Shrine* on the spot, made holy by the Miracle which had taken place. Each year, all the members of the parish process through the entire village, in remembrance of the Miracle of the Eucharist that was graciously given to this little town by Our Lord Jesus. Devotion to the Miracle goes on to this day, in this Chapel.

There is much documentation verifying the events of this Miracle, as well as generations of townspeople who have passed down what happened, the day the Lord sent a Miracle to their little village. This has not been a forgotten Gift from the Lord. To this day, *Eucharistic Adoration* is a strong part of the lives of the Faithful in the small villages surrounding Valencia.

One question remains unanswered. What happened to the Miraculous Hosts, rescued from the raging waters by the three Fish? We don't know for sure. What happened to the Fish? We are sure, they went back to their homes underwater, glowing from the touch of the Lord, thankful for the great Gift they were given. It would be nice to think that the Hosts were incorrupt, and still at that little church in Almacera, or in the Chapel in Alboraya. But that's not the important part of the Miracle or its story.

We have said, regarding this and many other Miracles of the Eucharist, *the Lord's work was accomplished.* If the Hosts, rescued by the fish in Alboraya, Spain in 1348, were consumed, it doesn't change the Miracle, at all. The Miracle happened! Word of the Miracle spread over that entire section of Spain; and eventually, all of Christian Spain knew of the *Miracle of the Fish.* Devotion to the Eucharist increased. To this day, there is still a following, still a devotion, still a procession in honor of the Miracle. Would it mean more if the Miraculous Hosts were in the Tabernacle in the Church, today, or *exposed* for everyone to see, and nobody cared, nobody went to visit Jesus in this Miraculous Form? We go back to the promise Jesus made to us in Scripture, *"I will be with you always, until the end of the world."*[8]

It's interesting that when we went into Scripture to find that passage, the very last sentence of Matthew's Gospel, what should be right before it, actually a part of the statement: *"All power has been given to Me in Heaven and on earth; go, therefore, and make disciples of all the nations. Baptize them in the name of the Father, and of the Son, and of the Holy Spirit. Teach them to carry out everything I have commanded you. And know that I am with you always, until the end of the world!"*[9] *"Teach them to carry out everything I have commanded you."* As the priests and the laity passed on the events of the Miracle of the Fish, [as with Juan Diego when he would tell the story of Our Lady of Guadalupe],[10] the Faithful, over the years have become more and more aware of what really happens on the Altar, during the Consecration of the Mass; and *Who* it is they visit and adore

---

[8]Matt: 28:20
[9]Matt: 28:18-20
[10]Read about Our Lady of Guadalupe in Bob and Penny Lord's book: *"Many Faces of Mary, a love Story"*

in Eucharistic Adoration. The Lord did not leave them. He remained with them, through the *ongoing* Miracle of the Eucharist, when bread and wine become His Body, Blood, Soul and Divinity, when He dwells among us in the Tabernacle, available to hear us, to talk to us, to console us, to be with us *"till the end of the world."*

What was this priest and the Church doing at this time, to cause Our Lord Jesus to give them, and us, the Miracle of the Eucharist? There's no denying, he was following the mandate, Jesus gave to all of us, just before he ascended into Heaven. Was Our Lord Jesus affirming what the priest and the Church were doing at this time in this place, to bring the true Faith back to the people of Spain, who had been loyal children from the time, Our Lady appeared in Zaragoza?[11]   Or was He insuring, this Faith would never die? *Nothing is by coincidence.* We can't believe Jesus, for no reason, just decided to give the people of this small village in Spain, a Miracle of the Eucharist, at one of the most crucial times in their history. Nothing, is by coincidence with the Lord.

You can trust in that!

---

[11]During her lifetime, the Lord asked His Mother to go to Zaragoza to tell St. James to return to the Holy Land to be martyred.

Boxtel-Hoogstraten - 1380

The Precious Blood

The Lord brings us to the village of Boxtel, in Holland, near Eindhoven and Bois de Lac, in the province of Nord-Brabant. Presently, there are about 20,000 inhabitants. Our Miracle takes place around 1379, in the Church of Saint Peter's. There had not been many Masses celebrated in the little Church. The Catholic Faith had not been popular with the local people, for some time. We must remember that this period was the beginning of the Renaissance. Europe was preoccupied with the new learning, which it thought was more important than, what they considered, the stuffy teaching of the Monks during (what had been referred to as) the Dark Ages.

Couple that with the Bubonic Plague. Calamity struck Europe on a major scale in the middle of the Fourteenth Century, in the form of a violent epidemic, called **The Black Death.** In a period of 100 years, some sixty million people were killed by this dread disease, for which there was, and there is still no cure. The world needed something to bring them out of that black period.

People began to think more of their physical and intellectual well-being, than their spiritual life. Church was something from the old days. They wanted something new, something exciting, something which would bring them to the depths of Hell.

Our Lord didn't want to see that happen to His people. No matter how unfaithful they were, He still loved them, and indeed still loves them. He would do then, as He will do now, anything

He can to save us from ourselves, from damnation. It reminds us a great deal of the parable of the 99 sheep, when Jesus left all the others to save that one sheep. We'd like to believe that this was the Lord's way of working in the same way.

The Miracle

A priest, Father Van der Aker, was celebrating Mass at the Church of St. Peter's on that special day, towards the end of 1379. It was at the Altar of the Magi, the Three Kings who had brought gifts to the Saviour of the world, *our* King, our Lord Jesus Christ. During the Consecration of the Mass, just after Fr. Van der Aker elevated the chalice, and said the words which would bring Our Lord Jesus onto the Altar, under the appearances of bread and wine, Father lost his balance, and jostled the chalice, overturning it, spilling its contents on the Corporal and Altar Cloth. *He gasped in amazement!* He had used white wine for the Consecration of the Mass, for reasons unknown to us. What was on the Corporal and Altar Cloth was rich, red Blood, in color and in substance!

Fr. Van der Aker was not happy about what had happened. He felt, he had done something terrible against God and did not know how to make the situation better. His parishioners were not aware that the problem was, *the priest had used white wine* and it had turned blood red after the Consecration. All they knew was that Father had spilled the Precious Blood onto the Corporal and Altar Cloth. Even the Altar server didn't realize what had happened. Fr. Van der Aker did nothing to let them know, either. He went through the motions of the Mass, although he was physically and emotionally shaken from the ordeal.

After the Mass, he ran to the sacristy, and began to wash the Corporal and Altar Cloth, in an effort to get the red color out. It wouldn't come out. He washed and re-washed it many times, to no avail. The color was in the Corporal and Altar Cloth for good. Fr. Van der Aker was distressed. He felt, he was a disgrace to the priesthood and to Our Lord Jesus. After the last attempt to wash out the red color from the Sacred Cloths failed, he sadly put it into a small valise, which he got from the sacristan, and hid the bleeding Cloths in the sacristy. He never said a word to anyone, until he was dying and confessed to his Pastor, Fr. Henry van Merheim. He also showed him the place where he had hidden the Sacred Corporal and Altar Cloth, still stained red by the Blood Which had spilled on them.

Fr. Van der Aker died that year, 1379, and the following year, 1380, at the request of William of Maerhem, Duke of Boxtel, Cardinal Pileo, the Apostolic Legate of Pope Urban VI, decreed on the 25th of June that the Precious Blood relic was to be exposed every year at that time, once a year. With the permission, came a brief history of the Miracle which constitutes strong documentation of the Miracle. We've got to remember that this decree, in effect a Papal Bull, came only about a year after the fact, less than a year after the priest, Fr. Van der Aker, had died.

There is another tradition that states that at the place in Boxtel where Fr. Van der Aker washed the Blood-soaked Corporal and Altar Cloth, a watermill and a well appeared, which was appropriately named *"The Holy Well"*. This also became a haven for pilgrims, who would draw water from the well, and pray to Our Lord Jesus, in petition for healings and favors requested. It is said that many miracles were attributed to the intercession of Our Lord Jesus through this shrine. The mill and the well don't exist anymore.

Once Cardinal Pileo had authorized the exposition and veneration of the Sacred Corporal and Altar Cloth, the people flocked to the Relics of the *"Precious Blood"*, as it became known. The little village of Boxtel became a Pilgrim's Shrine. The Faithful traveled from far and wide, in petition, in thanksgiving, in hope and prayer, to the Relics of the Precious Blood. Reports flooded the little parish office of Boxtel, of miracles, healings, incredible conversions. Nothing was too much to ask of Our Lord, at the Shrine of the Precious Blood. Although the Faithful were only allowed to revere the Miracle once a year, there was always a strong, steady stream of petitioners at the Altar in the little church, where the Miraculous Corporal and Altar Cloth were kept. But at that time, in June, when the Miraculous Cloths were exposed, throngs of people came from all over that part of Europe. *Satan was furious.* He was not able to dissuade the people of Belgium from believing in the Eucharist, number one, and the Miracle of the Eucharist, number two. Even when Satan reached out his long arm, using the Protestant Revolution in Europe, and this area was not spared from the onslaught, it didn't stop the people from believing. But Calvin's violence was ruthless; he not only attacked Catholics mentally and emotionally, but physically intimidated them into submitting, to the point of killing them, if they refused. Because of this danger, it was decided to temporarily stop the veneration of the Corporal and Altar Cloth of the Precious Blood, and to hide them.

It seems like a hundred years passed, where the Sacred Relics were not exposed for the Faithful to venerate and pray before. They didn't need the Miracle of the Precious Blood on the Corporal and Altar Cloth to be there, exposed. The church was still open. The Blessed Sacrament was there. The little chapel, where the Miracle had been kept during safer times, was still there. The people continued to pray in petition for favors needed, and in thanksgiving for favors granted. *"Blessed is he who does not see, and still believes."*[1] And the miracles continued to come. Nothing the enemy could come up with, was strong enough to shake the belief of the people.

In 1652, the Miraculous Corporal and the Altar Cloth of the *"Precious Blood"* were transported to Hoogstraten, south of Boxtel, on the Belgian border. The Relics were placed in a grand church there, *St. Catherine's Catholic Church* which had been built, only a hundred years before. It was a magnificent tribute to the glory of God, considered an architectural work of art. Here, as in Boxtel, the Faithful came in pilgrimage. There are four scenes in the Church, from the seventeenth century, which depict the Miracle of the Precious Blood.

---

[1]John 20:29

We don't know for sure, why the Sacred Relics were brought to Hoogstraten. In any event, for whatever reason the Corporal and Altar Cloth with the **Precious Blood** had been taken out of Boxtel. 272 years later, in 1924, the Sacred Corporal was returned to *Boxtel*, to its original home, the Chapel of the Precious Blood. But, the Miraculous Altar Cloth remained in Hoogstraten. The people from Boxtel never wavered in their zeal for their Lord Jesus in the Eucharist. Why was the Corporal taken away and brought back? We believe, one reason might be so that the people of this area, in Holland and Belgium, would never take Our Lord Jesus in the Eucharist, for granted. When we think of what has happened in Holland, how it is difficult to find a church Faithful to the Pope and the Magisterium, we could cry.

But in this one town, every year, to this day, there is a procession of the Miracle of the Eucharist on the Feast of Trinity Sunday. In Boxtel, the people come out. The Sacred Corporal is processed in the middle of a great multitude. They pay homage to their Lord in this Miraculous Form. They don't take Him for granted. You can bet, they will never let anyone take this prized Possession away from them again. Why do they have it? Because God loves them. Why do we have the Eucharist? Because God loves us. Don't ever take it for granted.

Why did this Miracle take place? This was during a very difficult period for the Church in these countries. Renaissance had taken over and the Lord knew, Luther and Calvin would not be far behind, ready to suppress the Church even more. The Lord had to prove to His children that what they had believed, what they had learned on their mothers' knees about the Real Presence of Jesus in the Eucharist was true. With this Miracle, people like Calvin and his ilk, could say what they want; they could not dispute what the eyes had seen, *a Miracle of the Eucharist*. With the kind of hell, Calvin would shell out, the Faithful would need to know they were not alone. A symbol could not help them. If what Calvin said was true, that Jesus was not really present in the Eucharist, then, they were all alone, Christ had died; He was in Heaven, and they were in these heretics' power. The people needed their Lord in the Eucharist.

There was a great fear that the Corporal would be desecrated during the worst of the Calvin times. It took a hundred years for the Corporal to be taken out of hiding, and returned to the Faithful. Why would the heretics want to destroy the Miracle of the Eucharist? Why burn the incorrupt bodies of Saints? Why did the infidels try to erase every trace of Jesus in the Holy Land? Was it to take away our hope in tomorrow, remove every vestige of Jesus present among us? They thought, if we couldn't see, we'd stop believing. Well, in countries where the Faithful were without the Church for hundreds of years, Mother Church was so deep in the hearts of her children, when the Church returned, the Faith was alive!

Do we need to know that Jesus is with us? In these days of the evil one's last hurrah, it can get frightening. Those we thought we could turn to, have turned against us. Has Our Lord sent us this Miracle to tell us, once again: *"Be not afraid. I am with you until the end of time"*?

Ettiswil - 1447

Victory over Witchcraft

One of the most powerful teachings, we have received from the Lord came through the work, He accomplished in Switzerland and Germany in the middle of the Fifteenth Century. The Lord's work was done in this particular instance in Ettiswil, Switzerland, but it was not only for this time or this place. The Lord was battling a powerful Satan, the Satan of witchcraft.

In our time, witchcraft in all its forms has been grossly understated. In our country, it has almost become a joke. We have cereals named after demons; TV animated cartoons, bad-breath commercials. It is so subtle, it's frightening. Archbishop Fulton J. Sheen, a twentieth century prophet, once said, *"Satan's greatest goal in this century is to deny his very existence."* From where we're sitting, he's doing a very good job. There are those outside the church, and sadly enough, inside the church, who are espousing that philosophy. There are priests saying there is no *personal devil*, in contradiction to statements made by Cardinals.[1]

But in the Fifteenth century, before we relegated demons to the ranks of neuroses, the priests and the laity took Satan, witchcraft and sorcery very seriously. They were able to recognize the power of evil very clearly and learned to fight it with all they were worth.

The Miracle of the Eucharist of Ettiswil, in Switzerland, is a

---

[1]Time Magazine, March 19, 1990 - pg 55

direct result of, and attack on satanic activities in northern Europe. The Lord takes us to Germany, in the area of Baden, in order to begin this account of a diabolical plot which spread its poison throughout Germany, and had its conclusion in Switzerland. It was turned around by the Lord, and in the end, He gave us a Miracle of the Eucharist. A nameless man, who practiced the occult and satanic rites, used dissatisfied, unhappy, ignorant Catholics to be the tools of his desecration against the Lord. All of his demonic activity took place around the Eucharist. We're told that perhaps it was because he didn't believe in the Real Presence of Jesus in the Eucharist, but we have to believe it was just the opposite. Our experience has always been that members of satanic cults truly believe in the Real Presence of Jesus in the Eucharist. That is why they are always insistent on obtaining real consecrated Hosts to desecrate; they realize the power of Jesus in the Eucharist. They recognize His willing vulnerability in the Eucharist.

And so, we begin the account of the nameless satanist who was able to enlist the services of an unhappy Catholic girl, Anna Vogtli, to do his loathsome dirty work. By using a Catholic, he not only was able to wound Jesus by desecration of the Eucharist, but he was also pretty sure he would be leading a soul into hell. We don't know what kind of reward he could anticipate when he arrived at the smoldering gates of hell, perhaps a hotter fire, or his own private furnace? Whatever the case, he used this girl to steal consecrated Hosts from the local church in the town of Bischoffingen, in the area of Baden. She did this once, successfully, and the satanist and his ungodly crew used the consecrated Hosts, the Real Presence of Our Lord Jesus, to desecrate Him, and perform disgusting acts, too terrible to describe here. But you can be sure, they believed; they truly believed that they were desecrating Jesus. Otherwise, it would not have made any sense. Think about it. Why go through this clandestine theft of Hosts, in order to perform satanic rituals, if they didn't believe they were spiting Jesus?

[Author's note: We were giving a weekend retreat in New Orleans a few years ago. We spoke about a Miracle of the Eucharist in Offida, which fought the satan of witchcraft. We touched on this question of whether the cultists believed that they were truly desecrating the Body and Blood of Jesus, or just a piece of bread. One of the retreatants took us to the side, and shared that she had been a member of a satanic cult in her younger days, and that there was no question in any of their minds that Jesus was truly present in the consecrated Hosts, and that the Hosts had great power.]

After the first successful theft of consecrated Hosts through the efforts of Anna Vogtli, the satanist's greed for more Hosts pushed him to recruit her once again. She went back to the church in Bischoffingen, stole more Hosts, and brought them to her contact. She was handsomely rewarded for her evil deeds, by the way. But what she was given, possessions she had always desired, never made her happy. She was always miserable.

It wasn't long before the satanists were again in need of the services of the unhappy girl. Don't you find it a little unusual that these devil's helpers never do their own dirty work? Why do you think it is that they're willing to pay a Catholic to be part of their satanic plots, rather than handle them themselves? The answer is really very simple. They're enlisting souls into their work, souls who will join them on their journey to hell. That's the most obvious to us. However, there may also be that fear that if they should enter a church, the walls might come down and crush them. Whatever the case, it was decided that they should not risk having Anna Vogtli go back to the same church in Bischoffingen again. It could be too risky. Surely, after two major thefts in a six month period of time, security in the church must have been beefed up.

So it was determined that the cultists would finance Anna to go out of the country, not too far, but far enough, so that the authorities in the church would not have heard about the thefts of the Eucharist in the Church of Bischoffingen. Ettiswil, in

Switzerland, not far from the German border, seemed like a perfect place. They sent Anna there, for the express purpose of stealing consecrated Hosts, which they would use for their sacrilegious rites. It was a small enough town, but not so small that she could not get lost. Also, she would not stand out as a foreigner to the town. *That's what she thought.* The parish church of Ettiswil was a good church to carry out their outrageous scheme.

According to the plan, Anna went to the church, and hid in the shadows of the side Altars until it was closed. It was the Thursday after the Feast of the Ascension in 1447. The Feast was still being celebrated because it was the octave of the Feast. As part of the Festivities, the Blessed Sacrament was carried in Procession every day for those eight days. To this purpose, the priest consecrated a large host every day for the eight days. We're not sure, if Anna and her cohorts were aware that a large host would be consecrated. We know, it would be a great bonanza for the cultists, in addition to having consecrated Hosts, to have the large Host, which is used for Mass, Eucharistic Adoration, and Benediction. Anna blended in with the crowd, but unbeknown to her, she was noticed as not being from the town by the local people. They didn't think anything of it at the time, other than the fact that they didn't usually have out-of-towners visiting their small hamlet.

When she was sure, the church was closed, and that everyone was out, she went over to the Tabernacle. There was an iron grille protecting a wooden door, inside of which were the consecrated Hosts being held in reserve, as well as the large consecrated Host which would be used the next day for the Procession. After she had pried the door loose, she took the large Host and six small Hosts, and went back into the shadows, to wait until the church was opened the following morning by the sacristan.

She had a fitful night, twisting and turning, then falling asleep and dreaming that she was standing before God on Judgment Day: He was asking her why she had persecuted His Son by stealing Hosts to be desecrated by satanic cults. She woke up in a cold sweat, shaking for all she was worth. Her breath was heavy; she couldn't wait to get out. As she looked around her, she could make out the images of Angels, looking at her with anger, waiting to pounce on her. When she would allow herself to doze off, she would be awakened by the sound of what she thought were the Avenging Angels coming after her.

At the appointed hour, she could hear the squeaking of the metal key grinding the lock, which would open the door of the church. Her heart pounded; she couldn't wait to get out. She thought for sure, Our Lord Jesus or His Mother Mary, the Angels or the Saints, would pounce on her, and destroy her. As the sacristan slowly wound his way up to the front of the church, towards the sacristy, Anna slowly and silently slipped out of the church, with her Treasure in the folds of a cloth kerchief. She headed in the direction, she had predetermined would be the best route of escape. Everything was going well. She looked around her. Nobody noticed her. She continued walking, not too quickly, so as not to attract attention.

All of a sudden, a strange thing happened. Her packet began to feel somewhat heavy. She thought it curious, but continued on her escape route. It became heavier as she walked along. In a few short moments, it was extremely heavy, and in less than two blocks from the church, it became too heavy to carry. Now she really looked around to see if she were attracting attention. She was carrying a small satchel, which had weighed her down so much, she could just about drag it along the ground. She knew that people would begin to notice her. She panicked. She didn't know what to do. She was near the cemetery, which is still there to this day. She dragged the little satchel, now weighing thousands of pounds, to her way of thinking. She saw a little area of uncultivated land, piled high with nettles.[2] Desperately,

---

[2]Prickly-type plant, whose skin has sharp needles which cut the skin on contact.

she dragged what was now her albatross, and pushed it into the pile of nettles. It didn't take much for it to sink to the bottom of the pile, it was so heavy. She looked around her. No one had seen her. It was very early in the morning. She piled more nettles on the heap, cutting her fingers in the process. When she took the Hosts out of the sack, she kept the Corporal, in which she had wrapped the Hosts.

[When she was finally apprehended, she had the Corporal in her possession. She couldn't explain why she had kept this incriminating piece of evidence.]

She left the scene, went quickly to the coach station, and took the next coach out of the country, back into Germany. She knew she had to leave Ettiswil; she feared she would be caught. She couldn't go back to Bischoffingen, because she knew the satanic cult would be waiting for her to return with the consecrated Hosts. She went instead to Triengen-in-Baden. Within a very short time, a matter of weeks, she was caught by the police, as the result of a few eyewitnesses from Ettiswil who had noticed that she, a stranger, had been hanging around the church, acting suspiciously, and then made off for the coach station like someone possessed.

When the sacristan entered the Sanctuary, he noticed the Tabernacle's grated gate had been pried open and the Hosts gone. As soon as the Hosts were reported stolen, an all-out search was made, not only for the thief and blasphemer, but most especially for the consecrated Hosts. Word drifted from Germany about the thefts which had taken place in Bischoffingen. The search party split in two: Half combed the area for the Hosts; and the other half, for the thief.

A young girl, Margarethe Schulmeister, was grazing her pigs near the cemetery of the Church. She was a very holy girl, and very poor. She was happy with her life, because she had the Lord. She loved to graze her pigs near the church, because she could feel the presence of her Lord and Savior there. On this particular day, she could not help but feel the strong presence of

Jesus around her. The pigs began to act strangely. She couldn't control their movement. They were near the fence of the cemetery. They stopped grunting. They began moving in different directions. Then, they wouldn't go forward; they wouldn't go backward. The pigs looked all around. One of them knelt; then all of them knelt. Margarethe called for help from another shepherd woman who was also grazing in the same area. Even with the two of them trying to move the pigs, they were unsuccessful. The pigs had taken on a posture of guarding whatever was there in the growth. Margarethe went over to what seemed to be the focus of their attention. She began to pull apart the nettles. They cut into her hands, causing her to bleed. She went as deep as she could. There before her, she saw a brilliant light coming from the nettles. She spread the weeds apart, to see six small Hosts in the shape of flower petals, with a large Host in the middle, forming the heart of a flower, the shape of a rose.

She gasped. She knew this had to be from Heaven. She was a very spiritual girl. She hadn't heard anything about the Hosts being stolen, but she knew Jesus was before her in a miraculous Form. Her whole body began to shake. She didn't know what to do; she knelt. Word, about these happenings, got to the volunteers who had been looking for the stolen Hosts. They immediately sent for the parish priest. Now, as he had not said anything about the theft to anyone, other than those he had enlisted to find Them, he knew this had to be through Divine intercession. He quickly vested up, and walked in procession, with the Processional Cross,[3] the volunteers carrying candles and the Altar boys torches. The church bells rang in praise of Our Lord Jesus, and although the people didn't know why the bells were ringing, they came out of their homes to follow the priest in procession.

It was only a short distance to the cemetery, actually at the end of the church property. When he approached the place where the Hosts were located, Margarethe was still kneeling in

---

[3]The Altar server carries this cross as he processes with the priest and other Altar servers toward the Altar, at the beginning of the Mass.

reverence. By this time, many others had come, and upon seeing *why* she was kneeling, they in turn went down on their knees in adoration. The priest came over to the place, and was awe-struck. He began to remove the consecrated Hosts from the ground, very carefully, so that they wouldn't drop back into the thicket. He was able to get the six Hosts out of the ground, although his hands began to bleed, as had Margarethe's when she attempted to remove Them from the thicket of nettles. He placed the six Hosts in a ciborium. But he had a problem with the large Host; he couldn't get it out of the ground. He dug deeper into the nettles, trying to pry the Host loose without breaking it. His hands began to bleed badly. The fingers were shaking from the pain. He couldn't grasp the large Host. He wouldn't allow anyone else to try taking the Host out of the ground. A number of the Faithful expressed verbally what was becoming very clear in his mind. ***Perhaps this is where the Lord wants this Miraculous Host to stay.*** Perhaps they were to make a shrine or a chapel out of this place.

A large stone was rolled over the spot where the Hosts had been found, and where the large Host was still in the ground. At the same time, a high fence with a gate was placed around the area where the Miracle had taken place. Within a few months, a temporary Chapel was constructed and consecrated on December 28, 1443, a year after the Miracle had occurred. Here, pilgrims would come and pray to Our Lord Jesus, at the place which He had chosen to prove He was with them in the Tabernacle and on the Altar during the Mass. Finally, in 1450, a more permanent chapel was constructed and finished on August 6, 1452. The Chapel still stands to this day, in honor of the Miracle of the Eucharist of Ettiswil which took place in 1447.

Why did they roll a stone over the consecrated Host? We were wounded at the prospect of Our Lord in the Eucharist being covered by a stone, until, after prayer the thought came to us: They rolled a stone in front of the tomb where they laid Jesus.

And from that tomb, Jesus would rise and we would know that we too would rise, someday, and have eternal life; we would share in Jesus' promise to the good thief: *"Amen I say to you, today you will be with Me in paradise. "*[4]

The priest went back to the parish church with the six small Hosts. Almost immediately, a precious reliquary was made to house this special Gift. It was a Monstrance of gold and silver, in which the pieces of the six Hosts were placed in the shape of petals, made available to the people who would come, hear about the story, and actually see the Miracle.

But the gold may have been too beautiful for those tempted by the glitter of gold, because a thief broke into the church and stole the beautiful Monstrance, as well as the Miracle of the Eucharist. All was not lost, however; the thief sent back the Miraculous Hosts to the church, but not the gold and silver Monstrance. A new Monstrance was built, perhaps even more beautiful than the first, of solid silver. But it was to have the same fate as the first. On May 27, 1555, thieves broke into the church again. This time, the Miraculous Hosts and the Monstrance were stolen, and never returned. It is not known what finally happened to the Miraculous Hosts. Sadly, it is believed they may have been destroyed.

The woman who was used by the satanists, Anna Vogtli, was arrested soon after the theft of the Hosts, in Triengen-in-Baden. Although the theft occurred in Switzerland, she was tried in Germany by a civil court, as well as by Church authorities. When they apprehended her, she was still carrying the Corporal, she had taken when she stole the Hosts from the church. This, plus the eyewitness testimony of those who had seen her in the church at Ettiswil, became damning evidence against her. She seemed almost relieved to be caught, and immediately confessed her crime, as well as the thefts in Bischoffingen, and her

---

[4]Luke 23:43

association with the cultists.

Her confession went far beyond the theft of the Hosts. She shared the plan of the satanists to cast spells on all who were their enemies, as well as high officials in the government and the Church. As part of her confession, she stated: "We *cast an evil spell on all those, we hated in order to ruin the fruits of the land. We did to the people every other sort of evil.*" (Had the plan to steal the consecrated Hosts from Ettiswil succeeded) "*We would have completely devastated the harvests, the vineyards and the other fruits of the fields....and with the Sacred Body of our Savior, we would have committed other abominable things. To speak of them is horrifying.*"

She told the investigators she had consigned herself to the power of the spirit of darkness, and been assigned to a spirit guide, who bore the name of Lux (Light in Latin, *Lucifer?*).

Anna Vogtli was convicted of witchcraft. She converted, confessed her sins, and was reconciled with the Church. Her last days were spent praising our Lord Jesus. Although she knew she had to die as punishment for her offenses, her heart was light. She was forgiven. When she went to her execution, she was completely reconciled with Our Lord Jesus. She was prepared to meet her Lord and Savior. Ironically, her cohorts, actually the satanists who engineered the whole plan, and were the cause not only of Anna Vogtli's crime, but of her final condemnation, were never caught. They probably went on to other areas of Europe to continue their satanic work.

Why did Our Lord Jesus give us the Miracle of the Eucharist in Ettiswil in 1447? What was he trying to tell us, prepare us for? Why did He choose the eastern boundary of Switzerland, and the western part of Germany? We know that at the end of the century, all the powers of Satan would descend on this part of Europe with Martin Luther's beginnings of Protestantism. Attacks on the Church and her teachings were spreading over the northern part of Europe, especially in this area. Jesus knew, we would need strength for the days ahead. There would be much persecution, and tearing down of our beliefs and values. Beliefs we had embraced from childhood, which had been given to us by our parents and grandparents, would all of a sudden be questioned and denied. We needed something from Our Lord Jesus to hold onto. We needed His Strength in a notable and extraordinary way. He gave us a Miracle of the Eucharist. One of Martin Luther's first attacks would be against the Real Presence of Jesus in the Eucharist. However, no one could deny the Miracle of the Eucharist of Ettiswil.

How do the circumstances of 1447 parallel the circumstances of 1994? All the beliefs we have treasured all our lives are being challenged. We're being told that our supernatural and moral codes are old-fashioned and out of style. Sin has become an alternate life-style. What was illegal under punishment of imprisonment five years ago is being defended by our country as part of our inalienable rights. Social behavior which was considered perversion is now forced upon us and our children, using equal rights under the constitution as a justification. Who has the rights and who doesn't? We're in the topsy-turvy world of Alice in Wonderland. White is black; black is white. Good is evil; evil is acceptable behavior. Does the Eucharistic Miracle of Ettiswil fit into today's world? Do we need a Miracle of the Eucharist? Will our Lord come down to us in our present state of sinfulness? Will He help us? Abraham said to the Lord, when He was anticipating the destruction of Sodom and Gomorrah, *"But Lord, if you only find ten good men, will you still save Sodom and Gomorrah?"*[5] Do we have ten good men? Do we have to apologize to Sodom and Gomorrah?

---

[5]Gen 18:32

Asti - 1535

The Host that bled out of love for us!

We are in the year 1535. Our story takes place in Piedmont, a region on the western-most part of Italy, bordering France. Piedmont encompasses such large cities as Turin and Milan, to mention a few. The people of that area speak an Italian greatly influenced by French and possess a spirit more German than Italian. They are industrious and hard-working, with values, very often, more of the world below and less of the World above.

Situated in the hills, south of Tanaro, we find Asti, an important town in Piedmont, noted for its wineries. Our Miracle of the Eucharist takes place in the roman-gothic church of Saint Secondo, Martyr and Patron Saint of the city. This Miracle has been authenticated by the traditions of the village and testimonies from the time it occurred.

It was Sunday morning, July 25, 1535. The Faithful of Asti were being blessed by the special gift of having a priest known for his piety, Father Dominic Occelli, celebrate the Mass. Father was a canon of the distinguished College of Saint Secondo in Asti, and well respected. The procession of priest and acolytes[1] marched down the aisle of the church. At the Altar, Father knelt, prayed silently, and then ascended the Altar, to begin the Celebration of the Mass. His eyes were focused on the large

---

[1]now called Altar servers

Chapel at the College of Saint Secondo in Asti, Italy

Crucifix above the Altar, the ongoing *Altar of Sacrifice.*[2] Being Sunday, the church was filled. At the moment of *"The Breaking of the Bread,"*[3] when the priest breaks the consecrated Host in two, Father was about to fraction[4] the Host, when It began to bleed. Drops of red Blood dripped into the chalice, spilling onto the Paten. The Paten, as well as the priest's fingers, was stained red!

The entire congregation witnessed what had transpired on the Altar. There, in front of all of them, the Host bled! Wonder and awe turned into trembling, when they realized that this might be *Divine* intervention, God bringing about a Miracle, in their church, in their presence, for them to witness! *Why? What did it mean? Was it the end of the world?* The priest turned to the acolyte,[5]

---

[2]read more about this in the chapters on the Mass

[3]According to the Catechism of the Catholic Church, on p. 335, sec. 1329: "this Sacrament (the Eucharist) is expressed in the different names we give It. Each name evokes certain aspects of It." One of the titles is "The Breaking of the Bread because Jesus used this rite, part of a Jewish meal, when as a Master of the table He blessed and distributed the bread, above all at the Last Supper. It is by this action that his disciples will recognize Him after His Resurrection..."

[4]fraction - "The breaking of the Bread: this gesture of Christ at the Last Supper gave the entire eucharistic action its name in apostolic times. In addition to its practical aspect, it signifies that in communion we who are many are made one body in the one Bread that is Christ (1Cor. 10:17)." It is a sign of unity and community. *The Catholic Encyclopedia* by Broderick

[5]Altar server

Bartholomew Carretto, and then to the Faithful present, and informed them what had just happened, that they had been blessed by the Lord that day, to be witnesses of a Miracle of the Eucharist; and they would never be the same. After a few minutes, everything went back to normal, the drops of Blood disappeared, and the Host returned to Its usual appearance.

The Mass ended. The words, we say, at the end of Mass, at Dismissal: *"Go in Peace to love and serve the Lord,"* come to our hearts. Do we realize, at this point in every Mass that Our Lord

Interior of the Chapel at the College of Saint Secondo in Asti, Italy

has brought us Himself, that we are united with Him and our whole Heavenly Family? Do we, in and through this unity, know Him more; and in knowing Him more, do we love Him more; and in knowing Him and loving Him more, do we desire to serve Him more?

The Lord had visited His people, miraculously! They wanted to savor this moment. How would they pass this down to their children and to their children? As an everlasting memory of the Miracle, the Pastor of Saint Secondo reverently preserved the Chalice and the Paten, and they have not been used for the Mass ever since that day. They have been available to be seen and venerated, from that time till today. The Bishop of Asti promptly informed his holiness Pope Paul III. Then, the Bishop compiled a notarized accounting of all that had transpired and sent a copy of the documentation to the Pope.

The Pontiff, with a Papal Brief dated November 6, 1535, responded, granting *plenary indulgences* to all those who, under the required conditions[6] visited the Church of Saint Secondo on the anniversary of the Miracle, and participated in the Eucharistic procession, that day.

"They will know them by their fruits!" A fruit of the Miracle of the Eucharist that further affirms the authenticity of the Miracle: Some Lutheran soldiers, of the Imperial Army of Charles V, came to Asti. When they learned about the Miracle of the Eucharist, they went to the church, to see for themselves. When they went before the Chalice and Paten of the Miracle, they knew it was the Lord! They converted to the Catholic faith! An inscription, dating back to that time, was placed above the Altar of the Sacred Heart, and reads, till today:

"Here, where Christ shed His Blood from the sacred
Bread, He drew powerfully to Himself, an unbeliever
from a misled Faith (of the heretics) to the True Faith,
at the same time, confirming the Faith of the people of
Asti."

Jesus, through His Body, Blood, Soul and Divinity, Present in the Eucharist, used this Miracle to bring back home some of those whom Luther and other protesters (Protestants) lured away from His Church. These two signs: the plaque that gives credit to the *miraculous conversion*, in particular, and the solid *faith* of the people of Asti, speak even more strongly than the evidence that can be seen till today. The story of the Miracle was passed on, vividly portrayed in a work of art, at the end of the XVI century. But *the* greatest Art, which portrays the Miracle, is the Son of the Creator Who is present at each Mass and in each Tabernacle in the world, Our Lord Jesus Christ.

---

[6]The Church grants such Indulgences under the following conditions: One must be baptized , a subject of the Church, free of excommunication and in a state of grace, and pray The Creed, The Lord's Prayer, one Hail Mary and a Glory Be, for the Pope's intention.

God was, through this Miracle affirming the priesthood and our priest, Father Occelli, who was very pious, as one can detect from his own written words, which appeared in the register of Saint Secondo College:

"October 8, 1532,

I, Father Dominic D. Occelli, entered the Society of the Most Holy Blessed Sacrament and because of my devotion to the Eucharist, I commit to celebrating a Mass, in honor of the Blessed Sacrament, on Thursdays of every week."

Before there was an acceptance of diabolical heretical teachings, expounding serious errors, by dissidents within the Church, the Miracle was looked upon as a Grace, a gracious Gift from God reinforcing devotion to the Eucharist by worthy priests on the Altar.

In the year 1536, passing through Asti, the Emperor Charles V, upon viewing the miraculous Chalice and Paten, ruled that they be carried in solemn procession under a canopy each year, on the Feast of Corpus Domini.[7] He requested, he be allowed to hold one of the poles of the canopy under which the Miracle was to be carried, in procession, in honor of the Triumph of the Blessed Sacrament.

The yearly Eucharistic Procession on the Feast of Corpus Domini had been preserved up until 1968, although it was reduced and limited to the processing in the interior of the church. Then in 1968, because the church was undergoing restoration, the traditional procession was suspended, completely. Finally, the work was completed, in 1975, and the church was reinstated to its full function. But the procession, which had been suspended for practical purposes, when the situation was resolved, was not reinstated. For all practical purposes, it has been all but forgotten.

People of the town and occasional visitors come seeking information on the miraculous occurrence which took place in the church of Saint Secondo, but because they cannot see a

---

[7]Corpus Christi

bleeding Host or a Host turned into a Human Heart, or Hosts that have not decomposed for almost three hundred years, they lose interest, and the great message that our Lord left us tends to diminish and lessen from neglect. But the perpetual memory of a miraculous event cannot be snuffed out. It remains etched in our minds, gnawing away at our hearts, so that when we see someone who is about to carry Our Lord out of the church, no matter what the price, we will run after him or her and ask that person to consume the Host or if necessary take the Host from the person and return It to the priest. With this, and all the Miracles of the Eucharist, have we been called to hold high the Holy Eucharist before the whole world, risking rejection, as Jesus before us?

Will we spend one hour with Him Jesus in adoration, remembering how much He goes through to bring Himself to us, miraculously, when our faith wanes? Will we adore Our Lord during the celebration of the Holy Sacrifice of the Mass, remembering that it is the ongoing Sacrifice of the Cross? Will we go to confession at least once a month so that we can welcome Jesus into a clean, sinless soul? Have the Miracles of the Eucharist inspired us to receive Our Lord frequently and to have a deeper devotion to this most special of all Sacraments and to honor The Eucharist with the adoration due our King?

Is the true message of this Miracle, and all others, that in the most Blessed Sacrament of the Holy Eucharist, Our Lord Jesus Christ is Really Present, that He comes and offers Himself to us in the Eucharist, through which the Church continually lives and grows?

"*To the everlasting fountain of the Savior must the soul run, to placate it's thirst for salvation*", as it is expressed in this stupendous prayer of Saint Bonaventure:

"*Oh sweet Jesus, pierced with hurts and wounds, I highly salute Thee, to fill the heart of my soul with Thy Love, so that it may truly burn, suffer, be consumed, and become less, it's only desire of Thee; that it may melt of love and be with Thee.*

"*That it may hunger only for You, Bread of celestial life, that has descended from heaven. That it may thirst for Thee, Font of life, Font of eternal light, Brook of real joy. That it may look for Thee, and in Thee, it may sweetly rest.*"

This evening, before you close your eyes, say this prayer that has come down through the ages, and remember that Jesus loves you and never leaves you alone.

"Soul of Christ, sanctify me.
Body of Christ, save me.
Blood of Christ, inebriate me.
Water from the side of Christ, wash me.
Passion of Christ, comfort me.
O good Jesus, hear me.
Within Thy wounds, hide me.
Never let me be separated from Thee.
From the malicious enemy, defend me.
In the hour of my death, bid me to come unto Thee,
so that together with Thy saints,
I may praise Thee, forever and ever. Amen."

Marseille-en-Beauvais - 1533

The Host Respected by the Snow

There is a saying, we use often in our Ministry, and the older we get, and the more we experience the majesty of the Lord, the truer it becomes. It is, *"The Lord works in mysterious ways, His wonders to behold."* The Miracle of the Eucharist we want to share with you now, may have been given to us for the express purpose of bringing you just a glimpse of the majesty and wonder of our mighty God, Who is in charge of all things, at all times.

I think we'll all agree that the world of today could very possibly be on a path of destruction with, as our Pope said, its *"culture of death"*. Our Church is being hurt as she is caught in its wake. It always appears as if the enemy is winning the battle. We see things happening inside the Church and inside our country that we never thought possible, and seemingly, they go unchallenged or unchecked. We worry about some of our priests and bishops, senators, congressmen, governors, president, wondering whose side they are on. Some of our brothers and sisters are traveling 50 and 60 miles from their home parish on a Sunday morning to attend a traditional Mass. We're fighting an intense battle; very often believing we're losing, and we're all alone. The laity is becoming stronger, while sadly, it seems the priests are getting weaker. It's at just these times that the Lord works very powerfully in some way, to affirm us, and whisper in our ears that we're not hopeless and helpless; we're not alone. Jesus made a promise; *"I will not leave you orphans; I will come to you." Does He not come to us? Is He not with us until the end of time*?

We have noted and stated many times, *"When the Church is in crisis, God sends us Miracles of the Eucharist to affirm us, to protect us, to let us know He has not left us, and that He is in charge.* " We believe, the Lord is giving us that message today, in the last decade of this second millennium, this Twentieth Century, by sharing a Miracle of the Eucharist which took place in a little town in the north of France in 1533. When the Lord wants one of His powerful Miracles to be known, nothing that the enemy can come up with, can stop that Miracle from being brought to the surface. He also usually lets us know, in no uncertain terms, the reason He has given us that Miracle.

The beginning to the middle of the Sixteenth Century, was a time of great struggle and even greater controversy for the Church. A roaring battle was waged for the souls of millions of Catholics who were lulled by the glamour of a new way, a Revolution, which the enemy chose to label Reformation. The heresies of an excommunicated Augustinian priest, Martin Luther, were sweeping across Europe, especially at this time, in Germany, France and the Scandinavian countries. As part of Satan's plan, Luther threw out all the Sacraments, the priesthood, and most especially the Eucharist.

The Lord takes us to Marseille-en-Beauvais, about 14 miles from Beauvais, some 60 miles northwest of Paris, on the way to Rouen, where St. Joan of Arc was burned at the stake, and Lisieux, the home of the Little Flower, St. Thérèse. Jesus chose the week of His Birthday, just a few days after that Holy Day when the Savior was born. We don't know for sure what the spiritual and political climate was, at that particular time, in Northern France. Had Luther's followers found their way into this little hamlet? Was the Church under attack here, or was this one of the last holdouts against a rising tide of anti-Catholic sentiments in Northern Europe?

We only have one positive indicator. We're told that the Parish Church contained consecrated Hosts, which were used to bring Viaticum (Holy Communion for the sick and dying). We have to believe that this was still a traditional Catholic Church, struggling to hold its own against that wave of unfaithfulness that had swept up so many churches across France, destroying the faith of the people. Is this why the Lord chose to give *this* Church the honor of a Miracle of the Eucharist? Whatever the Lord's plan, during the night, thieves broke into the little Parish Church of Marseille-en-Beauvais and stole the Pyx, which contained the Blessed Sacrament destined to go to the sick and dying. The Pyx was made of silver, and etched in gold. This was what the thieves wanted. They had no intention of taking the Hosts. Though they were thieves, they had a fear of the Blessed Sacrament, and the power in the Hosts. Were they remembering, way back when they used to go to church to worship the Lord? They carefully wrapped the Consecrated Hosts in the little linen pouch which had contained the Pyx. Then they took the pouch with the Hosts, outside the Church, and hid them under a bush. To ensure that the Hosts would not be found, they placed a huge stone on top of the packet, and went their way, a good night's work done, their evil deed covered by the stone and hidden in the dark of night.

At that time, January 1 was celebrated as the Feast of the Circumcision of Our Lord Jesus. On that holy day, Jean Moucque, a member of the Parish of Marseille-en-Beauvais, was on his way to Mass to celebrate that Feast. It was a cold day. Bitter wind whipped the fresh snow, which had fallen recently, into his face, causing a freezing chill to go through his entire body. He shivered from the cold. His face was covered with a woolen scarf; his head was tilted down to protect him from the fierce wind. In this position, he was able to see an unusual occurrence in the snow on the ground. There was a clear round opening in the snow on the ground, as if a very warm round object were laying under the grass. He looked at it, then continued walking towards the Church. His curiosity got the best of him, however, and he circled back to the spot and looked at it again. He bent down to see what was causing this warmth on the ground. Remember now, this was not the time of underground heating, or warmth coming from sewers. None of that existed at that time.

Jean Moucque moved the stone, and saw the Blessed Pouch, containing the Body of his Savior.

Jean ran into the Church to tell the pastor what he had found. The Pastor, Curé Prothais, had not told anyone about the Consecrated Hosts having been stolen. He had been praying fervently since the incident occurred, for the Lord to bring back the Hosts. He wasn't sure who the thieves were. Were they after gold or silver, or did they wanted the Consecrated Hosts for some horrible purpose? He knew the attitude of the zealous Protestants who would do anything to hurt the Church. They had utter disdain for the Eucharist. He was afraid of desecration of the Blessed Body of Christ.

When Jean came to him, and shared what he had found out in the bushes, a great sigh of relief went through the priest, and silent prayers of thanksgiving went up to Our Lord Jesus for sending back the Hosts, unharmed. He went in solemn procession, outside the Church, to the spot where Jean Moucque had seen the Hosts. He reverently picked them up and brought them back inside the Church. Word spread throughout the town about the Hosts that *even the snow respected,* and the Miracle was given that name. The ground was considered Holy Ground. Almost immediately, a fence was built around the spot where the Hosts had been buried. A Cross was erected in Honor of this Gift which the Lord had given the town and the Church.

People began to frequent the little wayside Shrine, praying for healings of all types of illness, and cures came about! The news spread quickly, and invalids came first from the area, then all of northwestern France, and then beyond, from the entire country. All the sick who came and prayed were healed of their illnesses. Healings of the spirit and the soul, took place. Conversions came about. People came back to the Church in great numbers. It was almost as if this one little church, in the middle of a very small section of Northern France, was single-handedly fighting the enemy of Lutheranism, whose power had encompassed so much of northern Europe.

The little Shrine in Marseille-en-Beauvais became a place of Pilgrimage. Gifts and offerings came in, and construction of a proper Chapel was begun. It was completed in six months. At first, it was a very simple structure, a wooden cross marking the spot where the miracle occurred, fenced in by blackberry bushes. This was in order to prevent the hallowed ground from being trampled on by those who did not know what had happened here, and also from those who did know, but would maliciously desecrate the place.

Miracles begin to happen through the Miracle

The Lord had plans for this special site. Pilgrims came by the hundreds at first, then by the thousands. Healings of body and soul were reported by the thousands. That's when the offerings came in. A *proper* Shrine began to be built. One of the first documented miracles was reported from the local priest of the nearby village of Creve-Coeur, Curé Jacques Sauvage. He had lost his speech and had an extremely painful illness, which attacked all his extremities. Nothing could be done about it. Everyone in the area could vouch for his impediment. He came to the newly constructed Shrine, and prayed to Our Lord Jesus in the Miracle, for a healing, if it were His Will, and was good for his (the Priest's) soul. The gift was granted, as much to the priest for his lifetime of loyalty to his God and to his vocation, as for the benefit of the doubting Thomases of the area, and the Protestants who would wish that nothing had happened.

One of the ladies, a blind woman, who had given alms to the construction of the Shrine, was given her sight back. She told a man from Autreche, who had an incurable wound on his leg. He came to the Shrine, and his wound healed almost immediately. One of the most memorable healings was another blind person, a man who came to the miraculous place in search of a healing. Record has it that upon being healed, he came back each year with a violin and played in thanksgiving for the return of his sight. This is a lot like the little drummer boy, who played his drums for Jesus, because that was the only gift, he could give to the Savior.

But Satan was waging war against God. The Miracle of the Eucharist was manifested in such a strategic area, it was dissipating the thrust of his revolution, begun by Luther, and continued by Calvin. The evil one placed two fallen-away clergy in the area. First, the Bishop-Count of Beauvais, Odet de Coligny, killed the Knight of St. Bartholomew, who had been sworn to protect the Miracle of the Eucharist. Then a Cardinal turned bad, and came against the Church. He embraced Calvinism publicly, and then proceeded to marry Elizabeth of Hauteville. His Vicar-General, Boutiller, followed suit, and embraced the same satanic philosophy as his superiors. It was he, however, who felt the most pressure from the Miracle of the Eucharist of Marseille-en-Beauvais.

The people kept flocking to the Shrine. Something had to be done about it, and fast. People were completely ignoring his Lutheran-Calvin jargon in favor of their God, manifested in the Miracle of the Eucharist. Boutiller sent one of his fallen-away priests to the Shrine of the Miracle of the Eucharist, in Marseille-en-Beauvais, with the instructions to consume the Miraculous Hosts (which had been hidden under the rock). The priest of the parish knew that this was not from the Lord, and tried to intercede, so that, what he considered blasphemy and sacrilege, would not happen.

But this was not the Lord's plan. He allowed the unfaithful follower of Calvin to come into the Church, and do his dirty work. The Pastor of the Church, the Faithful priest, praying to the Lord, trying to come up with some good reason why this was allowed to happen, was given the word, *"I can work through this for My Glory."* The priest knew this was the word of the Lord, and accepted it.

The unfaithful priest came to the small village, and went to the little chapel in honor of the Miracle of the Eucharist, whereupon he opened the Tabernacle which housed the Miraculous Hosts. He took them out, feigned a prayer for the sake of propriety, and consumed the Hosts. The healings and miracles stopped immediately. Perhaps this was a word from the Lord similar to what He said through His Servant Job. *"The Lord gives, and the Lord takes away. Blessed be the Name of the Lord."*

But veneration to the Miracle of the Eucharist of Marseille-en-Beauvais *never* stopped, praise You Jesus! The rock, under which the Hosts were hidden in 1533, was placed on a small niche in the Chapel. So even though the Real Presence of the Lord in His Miraculous Form was taken away from the people, the enemies of God were never able to take away the love and devotion to Our Lord Jesus in the Eucharist, nor the thanksgiving from the people for all the healings He had given them. They had something! They had the rock, and the rock was from the Lord, and that was enough for them!

But the fury and anger of the enemies of God would not let up. The Satan which was released through Martin Luther and John Calvin exploded into a rage during the French Revolution, when the enemies of the Church took their vengeance out on the People of God by killing or exiling every priest and nun in the country, and destroying every remnant of Christian devotion they could find. The little Chapel of the Miracle of the Eucharist in Marseille-en-Beauvais was no exception. During the French Revolution, some 225 years later, the Chapel was broken into, and the rock, which had been held in veneration (because it had protected the Body and Blood of Our Lord Jesus Christ), was thrown away.

But still they have never been able to destroy the memory of the gift, the Lord had given the people of that village, at a time when they needed Him so desperately. We're told that till today, a Mass of Thanksgiving is still celebrated, each January 2, which has been designated as the Feast of the *Miracle of the Host Respected by the Snow*. Jesus is telling us through this miracle, *"I will not leave you orphans; I will be with you until the end of time."* The followers of Islam, the Saracens could not destroy the Name of Jesus, for the hundreds of years they occupied most

of Europe. Although they tried, they could not kill the Lord Who
was deep in the hearts of the people. The Church rose again, as
her Founder before her from (what appeared to be) death.

There is also another key here, which is given us in the sub-
title of this miracle, *"The Hosts respected by the snow"*. The
key word is **respect**. We are in a time when the Eucharist is not
being respected. Many of our own practicing Catholics are
referring to the Eucharist, the Body and Blood of Jesus, as a
symbol. The Eucharist is not *really* Jesus, they tell us. There is
no respect. Priests barely raise the Lord during the Eucharistic
Prayer, at the moment of consecration.[1] Is the Lord telling us,
it's time to give back to the Lord, that which He so truly deserves,
*respect in the Eucharist, in the Word, and in the Body of Christ,
His Church?*

What are we doing to bring respect to the Lord? Do we
believe He is with us? Do we reverently genuflect before entering
and after departing from our pew? Are we kneeling throughout
the Eucharistic Prayer, when Our Lord comes to life on the Altar,
or do we follow the crowd and do what they do, even if we, in
our hearts, believe it is disrespectful to the Lord? Do we have
the awe and wonder, the people had for the Hosts, and then for
the rock that sheltered them when the Hosts were consumed?
Do we respect and praise Him for all He has done for us, as they
did for all the Lord had done for them? Do we have this love and
devotion for Our Lord? Do we believe? Do we have to lose Him
to believe? When we walk up to receive Our Lord really present
before us, in the Eucharist, do we meditate on *Who* we are about
to receive? Do you think *that* may be the reason, Our Lord wants
us to know today, that a Miracle of the Eucharist which took
place over 450 years ago, in a little hamlet in France, was taken
away from them, yet He never left their minds and hearts? *Why
not?*

---

[1]One priest told a meeting of Eucharistic Ministers "I'm not require to
raise the host during the consecration. Canon law says 'mostrare', not 'elevare',
and that's all I'm doing." P.S. That young man is no longer a priest.

Morrovalle - 1560

Miraculous conservation of a Host

There is a small Italian village called Morrovalle, located in a center of the Marches,[1] halfway between Macerata[2] and Civitanova Marche, on the Adriatic Sea, in the township of Macerata and the diocese of Fermo. The city is enclosed within a Medieval wall. As we enter through the gate called *Porta Alvaro*, in honor of the general from Aragon who was killed in 1445, in front of this gate[3] defending the Pope against Francis Sforza, we wonder how much if any, this little town has changed since 1568. The sign on the *Porta* reads *"Eucharistic City"*. When a visitor enters the gate to the city, the first thing he sees is the plaque pointing to the *Miracle of the Eucharist of 1560*.

†

Around 1210, under the pontificate of Innocenzo III, the first convent of the Franciscans was built in Morrovalle, in the Angels' Quarter. It was nothing like what we would consider a convent today. It was just a small hut where the Franciscans could headquarter, as they began their evangelization of the area. If the convent was not founded by St. Francis himself, assuredly it was founded by one of the friars close to him, considering the fact that the rule of St. Francis had only been approved by the Pope the year before. We know that St. Francis came evangelizing into this area the following year, in 1211, so the humble little headquarters may have been finished for his first visit. And knowing St. Francis, the more modest the convent, the more he liked it.

Around 1290, after the death of St. Francis, the Benedictines,

---

[1] a province in Italy on the Adriatic coast

[2] where another Miracle of the Eucharist took place in 1356. For more on that Miracle, read chapter on Macerata in Bob and Penny Lord's book: *This is My Body, This is My Blood, Miracles of the Eucharist - Book I*

[3] a monument was set up commemorating the General and the battle.

of the Abbey of Saint Fermano of Montelupone, gave the Franciscans a hospice, a more proper building which could be used for housing their community, as well as being their headquarters. This became the *"Convent of Saint Francis"*. Close to the convent was a church dedicated to the Holy Trinity.
[Special Note: The Portziuncola, the first church of St. Francis, which is located in the small village of Our Lady of the Angels near Assisi, was also given to him by Benedictines; although he insisted on not owning it and paid them one bushel of fish rent each year.]

Centuries later, there was a miracle which would take place in that church, that would be substantiated, so completely, there would be no doubt that the Lord had intervened for His children. So important was this to God and His plan for our salvation that less than *ten days* after the discovery of the miracle, the Pope would order an immediate investigation (the 40 page document is kept in the nearby village of Falconara). The Pope sent a special canonical committee to gather information. Four months after the canons arrived at their conclusive findings, affirming the Miracle, a Bull was issued by Pope Pius IV in which he solemnly recognized the authenticity of the Miracle, (the Bull is preserved in the parochial church of Saint Bartholomew, in Morrovalle).

The Miracle

It was Holy Week, April 1560. On Good Friday, the Church had been in total mourning. Our Savior had died! Not only had the lights dimmed in all the churches in the town, but also in the hearts of the people of Morrovalle. The church was an empty building; the Lord was not there. The Tabernacle was empty! They could feel the emptiness deep inside their hearts, as they knelt before the open, empty Tabernacle, that Good Friday. Their mood must have been like what the women had felt when they came and found the tomb empty. There was a cold chill in the church, as the Faithful entered on Holy Saturday evening for the Easter Vigil Mass. *[There is no feeling of loneliness like a church without the Lord present in the Blessed Sacrament.]* When, at last, the forty days of lent were over, and Light rose from the dark (the tomb), they rejoiced for the first time, *Alleluia, He is risen!* With dawn, a new day had risen with the *Light* of joy - It was Easter Sunday! [St. Paul said, *"If Christ has not been raised, your faith is futile and you are all still in your sins."* [4] And we are lost!]

Easter Sunday, April 14th, the Church had ended its sorrowful days of Holy Week with a new day and new hope. Now, the Faithful were celebrating Easter week. But at this moment, the entire village was sound asleep. It was Tuesday, two a.m. in the morning. The friars were in a very deep sleep having returned that evening from an apostolic pilgrimage bringing St. Francis' *"Pace e Bene"* (Peace and Good) to all, the cities, the villages and the countryside. Father Bonaventura, of the Friars of the Grey Penitents, was awakened by a loud crackling hideous shriek, like that of a madman. He shot up from bed. Startled, he ran to the window to see if he could spot the intruder. The dark night was suddenly lit up as if it was on fire. Huge, red clouds of smoke rose, filling the sky. Bright streaks of flames shot up, not too far in the distance. *"Oh my God,"* the priest thought, horrified, *"It's the church!"* Tongues of fire were engulfing the church, consuming and ravishing everything within.

Frightened, he awakened Father Superior, who sounded the alarm. Men, women and children from the village dressed quickly and ran, buckets of water in their hands, ready to help. Immediately, the friars organized the volunteers. More and more villagers flocked to the church, in an attempt to save her. But, despite the heroic efforts of everyone, it took *seven hours* to finally extinguish the fire. Blackened by smoke, tears running down their cheeks, lungs burning from the fumes, all the villagers could do was stare at the church, as if they could wish away the horror before their eyes. All that was left of their beautiful church was a heap of smoking ruins. The cause of the fire was never discovered. But we do wonder! Was Father not awakened by

---

[4] 1Cor 15:17

what sounded like a horrible shriek from a demon? Does this sound far-fetched? Did not the devil move St. John Vianney's bed from one side to another during the night, going so far as to set it on fire, another night?[5]

When the Provincial, Father Girolamo, heard the news, he hastened from Ancona to Morrovalle. Looking over the burnt remains of the church, and having determined the extent of the catastrophe, he decided, in accord with the Superior of the convent, that before clearing away the debris from the rest of the church, they had better go to the Altar where the Blessed Sacrament was and try to ascertain what damage had been done to the Hosts by the fire. He engaged Brother Illuminato and *Father Battista of Ascoli* to help him see to it.

The Papal Bull of Pope Pius IV speaks of Father Battista as a holy priest, a simple and good man of flawless reputation and a lifetime of integrity. Born of Jewish parents, Divine Grace enlightened him when he was still a boy. *[We have interviewed priests who have converted to the Catholic Church, and their testimony is pretty much the same. They will say, that upon entering a church, they felt the overpowering presence of Jesus and they knew! Mother Angelica once told us, it is by Divine Grace that we are Catholics. So it is not to our credit or a sign of our worth, but of God's love.]* He became a Christian, and then entered the Franciscan order and, thanks to his example, to the doctrine he preached, and to his convictions, he was able to bring to the Catholic Faith, 22 converts from the Hebrew Faith.[6]

Holy Saturday, three days before the fire, during the celebration of the Mass, Father Battista had consecrated a second large Host and placed It in the ciborium of the main Altar of the church. As the three Friars fought their way through the rubble, climbing over charred pews and smashed statues, choking at times from the lingering smell of smoke that covered the broken and

---

[5]Read about this and the Curé of Ars, St. John Vianney in Bob and Penny Lord's book: *"Saints and other Powerful Men in the Church".*
[6]Read chapter on The Old Law in this book

bruised remnants of their precious church, burning their fingers, arms and legs on the charred remains of pews, they struggled toward the Altar, praying, but not daring to hope they would find the Host intact. It became more and more evident that nothing had survived the ruthless fire.

But on April 27, it was to be different. It was exactly ten days after the disaster. Using great persistence, they began to remove huge pieces of marble that had once been the Altar. It was a devastating sight, almost as if a giant hand had smashed it, or the fires of hell had tried to consume it. Part of the Altar had fallen, blocking the wall where the Tabernacle had been. The Friars and their helpers lifted the heavy piece of marble. There was the cubicle, where the Tabernacle had been, but the Tabernacle had melted from the intense heat. All that was left were wood splinters and fragments of marble. Tears in their eyes, they reverently began to lift the fractured parts of the Lord's former palace, the Tabernacle. They gently brushed aside the mound of grey soft ashes that had collected in the opening. They could not believe their eyes. There was something gleaming! As they peered deeper into the alcove where the Tabernacle had been, Father Battista beheld the Holy Eucharist! There Our Lord was, in the middle of a cave, once again, unharmed as in Bethlehem. Only now, the swaddling cloth was the corporal, atop another linen cloth. The corporal was scorched and the second cloth burned more; but the Host rested intact under a light pall[7] of ash. The feet and the cup of the pyx, where Our Lord had reposed, had completely melted together from the heat of the fire; only its cover had resisted the flames.

They all fell to their knees in adoration. Their Lord was alive, and He was here with them! They were overcome, tears flowing down their faces. Recovering, they began to cry out: *There was a Miracle in their midst*! The other Friars hastened to broadcast the Good News! The bells tolled, announcing to all

---

[7]the Italian author uses this word which means the cloth that is used to cover a coffin

the surrounding region that Jesus was *miraculously* in their midst. Once again, the Good News went out, only now the Angels, who had heralded the Good News in Bethlehem, were using bells to proclaim that Our Savior was alive. Just as that *first* Good News would begin in a small village and travel to the whole world, so *this* Good News would spread from village to city, to countryside, to region, to you today. The bells kept ringing. As the Angels kept whispering in more and more townspeoples' ears, they flocked to the remains of the little church.

The Faithful took turns guarding the Miracle, kneeling in adoration, amidst the burned remnants of what had been the Altar. The Host was exposed for *three days*. Was Our Lord telling them, and us that what happens on the Altar is the ongoing death and resurrection of Our Lord Jesus? Was He telling them and us that He is alive on the Altar, after the Consecration, in the Tabernacle?

In the days that followed, the people of the village and of the region, in ever-growing numbers, came to see for themselves. Then upon seeing, believing; and upon believing, fell on their knees in adoration of the Lord in this Miracle. On the fourth day, the Superior having called him, Father Provincial Evangelista da Mora d'Alba arrived, and in the presence of the many Faithful who had gathered, and in the company of the Friars and the officials of the city, he celebrated a Solemn High Mass of *thanksgiving* for the Miracle received. After the Mass, he removed the miraculous Host from the area where It had been found, and reverently placed It in a Tabernacle, lent for the occasion by the Parish of the Collegiate Church of Morrovalle.

Afterward, the Host was placed into a vessel made of ivory and housed in a larger chest, for security purposes. They carefully safeguarded their Treasure, by locking the chest with three keys: two were consigned to the guardianship of the Priory and kept there, and the third was in the custody of the Friars.

A Feast Day was proclaimed, to announce the Miracle.

There are four documents that guarantee the veracity of the Miracle:

(1) Papal Investigation- May 7, 1560

Pope Pius IV, touched by the news of the Miracle but reserving judgment until further study, ordered an exact, detailed investigation. His priority was to choose a man endowed with integrity, prudence and doctrine. He called on his trusted brother Bishop, Lodovico, Bishop of Bertinoro. The Pope wrote, that the Bishop being an honest and prudent man, he trusted him to go to the place where the reported Miracle had occurred, and investigate *accurately* on the authenticity of the facts and to refer back faithfully to him, that which he discovered. Then the Pope invited the Bishop to guide the canonical process, granting him full faculties and authority.

(2) The results of the Canonical Process

Bishop Lodovico arrived in Morrovalle for the investigations, the 5th or 6th of May, less than a month after the fire. Taking care to be accurately informed of the facts, closely investigating all the possibilities, he then listened to the testimonies of eye witnesses. He presented his judgment to the Canonical Committee.

After careful deliberation, the findings of the Canonical Process were drawn up between the 16th and the 26th of May in 1560, and notarized by Christopher Bartoli of Apiro, chancellor of the Holy House of Loreto[8] and by Quirico Orsi, canon lawyer of the Curia of Macerata. Satisfied that he had all the facts, the Bishop diligently sent the results of what had emerged from the canonical process, to the Pope.

The Pope, for his part, entrusted the examination of the Bishop's report to a Commission of Cardinals. Five Cardinals of the utmost honesty and learning, verified the authenticity of the occurrences described, imparting to the Pontiff their favorable conclusions. Hence, having listened to their advice, and that of

---

[8]read about the Holy House of Loreto in Bob and Penny Lord's book: *Heavenly Army of Angels*

Bishop Lodovico, he declared that he found no fraud, no deceit in the incident, and that, therefore, one can conclude that the Miracle was a True and Real Miracle.

(3) The Papal Bull September 19, 1560

In his Bull, the Pope described the reported happenings of the Miracle, that following a violent fire that destroyed the entire church, reducing it to ashes, the Tabernacle of gilded silver was laid threadbare by the ferocious impact of the flames and almost liquefied. It further reported that only the cover of the pyx and the Eucharist remained intact, entire, unharmed, to the praise and everlasting glory of God and Our Lord Jesus Christ. The following is part of the declaration, concerning the Miracle, by His Holiness in his Papal Bull *"Sacrosanto Romana Chiesa"*:[9]

"The Holy Roman Catholic Church, before anything else, desires the purity of the Christian religion, as it keeps watch diligently, so as not to lead the Faithful to false miracles, in that way it urges, that we always remember, with piety and devotion, that which Our Savior, in His mercy toward mankind, deigns, at times, to operate through Christians, for His praise and glory, and exaltation of the Catholic Faith."

The Pope described in his Bull the full story of the Miracle and the findings of the Commission.[10]

The Pope said in addition: *"In order to adequately honor so great a Miracle, given to us through God's Divine Will, in our time to strengthen our belief toward this great Sacrament, which at this time through diabolic prompting (instigation), comes torn and profaned, we proclaim that all believers must know this Miracle and celebrate It with all the affection of their hearts."*

And because he felt so strongly about the Miracle, the Pope granted a Plenary Indulgence to those who are sincerely sorry for their sins, and having gone to confession (or will, in the period prescribed by the law of the Church), visit the Franciscan church on the anniversary of the fire, the 16th of April, and of the

---

[9]Holy Roman Catholic Church
[10]which we related at the beginning of the story.

miraculous manifestation the 27th of April.

The Supreme Pontiff granted, in addition, special permission for the Divine Office of Corpus Domini to be said, on those same days, in the same church.

The Pope put his signature to this Bull, September 19th, 1560. The parchment which contains the original Papal Bull is conserved in the Parochial church of Saint Bartholomew in Morrovalle.

(4) The letter written in 1568, informing Pope Pius IV of the Miracle.

A subsequent proof in favor of the Miracle is the official letter written on parchment, that is kept in the Archives of the town of Morrovalle. In it, are instructions to the envoy, sent to Rome, who was given full authority to advocate the cause for the Miracle, before the Pope. In it, he is told to present himself to the Pope and inform His Holiness of the holy and wonderful Miracle manifested in the church of St. Francis, and to extol the laudable and praiseworthy accounting of the Miracle.

There were articles printed in Ancona, on the Miracle of Morrovalle taking up eight books and 523 chapters. The first book that was written, containing 22 chapters, articulated on the Divine Worship, the veneration of the Saints and on the Mass. All this centered around the Miracle of the Eucharist of Morrovalle.

The following events of the sanctuary and of the miraculous Host

The sanctuary of the Miracle was restored, more beautiful than before, now in the form of a Latin cross. This was through the generosity of the deeply Christian population, who although many were of humble circumstance (like the widow and her mite in Holy Scripture), gave all they had to build their churches, with special mention made of the Lazzarini, Marchetti and Colleterali families, who contributed magnanimously. [It is for this reason, we cry and take issue with anyone tearing down the beautiful traditional churches that our ancestors have built with the offerings from their very substance.]

So many came, the church became soon too small for all the worshipers. It had to be enlarged. It was a time of glorification of the Lord in His Blessed Sacrament and in His Church. *But all good things come to an end, or do they?*

In 1742, the first calamity hit the church. The deadly tremors of an earthquake seriously damaged the Franciscan church of the Miracle. The church had to close, because the earthquake had not only damaged the structure, it had weakened the walls to a point of being dangerous. The Faithful prayed and the church was to reopen. As they celebrated Masses of Thanksgiving, little did they know that a worse hardship would face the church.

1808 came and disaster with it. Satan had attacked, using Mother Nature against God's children. Now, he would use fallen man. Napoleon Bonaparte marched through this part of Italy, and brought with him, the suppression of the Church. The Friars were forced to abandon the church and convent. But through the pressure and insistence of the Commune of Morrovalle, the Sanctuary was left open to those desiring to visit the Miracle and venerate Our Lord. The Shrine became an annex to the Church of St. Bartholomew, and the priests there helped to keep up the church.

In 1824, the convent and church were returned to the Friars. But a new tempest would come to disturb the peace and good of the Friars and the cloister, 37 years later.

Just when you think things cannot get worse, another year and another attack. It is 1861; the big Church and the small church (of the Miracle) are under attack. Sadly, the Church has always been the recipient of wounds from the world. Our Church is called to live the Gospel life. As Our Lord Jesus said: *"I am not of this world."* And we know, the world tried to kill Him, and it will always try to kill Him, only now, through the death of His Church. The world, in its sinfulness, has always turned against itself, and the Church in its wake.

When you visit Italy, and travel to the different Provinces, you will notice a marked difference in the way they cook, they pronounce different words, with attitudes as different as the way they bake bread and cook sauce. You find an almost exaggerated pride in their *Region* over their country. It is because, at one time, they were a mass of over 27 different little kingdoms, with their own languages, dukes and desires on the kingdom next door. As you drive through the breathless hills and mountains of Italy, you cannot fail to see the fortified cities on the hillsides, surrounded by medieval walls, their towers rising high above the other buildings, reminders of days when they housed lookouts, as well as the duke of the village.

This is what greets us in 1861. We are in the midst of a bitter struggle between the Papal States and the Italian States. The people of God have always paid the price for the greed and avarice of the few; and the Church, committed to the lost and hungry, has always been a threat to those who would exploit them. There has always been a battle waged between good and evil. The Church preached hope and new life, and the dignity of man, quoting Jesus that we are no longer slaves. This did not agree with the Feudal times of serfs and masters. Besides, the Church had property that the Italian States wanted for their own. The demon of greed can never be satisfied. The Church became alienated from the Italian States. And so, the Italian States confiscated all the holy, clerical and religious items from convents and churches. The Italian States attacked convents and monasteries, and cast out their Religious, as well as stole everything that was not nailed down.

In 1867, the Franciscan church (of the Miracle) was ransacked and desecrated, reduced to a barn, and, up to the present, remains desecrated and used for other purposes, such as museums and etc. With the permission of the Holy See, the Feast of the Portziuncola pardons[11] was transferred to the Church of Saint

---

[11]More widely known as the Portziuncola Indulgence, originally attached to the Chapel that was dedicated on August 2; thus the indulgence may be gained as a plenary indulgence as often as the conditions are fulfilled.

Bartholomew.

In 1960 they solemnly celebrated the fourth centenary of the Miracle and, on that anniversary, the town council of Morrovalle, unanimously decided that on the facade of the principal door of the city, be placed the inscription: "Civitas Eucaristica," City of the Eucharist.

Each year, during the month of April, remarkably large crowds would flock to the Sanctuary in Morrovalle, to obtain the Plenary Indulgence granted by Pope Pius IV. Today, on the historic two dates, April 16th and 27th, they no longer make great celebrations: it's limited to the exposition of the Blessed Sacrament and of the Monstrance containing the relics on the main Altar.

The Church of St. Bartholomew in Morrovalle

The pyx that contains the cover of the pyx of the Eucharistic Miracle of Morrovalle, Italy

It is not known what happened to cause the Faithful to cease celebrating the Feast Day of the Miracle. Was it because the Host of the Miracle was no longer there? *It happened!* as the Papal Bull and all the documents verified. Our Lord *did* bring about a Miracle to reach the hearts of His people. When we think about it, though, this proves, equally or even more-so that the Lord is Really Present in the Eucharist, in our church after the priest consecrates the bread and wine into the Body, Blood, Soul and Divinity of Christ, and in the Tabernacle. The cover of the pyx is a remembrance, a symbol, not a reality of Christ's Presence, the way the miraculous Host was. Where the Host of the Miracles of the Eucharist are present, whether in Their original Form (as Hosts), or miraculously changed (into a Heart as in Lanciano) the Lord is there, in our midst and it is He Who holds us, and brings us back. Here, is it because only a symbol remains that devotion to the Miracle has declined? Is this why our brothers and sisters in Christ, who are separated from us, go to church after church seeking Jesus? Is it because, they have only a symbol and not the Eucharist, the living Jesus in their midst?

No one knows what happened to the miraculous Host. It is believed that possibly, when they broke into the church, the Host was stolen. All that remains is the cover of the pyx and the relics which remain intact. It is now encased in a crystal vessel, with the Bishop's seal attached, on view in a beautifully ornate Monstrance. The relics and the Papal Bull of Pope Pius IV, dating back to the sixteenth century, is kept in the parochial church of Saint Bartholomew. By special grant (permission) of Pope Leo XIII, one is able to earn also the indulgences granted by Pope Pius IV for the remission (of all temporal) sins, on the two Feast Days in April.

The first of June, in 1981,[12] when our Pope John Paul II was questioned by the youth in Paris, he shared confidentially that the most important thing in his life was not to be Pope and Bishop, but to be a priest, a *"Minister of the Eucharist."* He said: *"It is indeed the Mass the true identity and profound (searching) of the priest and, may we add, of the Christian. It is the Memorial Sacrament of all the Mysteries of Christ: evocation,[13] realization, invocation[14] of His Blessed Passion, glorious Resurrection, secure in the confidence of His coming."*

---

[12]the year Father Giannini told us to give him a copy of our book when we were finished writing it. [It did not get written till 1986.]

[13]calling forth

[14]petitioning

El Escorial - 1572

Our God Reigns

We were bringing a group of pilgrims on a Journey of Faith through Spain, when we stopped in the main church of El Escorial. We were on our way to the shrines of Saint Teresa, in Avila and Alba de Tormes. We had visited the Shrine of

Shrine - Royal Monastery of El Escorial

the Miracle of the Eucharist in Daroca, prayed at the Shrine of Our Lady of Zaragoza, and continued across the country to Madrid. Now, the next day, we were heading towards Avila. But between Madrid and Avila are a memorial and a shrine not to be missed. The memorial is called *The Valley of the Fallen*, a tribute to those spanish soldiers who had fallen in the Spanish Civil War of 1936. You can tell that you are approaching it, when you see an immense cross (430 ft. of reinforced concrete) looming majestically in the sky, miles in the far distance. There is a huge underground church there which is beautiful. There is also Franco's tomb, his final resting place. But what we want to tell you about, is to be found in the magnificent Shrine of the Royal Monastery of El Escorial.

We arrived early in the morning at the Monastery of El Escorial, having left Madrid before the rush-hour traffic began.

We walked through the big church to the sacristy, to arrange for our priest to celebrate Mass, for our group. This day, the very first time we ever visited the Sacristy, the Lord would give us a very special gift. Because we were not a large group, only about thirty or so, they told us to celebrate Mass at the little chapel in back of the sacristy. While we were waiting for our priest to vest up, we looked at the various paintings on the walls of the sacristy. One of them portrayed the theft of some Consecrated Hosts. Another showed a large assembly of dignitaries. One of them, perhaps a Bishop or Cardinal, was presenting a King with a Monstrance, inside of which was a Consecrated Host. There were two unusual things about one of the paintings in the sacristy. One was that everything that was taking place, in the room in the painting, appeared to be happening in the sacristy in which we were now standing. The other was that the Host in the Monstrance, in the painting, had three red dots on It.

We asked the priest in our broken Spanish what was the significance of the two paintings. He told us, the one took place in Holland, and portrayed heretics desecrating Consecrated Hosts. The other, showed a Monstrance with the Miraculous Host being adored by the King of Spain, here in the sacristy of El Escorial. We asked where the Miraculous Hosts were kept, now. The man pointed to the Altar in front of us, the very Altar where we would be celebrating Mass. Well, you have never seen such a group of excited, happy pilgrims as we. We were given the gift of celebrating Mass at the Altar of the Miracle of the Eucharist, and to venerate the incorrupt, bleeding Host.

What is El Escorial?

It was originally a grand monastery, the Royal Monastery of Spain in honor of the Spanish Martyr, San Lorenzo, or St. Lawrence. The concept of this masterpiece of Spanish architecture came to King Philip II, as he fought a fierce battle against the French in St. Quentin, France in 1557. He vowed, if he were victorious, he would build a splendid Monastery in honor of the Saint, on Spanish soil. Actually, he accomplished a double task with one action. He had also promised his father, Charles V, that he would provide a burial place for him and his ancestors to come. The cornerstone was placed on April 23, 1563. Four years later, on the Feast of the Holy Innocents in 1567, the first six *Religious brothers* were admitted to the Monastery as custodians.

It became the pet project of King Philip of Spain. Various queens and princesses were the first to be buried inside the tombs of the Monastery. During a visit of the King to the Monastery, on June 14, 1575, the foundations of the main church were begun. The same month, the King donated the Library to the Monastery. It contained 4,000 volumes. And then the *King* was given a special Gift, which he in turn, gave to the Monastery of El Escorial. It was a Miracle of the Eucharist.

The Story of the Miracle of the Eucharist of El Escorial

The lies and errors of Martin Luther spread rapidly throughout Europe. Bad news has always drawn more attention and been more popular than Good News. In Switzerland, his followers were led by a man called Zwingli. Their influence spread outside the borders of Switzerland and spilled into Holland. We go to the Cathedral in Gorcum, a town in southern Holland. This is where our story begins in 1572. The followers of Zwingli hated the Eucharist, more than their mentors, the followers of Luther and Calvin, if that's possible. Wherever

The Miracle of the Eucharist of El Escorial

feasible, they did whatever they could to attack the Church, and desecrate the Eucharist. Their goal was to take away all that Catholics held dear, whether by ridiculing all they, and their ancestors before them; believed, or by debilitating them, showing their disdain for Jesus in the Eucharist, profaning Consecrated

Hosts, every chance they had. Their hatred for Jesus in His Eucharistic Form held no bounds. Why did they hate Him so very much, if they did not believe He existed? There is no logic in desecrating a symbol. If they truly, sincerely believed that the Eucharist is merely a piece of bread, then why did they go out of their way to destroy Consecrated Hosts?

These heretics broke into the Cathedral of Gorcum with the intention of desecrating the Presence of Jesus in the Blessed Sacrament, in whatever way they could. They stole into the Tabernacle. They opened the Monstrance, and took out the Consecrated Hosts. The more *contemptible* and horrible their vile actions became, the more excited they got, the more outrageous their behavior. It was an escalating madness, a craze which accelerated, the more they profaned the Eucharist. They built up this great fever, and smashed the Hosts with a vengeance. It was the scourging of Jesus once more, at the Pillar, the crowning with thorns, the mockery He and His Mother endured at Calvary. The final blow came when one of the heretics threw a Consecrated Host on the floor, and stomped on It with his boots. The bottom of the boot had spikes on the sole, to help grip the road when there was mud on the ground. The spikes punctured the Host in three places, and *small drops of Blood emerged from the Consecrated Host.*

The attacker went into shock. He couldn't believe his eyes, the sight before him. He looked around. His companions behaved in the same way, staring in amazement at what had happened. He went down on his knees to pick up the Host, but was afraid to touch It. He knew *now* that there was a living Being inside that Host, and that Being was God. He began to sob loudly. He got up and ran for all he was worth. He wanted to put as much distance between him and what he had done, as possible. His friends followed suit, and in a matter of minutes, the Cathedral was as empty and silent as it had been before the molestation had taken place. There was only one big difference now; a bright shining Host was laying on the floor, with three drops of crimson blood slowly oozing from it.

Once in the vestibule of the Cathedral, the heretic and perpetrator could go no farther. He didn't want to be here; his friends didn't want him to be here. They kept warning him that they needed to escape or the authorities would be coming soon. But try as he might, he couldn't bring himself to leave the Lord alone in that condition. He had to do something; tell someone. The Lord was melting his heart of stone. Did he see the Lord bleeding instead of a Host? He shrugged off the warnings of his friends, and went in search of a priest. He found John Van der Delft, a Dean of the church. He confessed his crime to the Dean. Together they went back to the Altar, where the Body of the Savior lay on the floor, gleaming in the light, the red blood spots glistening against the moonlight which poured in the window.

Both men realized that it would not be safe to leave this miraculous Form of the Body of Christ here in this church. The climate of the city was so anti-Church, they were sure the Host would come to harm. They got on their horses, and left the city, the Miraculous Host wrapped carefully in a sack. They went through the dark night to the imperial city of Malines, and the convent of St. Francis. Fortunately, or unfortunately, the Miracle of the Eucharist of Holland became very famous. People came to the Franciscan convent from all over the country to pray before the Blessed Sacrament in this Miraculous form. That was the fortunate part. The unfortunate part is that It became too celebrated, too well-known for Its own safety. The custodians of the Miraculous Host knew they had to protect It from those who would destroy It and the Church.

After two months, the situation became turbulent in Malines. There was a great hostility against the Church. Also, those heretics who had *not* converted over to the Faith had heard about the Miracle which had taken place in the Cathedral at Orcum, and wanted to get their hands on the Miraculous Host. They wanted to desecrate It horribly, and then destroy it. It had become an obsession with the heretics by now. The Dean and the Franciscan took the Miraculous Host from Malines into Anvers in Belgium. It was thought that, at least *temporarily*, the Host would be safe in Anvers. Again, in the dark of night, with the Angels as protectorates, the vulnerable Jesus was brought to Anvers, Belgium by a trusted, pious man, Andres de Horst.

The plot thickens. A German noble, very influential in the court of Vienna, heard of the Miracle of the Eucharist. He wanted desperately to have the Miracle of the Eucharist in his possession. You've got to remember that there was a great deal of prestige for a city, or a country, or even an individual to have in their possession, these great relics, such as the bodies of incorrupt saints, and in this instance, a Miracle of the Eucharist. This German noble, Ferdinand Weidner, argued that he needed something, as powerful as a Miracle of the Eucharist, to use against the non-believers who were running rampant in Germany. He may have been sincere, and that may truly have been his reasoning. At any rate, he pressured the same holy, pious man who had brought the Miracle of the Eucharist to Anvers, Andres de Horst, to get the Host out of Belgium and bring it to him in Vienna. He even used the influence of the custodian of the Franciscan convent in Malines, where the Hosts had been brought *originally* when it was determined they were in danger. So, very clandestinely, the Miracle of the Eucharist went once more in the same year, 1572, to *another* country, Austria, and *another* city, Vienna.

From 1572 to 1579, the Miraculous Host remained in Vienna, hopefully converting unbelievers by the miraculous evidence of Jesus physically present, through His drops of Blood on the Host; and the fact that the Host had not decomposed after seven years. There was power in the Eucharist, for all to see. We know the Lord allowed Himself to be brought to this country for a reason. We know that all hell had broken loose in the earlier part of the century because of Luther and the German princes. And it was accelerating wildly, *especially* in the Germanic countries.

Now, from 1572 to 1579, was a crucial period for the Church

in that area. A Miracle of the Eucharist, with the power to change mens' hearts, even in the highest circles, was needed in the front lines. There's no question about that. The only fear, or apprehension we have is for the safety of the Body of Christ in that atmosphere. Who was taking care of the Lord? He was most likely in the hands of the German noble, who, while he probably had the best intentions, was not a priest. Was the Miraculous Host reserved in a Tabernacle with a priest, a bishop or a religious safeguarding It? We don't know. That's the scary thing; we just don't know.

But one thing we do know, God's in charge. He's always in charge. He can turn anything around, and in this instance, we're sure He used the power of His Presence in the Miracle to melt mens' hearts of stone into hearts meant for Him alone. At a given time in 1579, or the early part of 1580, it was part of the Lord's plan for the Miracle of the Eucharist to leave Vienna, and be brought to Spain. Ferdinand Weidner received a visit from an old friend, also a noble and ambassador, Baron Adam Dietrichstein. With him was a very powerful and persuasive lady, Doña Margarita de Cardona, of the noble Spanish family of the Duchy of Cardona. The two, but especially Doña Margarita, expressed a sincere interest in the Miraculous Host. They put a great deal of pressure on Ferdinand Weidner to let them have the Sacred Species. It was intimated that they intended to bring It back to Spain, as an offering to King Philip II of Spain. They let Weidner know in no uncertain terms how appreciated this would be, by them and the King, and how they would spare nothing to show their appreciation to Ferdinand.

Weidner felt the great pressure coming from his two guests, but didn't want to give in to it. However, it never let up, to the point where he felt himself in a no-win situation. He had no other choice but to let them have it. Seeing as he was in this situation, he decide to make it work for him. He made a great, noble gesture, explicitly designed to insure him of receiving the greatest reward for his generosity. He stated, he would not relinquish this priceless treasure to anyone but them, and of course the King. He shared with them the danger and great cost, involved in getting the Miraculous Host, in the first place, from the Dutch. He told of clandestine meetings, and exchange of bribes, and life-threatening near-misses with the heretical Protestants who would kill to get their hands on the Miraculous Host. His guests gave him the proper amount of attention and importance, consoled him, cajoled him, and then promised him that the King of Spain would be made aware of all that Ferdinand Weidner had done to preserve the Miraculous Host.

Grasping the moment, lest he repent and go back on their agreement, they then proceeded to take the Miraculous Host quickly from Ferdinand Weidner and go directly from Vienna to their home in Prague, Czechoslovakia. We do not know if the original intention was to keep the Miracle of the Eucharist for their own veneration and adoration; and then use It later as a political tool. Or was it, rather than rushing off to Spain to give It to King Philip II, they would wait until the time was right. We're sure that in the back of their minds, they truly intended to bring it to the King, someday, but not just yet. *As a matter of fact, not for thirteen years.*

Now we know the Lord had a plan for this Miracle of the Eucharist. It wasn't just to convert the violent heretic in Holland who brought about this heinous act, many years before, although that was accomplished. There was more to it than that. We don't know if the long trip from Holland to Vienna to Prague was part of the Plan, or just tolerated by the Lord, a detour which He would use to glorify His Holy Name. And while we believe the Lord is not limited by time and space, has all the time in the world, and is not pressured by anything to have His will accomplished, it may have become a time for action, especially after thirteen years. We're sure mass conversions took place in Germany and Czechoslovakia during the time the Miraculous Host was adored and venerated by the local people, but they were such a select few. What we considered the enemies of God, the people who had originally set out to destroy the Eucharist, and the Church, these were the first ones whom the Lord wanted evangelized. Although He was saddened by the harm they had done to themselves and the poor sheep who unwittingly had followed them, He still loved them. He had died for them, too, and he wanted them to come back home to His Church. We don't think it was happening to the degree the Lord had intended, in that very nice, socio-political atmosphere in Prague. And so, like the Holy House of Loreto, the Miracle of the Eucharist had to move again.

The Lord began working on Doña Margarita de Cardona. She was inspired to send the Miraculous Host to her daughter, the Marquise of Navarre. She had to be very cautious about how to get the Miraculous Host out of the country. *It had to be politically correct.* The only way that this could be done would be to make believe it was a gift from Rudolph II, Emperor of Austria and King of Hungary. In this way, the people of Prague would not be as upset about losing the Miraculous Hosts and she would have clear entry to the King of Spain.

But before she did this, the Lord inspired her to document the Miraculous Host, and Its journey: from whom she received it (Weidner), and from whom he received it (the custodian of the Franciscan monastery at Malines), and from whom he received it (John van Delft). This was notarized, and became a crucial part of the history of the Miracle. Once this was done, Doña Margarita had a beautiful silver chest made, into which the Miraculous Host was placed on a felt bed, with the documentation tucked in the back.

Now here's where it becomes like a ballet. Doña Margarita was sending the beautiful gilded silver box to her daughter, the Marquise of Navarre. The daughter then had the Austrian envoy to Spain, Baron Quevenheler take it from her, and bring it directly to the King. As a high dignitary of Austria, he had clearance to the King, but as bearer of so precious a gift from his King to the King of Spain, the doors would swing open, wider, more quickly expediting his meeting with King Philip II.

Now, the King was at his Royal Monastery in El Escorial. It had been ten years since he had begun construction on it, in thanksgiving to Our Lady for having defeated the French at San Quentin. King Philip II was a very holy man. He had his apartment right next to the chapel in the Monastery of El Escorial, actually in a place which would normally have been reserved for the sacristy. In this instance, the sacristy was placed on the other side. Philip wanted to be able to attend Mass privately from his room, especially when he was ill. Thus, we have a justification for the apartment next to the Chapel. He was very spiritual, and desirous to surround himself especially here, with as many relics and spiritual things, as possible.

When word came to the King that Baron Quevenheler of Austria was coming to present him with an actual *Miracle of the Eucharist*, he became elated. The King of kings, His Lord and Master was coming to his palace, to dwell with him. It was more than the holy man could do to contain himself. To think, the Lord would be coming there! He planned a formal grand affair, for the welcoming of the Miraculous Host to the royal court. There's no question that Doña Margarita became known as the person who actually engineered the gift being given to the King, and that she became a person very close to the King, as a result of this magnificent gift.

The Miracle of the Eucharist became the most prized Treasure of King Philip II. He prayed often for the Lord's intervention in aiding him how to rule over his kingdom of Spain and its people, and implored His help in handling all the problems in which the Church and state found themselves, especially in the New World, America, and in the problems of the Inquisition, which had flared up again during his monarchy. Philip gathered a great deal of comfort from having this radiant Miracle of the Eucharist at his side, and kept The Host exposed in the beautiful case which Doña Margarita had designed for the Miracle. Four and a half years, after the Miraculous Host had been delivered to

King Philip II, he died, his confessor by his side, and the Miracle of the Eucharist before him, in plain sight. He had spent his life protecting and defending the Church. At his last moments, his Church and his God protected him from the enemy, through the Sacraments of the Church he so dearly loved, as he prepared to enter into the Kingdom.

The Miracle of the Eucharist, still incorrupt, was kept in the Shrine of the Annunciation in the Basilica, in the same reliquary in which it had been brought from Prague to the King. The Lord gave us another great believer in the power of the Eucharist, and

Charles II, King of Spain venerates the Miracle of the Eucharist of El Escorial

the Miracle of the Eucharist in King Charles II, the last of the Austrian kings in Spain. He had a great devotion to the Miracle of the Eucharist, which he had been privileged to pray before, many times, being of the Royal family. But he wasn't satisfied with the silver chest, nor the place of veneration of the Miracle. He wanted the people to be able to view and venerate the Miracle of the Eucharist. He ordered an exquisite Monstrance to be made which would better show the Miracle of the Eucharist to the Faithful. Feeling the need to build a more splendid chapel in honor of the Miracle, he began construction on the *"Chapel of the Sacristy"* in the main church. The chapel in the sacristy was made of precious marble, fine woods and decorated in brass and gold leaf. The philosophy of the King was that this had to be the most magnificent chapel to venerate the most precious gift the country had ever been given.

It is a beautiful chapel, in which the Miracle of the Eucharist has a prominent place of honor, although it's only on display to the Faithful twice a year. It was in 1684 that the great translation of the Miraculous Host, in its new Monstrance, was transferred from the chapel of the Annunciation in the Basilica to the new chapel in the sacristy. The painting, which shows King Charles II adoring the Miracle of the Eucharist, is the major painting on display in the sacristy. Great devotion to the Miracle of the Eucharist took place under King Charles II. At his own personal cost, candles were always to be lit on either side of the Miracle at the main Altar. The two days devoted to public veneration of the miracle are *September 29th*, Feast of St. Michael the Archangel, St. Gabriel and St. Raphael, and *October 28th,* Feast of St. Jude, patron of hopeless cases. A *plenary indulgence* was given on those two days.

Satan strikes again

We can't say the wrath of Satan, which was unleashed on the European continent in the last decade of the Eighteenth century, was because of the Eucharistic Miracle of El Escorial alone, but we're sure it had something to do with it. There may have been too many signs of the Lord here on earth to suit the evil one, so he let loose with the French Revolution in 1789, which dealt a devastating blow to the Church. The Reign of Terror was followed by the reign of Napoleon Bonaparte, who, while he never said he was against the Church, may have caused more damage in (his way of) not persecuting the church, than the French Revolution did (in their way), persecuting the church.

Napoleon and his French troops descended on Spain, their neighboring country to the south, and sacked and looted and raped anything in their path. It was one of the most despicable acts taken against priests and nuns, all in the name of *Liberté, Egalité and Fraternité*. We can never figure out, however, whose liberty, equality and fraternity we're talking about, and why liberty, equality and fraternity have to be bought at the cost of attacking another country and always the Church. So we must give credit where credit is due, to Satan. In this vein, with this pretense, the

French attacked Spain, looking for as much loot as they could possibly find, and what better place to look than in El Escorial, reputed to have more riches than any complex in Europe, with possible exception of the Louvre and the Vatican.

They descended like locusts on the holy place. Thank God, the custodians of the Shrine had advance warning of the onslaught of the French which was imminent. They began hiding things, especially expensive art-work, statues, anything which was not replaceable, in the attic between two beams above the crucifix near the door where the processions entered. The Miraculous Host was also hidden in a place which was out of the line of fire. The Miraculous Host, along with items of less importance, was left in that attic-type hiding place for 18 months, and then some. Then it was removed and put in a hideaway in the office of the Custodian, for another four years.

During this time, care had to be given also to living *human* treasures, the Friars, who had to be hidden, and it was not as easy as with the gold and silver, and even the Miracle of the Eucharist. The brothers needed to be hidden in a place where they would be safe from the enemy, and could also function, breathe, eat, sleep, and all the little things that make up a person. They needed a place to stay, out of the reach and sight of the enemy. The Lord provided this as well as for the brothers. He gave them a chapel, where fourteen friars lived in hiding until the Napoleonists left.

After Napoleon's defeat, much of what was stolen was given back to the Monastery of El Escorial, but no gold, jewels or precious stones. The chapel of the Sacred Host was refurbished, and devotion began again. But Satan was not finished yet. In 1837, there was a suppression of religious orders in Spain, yes, *Catholic Spain*. The two day Feast of the Miracle of the Eucharist, begun by King Philip II in honor of graces granted to him and the people of Spain, was reduced to a simple adoration and exposition after the High Mass with perhaps a homily, and a benediction afterward. This practice remained in El Escorial for almost half a century. The original devotion to the Miracle of the

Eucharist was reinstated under King Alfonso XII in 1885.

Once again Satan reared his ugly head in this century. From the years 1936 through 1939, the period of the Spanish Civil War, the chapel of the Miracle of the Eucharist was closed, and devotion of any kind was forbidden under pain of imprisonment, and punishment. The Augustinian community at El Escorial, all 106 members, were taken from the monastery, and brought to Madrid where they were subjected to night and day interrogation and harassment by the head of Secret Service. In 1939, after the hostilities were over, a few people, grateful for the gift of being alive, went back to El Escorial, and began devotion to the Miracle of the Eucharist.

There had been a beautiful Monstrance given to the Miracle of the Eucharist by Queen Isabella II, and Francesco d'Assisi,[1] her consort. It was stolen during the Spanish Civil War, and never returned, along with many other jewels. The thief, who really had a fear of the Lord, left the Miraculous Host in the little chapel, where they had hidden It during this skirmish. A new Monstrance was built again, only this time, they were more cautious. They built a safe, as well. The Miracle of the Eucharist is still only on display those two days a year, September 29th, and October 28th. The rest of the time, it reposes in back of the sacristy, where there is a very small chapel.

There is a beautiful Crucifix with two Angels and a Tabernacle for the Miracle, which is in its beautiful Monstrance. The painting which tells the story of the desecration of the Hosts, comes down and covers the Altar of the Miracle of the Eucharist. When you celebrate Mass at the little chapel in back of the Sacristy, you can see the Altar with the crucifix and Angels, but the Monstrance is not there, visible.

The miraculous Host is incorrupt to this day, over four hundred years later.

---

[1] Named after St. Francis of Assisi

Why is the Miracle of the Eucharist of El Escorial so important to us today? What is the great significance? We really believe that Jesus is telling us, He is with us and will be with us till the end of the world, through wars and plagues, never giving up on us. By the evidence of the Blood He left us on the Host, the three drops of His Blood, He is telling us *perhaps* that He is once again bleeding for us, taking the blows due us, out of love for us. We believe He is also affirming that the Trinity is present on the Altar, as Jesus once again offers Himself to the Father for us. The sign of the Three drops of Blood could be Our Lord reminding us of the three days He spent, from the time of His death to His resurrection, reassuring us that we too will rise with Him.

He is telling us to be not afraid! He is with us. Satan can bring out all his best guns, over a period of what seems like forever, yet the Lord won't be defeated. We need this Miracle of the Eucharist today. We need the courage to know that no matter what guns are aimed at us, we'll prevail. We go back to Scripture, *"And these signs will accompany those who believe: in My name they will cast out demons; they will speak in new tongues; they will pick up serpents, and if they drink any deadly thing, it will not hurt them; they will lay their hands on the sick, and they will recover."*[2] Might we add to that, ***"In My name, they will have courage!" Why not?***

---

[2]Mark 16:17-18

Faverney - 1608

Lift Your Hearts to the Lord!

"When the day of Pentecost had come, they were all together in one place. And suddenly a sound came from Heaven like the rush of a mighty wind, and it filled all the house where they were sitting. And there appeared to them tongues as of fire, distributed and resting on each one of them. And they were all filled with the Holy Spirit and began to speak in other tongues, as the Spirit gave them utterance."[1]

Miracle of the Eucharist of Faverney, France

Pentecost is called the *Birthday of the Church.* It is that most powerful time, when the Holy Spirit descended upon Our Lady and the Apostles, and they were filled with courage and zeal and inspiration. They were on fire! The Apostles charged out of that upper room into the streets of Jerusalem and evangelized to the Jews in the streets. We're told that about 3,000 Jews were baptized that day.

Throughout our journey, doing research for this book, we found that many of the Miracles of the Eucharist were Gifts given to us by Our Lord Jesus, during the time of Pentecost, either at Pentecost, or near Pentecost. *"It is the Spirit who gives life."*[2]

---

[1]Acts 2:1-4 Ignatius Revised Standard Version-Catholic edition
[2]John 6:63 Ignatius Revised Standard Version-Catholic edition

159

We will see the power of the Lord, as He battles the evil one in the Miracle of the Eucharist of Faverney, France, which took place in 1608. The area the Lord chose, to give us this Miracle, Burgundy,[3] has been a battlefield between God and the devil for centuries. It has always been overrun with foreign warriors wanting to take over the province. It is the birthplace of St. Joan of Arc, who in the mid-Fifteenth century, had to flee her home in Burgundy and hide out with her parents to avoid the raids of Burgundian freebooters,[4] who were renegades of that time.

After the death of St. Joan, and ultimately the Dauphin, Charles VII, Burgundy came under Spanish Rule, and was governed by the daughter of King Philip II of Spain, the Infant Isabella and her husband, Archduke Albert of Austria. This may have been the best thing to happen to Burgundy, for Queen Isabella followed the lead of Spain, fidelity to the Church, as she fought against Protestantism in France. In 1598, the Huguenots[5] were allowed to freely practice their heresies, and so they were gaining strength throughout Europe, especially in France, but not in the principality of Burgundy, in which Faverney found itself.

That's not to say that all was wonderful in Faverney. There was a Benedictine Abbey in the town which was no better than many of the Abbeys from that period, that had fallen into decay: no more community life, their life more secular than religious, an absence of poverty, the Divine Office rarely sung, all in all very lax living the Rule of the Order. As a matter of fact, there was no longer any Rule in the Order. They not only didn't follow the Rule of St. Benedict; they probably didn't have a clue as to what it was. They lived in idleness and were totally lukewarm. In the church, the vestments, the books and sacred vessels that still remained were worn out. Theology was ignored, as they paid little attention to the teachings of the Church. They didn't

---

[3]now a part of France, but not at that time. At the time of the Miracle, it was its own country.
[4]plunderers, pirates, buccaneers - Webster's New World Dictionary
[5]French Protestants

even have a library in their monastery.

Pentecost Sunday, 1608. The Benedictine community was in charge of the little church in town, which boasted a statue of Notre Dame de la Blanche, or the White Lady. She, and the church named after her, were the only part of the Church, they maintained a live devotion to, the only thing that kept them from losing their faith altogether. The devotion to the Lady brought pilgrims here to Faverney, to petition the Lady for favors, and giving thanks for favors received. The day of the big indulgences at the Church, was the Monday and Tuesday after the Feast of Pentecost. That was also the day that the Blessed Sacrament was exposed twenty-four hours.

So you see how the Lord is working, using everything He can to bring not only His people back to the fold, but also, and maybe more importantly, His Religious. Can't you just see the Holy Spirit, waiting to zap those Benedictines after the Miracle has come about? We really believe, this was the Lord's plan in the first place. And the most amazing thing about it is, it worked. It always works! The Lord would not give up on this area of France, this Burgundy, and the miracle we're about to behold is one of His ways to be sure that He holds onto it.

The Miracle

As the Feast of Pentecost was approaching, the sacristan of the Church, Dom Garnier, made a special repository for the Blessed Sacrament, for the time when Our Lord Jesus would be exposed to the Faithful. He did the same thing every year; but this year, he made it just a little more special. He set up a small Altar, in front of the choir rail, by placing a table on the Gospel side of the Church. He covered it with a table cloth on which he placed a Tabernacle. On the Altar, he placed a corporal with a silver Monstrance, whose base was attached to a sacred stone,[6] upon it. He attached the small Altar to the choir rail, to provide strength and security. In back of the temporary Altar was a red cloth, which hung for the entire three days. In front of the table, attached to the table cloth was the Papal Bull from Pope Clement VIII, granting the indulgences, and a letter from the local bishop, Msgr. Rye, which authorized the publication of the indulgences. There was also a relic of the finger of St. Agatha.

On Saturday evening, May 24, the evening before the big day of Pentecost, the prior of the community, Dom Sarron exposed the Blessed Sacrament. Actually, he placed two *Consecrated Hosts* from the morning Mass into the lunette,[7] because the Hosts were too small. Apparently, the priest didn't have a large Consecrated Host, or had not consecrated a large one that morning for Adoration that evening. Whatever the case, he put the Monstrance on display with the two Consecrated Hosts in it. The services began.

At 8 p.m., Dom Garnier, the sacristan blew out the candles, leaving only the two oil lamps lit, one on either side of the Monstrance containing the Blessed Sacrament, and closed the church. Nothing happened. The following day, Pentecost Sunday, there was a much larger gathering of the Faithful, to take part in the service and adore Our Lord Jesus in the Blessed Sacrament. The priest, Dom Sarron, had worked all Saturday evening to prepare a proper homily for the Feast of Pentecost. Was the Lord working on him, bringing the readings of St. Luke, in the Acts of the Apostles, to the forefront of his mind and spirit? Was Jesus speaking to him? Was the Holy Spirit whispering in his ear? Was Notre Dame de la Blanche trying to get his attention?

That evening, the Mass had been beautiful. Dom Garnier

---

[6]this is from the early days when they had a sacred stone Altar they could easily transport from place to place, because the church, being underground, had to be prepared to move on, in case of discovery - covered in our chapters on the Mass.

[7]Small, crescent-shaped clip or circlet, which holds the Consecrated Host. It is slid into the monstrance along a groove or track to hold the Blessed Sacrament for exposition.

had felt the Holy Spirit filling him with power during the homily. He felt different! He had celebrated the Feast of Pentecost, many times, but He had never felt this way, before. But it was a good feeling! He went through the Benediction with the Blessed Sacrament, extinguished the candles, lit the oil lamps, and left the church. When he went to sleep that night, the warm feeling, he had felt when he had heard the powerful homily about the Holy Spirit and Pentecost, was still with him.

Now, no one knows why, but Dom Garnier returned to the church about three in the morning. As he approached it, he noticed something strange. There was a glow surrounding the Chapel where the Blessed Sacrament was exposed. He couldn't make out what was going on; all he knew was, he had never seen anything quite like it before. His pace began to quicken. He was becoming anxious. When he entered the church, he gasped at what he saw. The church was full of smoke, so bad that he had to open all the doors, just to be able to breathe. The source of the smoke was the little Altar where the Blessed Sacrament was exposed. There was nothing left of the Altar but a pile of ashes.

He left the church, immediately and ran for all he was worth to the monastery, to tell the monks. Then, together, he and the monks all ran off to awaken the villagers, to draft their help in putting out the fire in the church. He returned to the church with Brother Brenier, to the center of the disaster. He got hold of a young novice, Gabriele Hudelot and told him to get tongs, so that they could look through the rubble, to find whatever may be left of the Monstrance. The smoke was so thick, they could hardly breathe, and it was too dark to see anything.

But all of a sudden, the young man, Brother Hudelot pointed into the air. He couldn't believe what he was seeing *"Miracle!"* he shouted, *"Miracle!"* All eyes followed his arm, up into the air, above the Altar. The monstrance was suspended in mid-air, right above where the Altar had been, but now without any visible means of support. It was slightly bent forward, and the left arm of the small cross on top, seemed to touch the bars of the gate of the choir railing. It was unbelievable. They couldn't believe what they were seeing. As the smoke began to clear, and their eyes adjusted to the scene before them, it was a paradox. Below, on the ground, were broken and twisted candlesticks. The sacred stone which had been attached to the Monstrance was shattered in three pieces. All that was left of the table was four charred legs. The Tabernacle was melted. Yet the Monstrance with the two Consecrated Hosts were perfectly intact, floating safely above the broken fragments. Another interesting, and completely unexplainable thing was that the two documents, made of paper, the Papal Bull and the letter of the bishop, were completely unharmed with the exception of the bishop's seal which had melted somewhat, having been fused together by the extreme heat of the blazing fire. But other than that, the documents were in perfect shape, also. In addition, the relic of the finger of St. Agatha was saved.

What now?

After the initial shock wore off, the monks dropped to their knees and knelt, in adoration of their Lord and King who had visited His undeserving servants, through this true Miracle of the Eucharist. They folded their hands together, for the first time in maybe years, tears coming to their eyes, praising the Lord not only for loving them so very much, He would grant them such a powerful Gift, but for accepting them back again. They were home, like the prodigal son, and it was so good to be in the arms of the Lord and His Church. They felt as if they had been on a desert and an Oasis, the Real Presence of Jesus Christ, had miraculously come to *them.* And they knew, they would never be the same, again, as they prayed in thanksgiving to their Faithful God for the Gift of Himself.

After they prayed for a long time, they began looking at each other first, then at the Monstrance, suspended in mid-air. What do they do now? One of the monks had a brilliant thought. Call the Capuchin monks from Vesoul, a few kilometers away. Have them come to witness the miracle which had occurred in the church. They sent one of the monks, Dom Noirot, to tell the Capuchins about the Miracle. But on his way to the Capuchins, he passed the early-morning pilgrims heading for the Church to pray for the Plenary Indulgence. He had to stop them and tell them about the miracle.

The word went out like wildfire over the entire area. Pilgrims, on the way to the church, reached out to everyone they saw on the road, and the numbers became larger and larger. That afternoon, they had the largest gathering of pilgrims, they had ever had in the church. There wasn't enough room inside the church. They had to wait outside, and form a line to get in to venerate the Miracle of the Eucharist. The Capuchins arrived, just before the evening service, and praised Our Lord Jesus for the powerful gift He had given the people of Faverney. After the evening service, they began their own investigation.

This night, there was no blowing out of candles and closing of the church. There was no way to get the pilgrims out. Granted, they were not all believers. There were the skeptics, the heretics, the Protestants, the curiosity-seekers. But we can be sure that many of them were converted, despite the disbelief they registered when they first arrived at the church. They came to ridicule and put the hoax down; they stayed and revered the Lord, in this Miraculous Form until the early hours of the morning.

The following morning, there were many Masses scheduled. This was not really unusual, because they had been scheduled for the Plenary Indulgence attached to Notre Dame de la Blanche. But it seemed like there were an extraordinary amount of Masses to be celebrated that Monday morning. The first Mass was that of the community, followed by the Capuchins, and then those of the pilgrims. At the ten o'clock Mass, a priest from a nearby town, Menoux, was the celebrant. His name was Fr. Aubry. To give the pilgrims credit, they tried to concentrate on the main Altar, where the Mass was being offered, as opposed to the side Chapel, where the Monstrance was suspended in mid-air. It became especially difficult during the Holy, Holy. One of the candles to the right of the Monstrance went out. Dom Garnier, in his role as Sacristan, went over and relit it. It went out a second time, and then a third time.

Now, the pilgrims couldn't take their eyes off the side Altar. But then when the Consecration of the Mass began, they refocused their attention back to the main Altar. However, at the moment of Consecration, while the Host was still elevated, an awesome vibration was felt, like that of a silver blade when it vibrates. All eyes went back over to the direction of the Monstrance, which was still tilted in mid-air. As the priest was lowering the consecrated Host, the Monstrance began to straighten out, and as the Host was placed back on the paten, the Monstrance slowly, very gently lowered Itself and rested on the table which had been brought in, to take the place of the one which had burned. The Miracle was over. The Miraculous Monstrance and Hosts had been suspended for thirty three hours, the exact age of Our Lord Jesus when He ascended into Heaven, after which the Holy Spirit came, on the first Feast of Pentecost. We might say the cycle was complete, starting with the Feast of Pentecost[8] and ending with the Feast of Pentecost.[9]

Everyone in the church was thoroughly, visibly shaken, everybody, that is, except the priest, Fr. Aubry, from Menoux. He continued celebrating the Mass. He knew all along that Jesus was there. He didn't need a Miracle to tell him He was there. But we're pretty sure that after he left the Altar in a very dignified manner, and entered the sacristy, his knees began to shake, as had everyone else's. Also, as soon as he left the Altar, a mad dash of pilgrims ran up to the table where the Monstrance, containing the Miraculous Hosts, was waiting. Looking from

---

[8] The Holy Spirit came the first Pentecost, and empowered the Apostles, converting them, changing their cowardice into courage to the point of martyrdom.

[9] The Miracle occurred on the Feast of Pentecost, and changed the stony hearts of the apathetic, lukewarm, irreligious monks to adoring hearts that belonged to their Lord.

the outside in, one could see the King sitting on His throne, while all His subjects came up and paid Him Homage.

Do we give that reverence to Jesus in Perpetual Adoration? We have to stop here, in the middle of this account, to ask the question above. In this miracle, our Lord, in His Eucharistic Presence, gave us a physical sign that He was truly there in the Monstrance. Thousands of people, who had witnessed this Miracle, came around the Altar, and stayed for hours, praying to Jesus in His Miraculous Eucharistic Presence, petitioning Him and thanking Him for favors received. They never left. They were on their knees, all the time they were there before Him. Who even knows if there were enough kneelers for all the people. It didn't matter. Jesus was there, and they knew it. No kneelers, you can bet, they knelt on the hard, concrete floor; they stayed; they prayed.

Do we do that? First off, *do we even show up for Eucharistic Adoration?* In our little town, we have two churches that have 24 hour Eucharistic Adoration, and they are hard-pressed to get enough people for one person to cover each of the hours. We never see the great crowds that we're talking about in this Miracle. And yet Jesus is no less present at Exposition, and Adoration, than He was when He let everybody know, in no uncertain terms, in Faverney, it was He who was among them. Where are we, and why aren't we at the church, on our knees? We still have kneelers in most of our churches. They're soft and cushy. And even if they don't have kneelers, go on your knees. *It's your Lord!*

What are we talking about here? We're talking about piety; we're talking about *desire*; we're talking about giving praise and *honor* to our God. But it works both ways. As we give praise and honor to our God, He takes care of our needs; He answers our petitions; He blesses our families. Jesus asks you to spend one hour with Him; He asks you to adore Him in His Eucharistic Presence. But He also gives you power and strength through Eucharistic Adoration. Are you aware of the extra blessings a Parish receives when there is Eucharistic Adoration? Why do you think the enemy is constantly fighting, trying to block Eucharistic Adoration from blossoming in your Church?

How many times have you tried to get Eucharistic Adoration off the ground in your parish, only to be shot down by any one of a number of authority figures? There is no coincidence. It's the enemy attacking your parish. This is more reason why you should spend time before the Blessed Sacrament. If you can't get the Blessed Sacrament exposed, begin by adoring Our Lord in the Tabernacle. Keep praying for the Lord to soften the hearts of those who are blocking Eucharistic Adoration. Practice fasting. Do penance. These are tried and tested methods the Lord has given us over the centuries. They worked then; they work now.

Read about the power of Jesus in His Eucharistic Presence. Pay attention to how He blesses those who honor Him and venerate His Body and Blood in the Eucharist. Fight for all you are worth to bring this Gift of the Lord into your Parish, and once It's there, don't ever take It for granted. Work at making Eucharistic Adoration successful in your Parish.

Back to the Miracle

Two days after the Miracle had ended, Thursday, May 29, the official investigation was begun. Fifty four testimonies were taken. They included the eight religious of Faverney, the three Capuchins of Vesoul, the priests of Faverney and Menoux, especially the one who celebrated the Mass that day, farmers, workers and politicians, including the magistrate of the town. They could have interviewed thousands, because thousands had witnessed the Miracle at some time in the thirty-three hours. But they felt that they had a good cross-section of the people represented in the fifty four witnesses.

It took the Archbishop of the diocese less than two months to come to a conclusion that it was truly a Miraculous visit from Our Lord Jesus in His Eucharistic Presence, affirming the gifts of the Holy Spirit, the Feast of Pentecost, and the importance of Eucharistic Adoration. On July 10, he gave his stamp of approval on the authenticity of the Miracle. On July 27, still less than two months from the time the Miracle occurred, the letter of the Archbishop was read at all the Masses in all the churches of the Diocese. On September 13th of that same year, the Papal Nuncio to Brussels advised Pope V of the extraordinary occurrence that came to pass in Burgundy.

The three parts of the Miracle which had the utmost importance, especially at that time, when the flames of Protestantism were being fanned all across Northern Europe, were the Eucharist, the Papal Bull, and the relic of St. Agatha. These truths, the Real Presence of Jesus in the Eucharist, the authority of the Pope, and the veneration to the Saints, in the form of the relic of St. Agatha, were being denounced by the followers of Luther, Calvin and their followers. The Huguenots were the most radical of the Protestants in France. In addition, the church was in honor of Our Lady, being dedicated to Our Lady of White, and it was a Monastic church, run by a Religious Order, which was also under great attack by the Protestants.

The immediate results of the Miracle were truly Pentecost revisited. Prominent Huguenots in the town, who were very influential, could not help but convert to the Faith, after the undeniable proof of the Miracle of the Eucharist which they had seen. They couldn't help but witness it; everyone in the town, and then some, witnessed it. One of the people, Francis Vuillard, went in and out of the church more than thirty times in the course of the thirty three hours. These men who had so vehemently attacked the Church, came back and with them, their families. Not only did they return, but in and through their fire, they brought hundreds of Huguenots back to the Church. Like with St. Paul, these former Huguenots, former enemies of the Church, became the strongest enemies of the Huguenot movement in that part of France.

The most precious parts of the Miracle were the two Hosts and the Corporal on which the Hosts had been consecrated, and on which the Monstrance had rested. The Lord decided that it was best that these gifts be shared with other areas, rather than be just for this church. When it was requested, The Corporal was freely given to a Jesuit priest, Fr. Ayrault, rector of the Jesuit college at Besancon, a distance to the south.

The Gift, requested by the church of Dole, was a different story, altogether. It would not be easy in coming. They had begged for one of the consecrated Hosts which were part of the miracle. It took some time before they could get any kind of answer from Faverney, and it was not positive. They begged even harder, exerting whatever influence they could to have the desired prize in their church. We truly believe that it was not for the glamour, or the prominence of having a Miracle of the Eucharist in their church, but that it was because they wanted to be able to venerate Our Lord Jesus in this miraculous Form. Proof was in the welcome that was given the Eucharist, by the townspeople when they finally wore down the custodians, at Faverney, and were given the gift of one of the Hosts.

On December 17, 1608, in high solemn procession, the Eucharist was placed on a luxurious litter, escorted by priests singing Psalms, musicians, Altar boys with candles lit, and a cortege from the army. That was the assemblage from Faverney. On the other side, the caravan from Dole outdid their brothers and sister of Faverney. They went about three miles outside the city to wait for the arrival, and processed with the procession from Faverney. As they arrived at the city of Dole, the city was all decorated in honor of the Miracle, and an arch of triumph was made under which the Miraculous Host was carried through the city, into the church.

The Host remained in a position of prominence in the church of Dole for almost two hundred years. The people of Dole venerated the Miraculous Host at every possible occasion. But the Protestant Revolution, which spawned the Huguenots, gave birth to the dissension which brought us the French Revolution. A few years into the French Revolution, 1794 to be exact, anticlericals broke into the church and stole the Host, and most likely destroyed it. But they never were able to destroy the power behind the Eucharist. To this day, the miracle is venerated in Dole, in spirit, if not in Body.

In Faverney, a special chapel was created to house the Miracle of the Eucharist that had remained with them. Undoubtedly the Lord was telling His people that as long as they were willing to respect Him in His Eucharistic Form, and give thanks for the Miracle, He gave them, He would continue to protect them. Twice in the Eighteenth century, 1726 and 1753, fires broke out which could have destroyed the little town of Faverney. And twice, the Miracle of the Eucharist was credited with having stopped the fires. When the frenzy of the French Revolution invaded this peaceful, God-loving town, the first thing they wanted to obliterate was the Miracle of the Eucharist. But the Lord used a brave Christian, who took the initiative to take the Miracle and hide it from the enemy. In 1795, still during the Revolution, the Miraculous Host was brought to the Abbey church, and kept there. The Abbey church has since become the Parochial church of the town.

In 1862, the Congregation of Rites authorized the celebration of the Miracle of the Eucharist as a local Feast Day in Faverney and the diocese. In 1912, the little abbey church was raised to the level of a Basilica. There is still a shrine to the Miracle of the Eucharist there. The Host has decomposed, at which time we believe the Real Presence of Jesus is no longer in the substance. But that has not stopped the veneration to the Miracle of the Eucharist. Eucharistic Adoration is still a major part of the Basilica of Notre Dame de la Blanche, our White Lady, in thanksgiving and remembrance of the Miracle that was given to the people at Faverney. The Chapel is still there, and a symbol of the Miraculous Host is venerated there.

We'd like to end our account of the Miracle of the Eucharist of Faverney, France, with an excerpt from the Pastoral Letter issued by Bishop Rye on July 10, 1608, when the Miracle of the Eucharist had first been approved:

"We exhort each to bless and praise God in all His works, particularly in this one so miraculous; to strengthen their own faith and reverence towards this Most Holy Sacrament; to become worthy of the graces and of the favors that are ordinarily communicated to those who frequent this Sacrament with proper preparation. We recommend, moreover, to all the prelates, shepherds of souls, and other ecclesiastical figures, as well as the laity, to be very vigilant in that which concerns the worship and piety towards the Blessed Sacrament."

We believe, our Bishop was pleading with the people not to get caught up with so much of the modern day world, that it fogs our minds when it comes to recognizing Jesus in the Eucharist, and adoring Him. These words were written over three hundred years ago. They might just as well have been written yesterday, or for today's homily. The people of that time listened, and cooperated with the Lord in keeping the gift/weapon of the Eucharist alive in their day, so that the Eucharist would be a strong weapon for us today. Our job is to keep that light of the Holy Spirit, that gift of God, alive and bright for the people of the Twenty Third century.

We can do it. Just keep your eyes on the Lord! He will be there on the Altar, at the moment of Consecration during the Mass. He is always there in the Tabernacle. He is waiting for you, in the Monstrance when He is exposed for Eucharistic Adoration. Did you ever desire to have been with Jesus in the Garden of Gethsemane when He sweat Blood and Tears over the sins of the world, to comfort Him when His trusted Apostles could not stay awake with Him? Do you have an hour to spare, now? Jesus still sees the sins of the world and He still cries. *Do you have an hour to spare?*

Turin - 1640

Miracle of the Mountain

We invite you to come with us in our helicopter, way up in the sky, close to Heaven. Look down and try to visualize the scene that Our Lord Jesus, His Mother Mary, and any of our Heavenly family would have if they looked down at

The Mountain of the Capuchins

us here on earth. The area is northern Italy, Turin in particular. This has always been a hotbed of secularism and materialism. Industrialization always finds its way there. We wrote not too long ago about Don Bosco[1] a saint and prophet of the Nineteenth century, who evangelized the homeless waifs, the children left abandoned by the Industrial Revolution in Turin during that time. Satan was having a field day with our young people, until the Lord sent the mighty St. John Bosco, God's acrobat, to save the day. St. John Bosco was born in this same area, near Turin. Again we see the Holy Clusters of the Lord.

---

[1]*Saints and Other Powerful Men in the Church*

The year is 1640, and the Lord brings us back to Turin, which is again highly industrialized or should we say *still,* and the situation is bad. The city, at that time, was composed of unhappy people who left their farms in the southern regions, seeking a better way of life in the big metropolis, only to lose their souls in the process, forgetting all the simple, faith-filled lessons, they had learned on their peasant mothers' knees about the Lord and His Mother. Lost in the noise of the city, whatever seeds that had been sown, were now choked out by the glamour of evil that the city had to offer and the price one had to pay to achieve it.

But the Lord takes us away from the dirty city, to a hill, peaceful and sloping. The history of this hill, very dear to the people of Turin, mixing and blending legend[2] with authentic history, reverberates with the *pain* of the dying and the *tears* of the living. This mountain, this summit of stony silence, is a place of contradiction. When war and death scarred this peaceful countryside, it stood still and waited, appearing lost in serene calmness, but gently, patiently living out the philosophy of its people, *"This too, shall pass."*

But let us journey back to the year 1583. We find ourselves on the hill, birds calling to us and to one another, the sweet fragrance of the hope of springtime filling the air, almost dizzying with its promise of new beginnings. The rolling pastures seem to flow with the tall grass that moves with the gentle wind, a ballet, God and His creation dancing as one. Even the sky seems to bend down to caress the hillside.

A safe distance from the world of commerce below, the only hint of what hell might have gone on, in times past, to upset this innocent peace, are the remains of a *Bastia*, a fortress. Its bastions and moats, foreboding and ominous, distorted by the cruel jagged towers, beaten by time and ruin, tarnish the calm sky, a coarse intrusion on God's gentle, peaceful masterpiece. Its ramparts, stained by the blood of archers defending the fort, assail not only

---

[2]legend does not mean myth, but a teaching

the memory of those mothers' sons they killed, but God Himself who had another plan for this piece of Paradise. The walls, still soiled by the boiling oil, poured down on the enemy as he attempted to storm the fortress, left stains that time and weather could never erase.

Wars fought and won, and then lost again, the mountain and the fortress ended up as the private property of two families. Finally, in 1583, the Capuchins settled here. From that time on, its popular history of battles fought and won, was supplanted by the *pace e bene*, peace and good of the followers of the Little Poor One, Father Francis. There was on the mountain, at that time, a Chapel devoted to the *Blessed Mother of the Mountain*, Santa Maria del Monte, where an ancient image, carved of wood, had been venerated for centuries. The Duke of Savoy, had a strong devotion to Our Lady, as had many other knights of the time. He had the inspiration of placing the statue of Our Lady in a Chapel worthy of her Queenship, a grand Sanctuary which he would place under the custody of the Sons of Francis.

Work on the project was begun immediately by the famous architect Ascanio Vittozzi, and in the year 1634, the Sanctuary was completed in the splendid baroque style, in the form of a Greek cross. Its walls were ornately sculpted in plaster framed by precious marble, the finest home for Our Lord Jesus to dwell in, a *Castle on the Mount*,[3] a home befitting a King!

The work completed, the Sanctuary's walls resounded with the prayers of humble unknown monks, as well as with those of Saint Francis of Sales and of Saint Lawrence of Brindisi, both Doctors of the Church, and of all the Piedmontese Saints, the Capuchins trying to put in words, the yearning of the soul to know and adore God, as their voices reached for Heaven.

---

[3]as King Victor Amedeo called the Sanctuary

The Convent

At the request of Charles Emanuele, The Duke of Savoy, and with the approval of Heaven, itself, the convent was erected in 1583. It is documented in an ancient text:

"As the cross was being carried to the convent, the Archbishop from Turin and his Highness, the Duke, leading the procession, the monks and many people following, there appeared a grand celestial splendor of Heavenly Angels encircling the top of the Mountain. They continued, their wings fluttering happily, sparkling from the reflection of the sun, glorifying the Lord, until the procession entered the church, and the Cross was placed above the Altar. Rich and poor, famous and unknown, proud and humble, they all witnessed the presence of the Heavenly messengers."

As this became home for the band of Capuchins, it also became the headquarters and command post for the Heavenly Host of Angels, another mountain claimed by Michael and his Angels. And this awesome, celestial army continued to surround and accompany the Capuchins, especially when they descended the mountain, to condemn and fight the heresy that was crushing the Church in the Dukedom of Savoy. The tentacles of disobedience and dissent, caused by the infectious cancer of Martin Luther, spread like a wave of terror into the northern body of Italy from Germany and Switzerland, and ate away at the faith of uneducated priests who followed the Judas Goat to slaughter, and with them the unsuspecting faithful. As Luther and Zwingli and Calvin, to name a few, went at each other, fighting among themselves, the faithful in Europe fell victims. What Luther began, to do away with one Pope, became the birth of many false popes, one disobedient Luther fragmented into hundreds of Luthers.

As if being carried by silent invisible angels, our Capuchins descended the mountain to fight yet another plague, now one that attacked the body and not the soul. They appeared as angels of mercy in rough, poor habits, sent to comfort the helpless victims of the epidemic of 1598. Sadly, one of their own, the first Superior of the Mountain, fell victim, died and was buried at the foot of the cross. This did not stop the Capuchins from ministering to the poor and the afflicted. In 1630 they resumed their heroism, caring not for themselves and the possible loss of their own lives, to this relentless killer epidemic. One of the friars wrote: *"I'm not worried; I don't fear dying any more than I did, the last time I served my neighbor."* Although this is what *one* of the Capuchins wrote, he expressed the sentiments of *all* the friars. More than one hundred Capuchins died, as the result of the epidemic. Unfortunately, the political revolution expelled the Capuchins from the Mountain two times, once in 1802, and then in 1867. But the respect of the Sovereigns, and the thankfulness of the people who remembered the kindness and selflessness of the friars, and desiring the return of the traditions of the Church, brought them back to the Mount, after a period of time. They are part of this story and the history of Turin.

Miracle of the Eucharist of the Mountain of the Capuchins

Because of its strategic position, the Mountain remained a target for invaders on Turin, involving the Capuchins and the inhabitants of the mountain in the various sieges on the city, as is evidenced by the bullets still encased on the facade of the Church till today. Highly respected citizens of the Mountain, in 1640, attested to the Miracle of the Eucharist of the Mountain.

Our story begins on May 10, 1640. There was a war on, again. Thomas of Savoy's soldiers were being chased by the French, who were allied with the Queen Mother Christina. They were pushing forward, together with the entire population of Borgo Po, toward the Mountain, which remained completely isolated. The Church of Santa Maria del Monte was crowded with refugees; as well as many of the homes on the Mount.

The French, from a tall bunker, answered the artillery that attempted to resist, with an unmerciful battery of gunfire, weakening the brave resistance of the soldiers of Thomas of Savoy.

On May 12, a traitor opened the doors of the church to the

French. It was a dreadful massacre. An eye witness testified: *"I saw a soldier go towards the Main Altar where the Blessed Sacrament was kept. He mounted the Altar and when he was there, I saw him attempt to kick in the door of the Tabernacle and when that failed, he pried it open with a piece of iron. Having opened it, he put his arm inside to seize the Blessed Sacrament. In that instant, from out of nowhere, a deluge of flames quickly shot throughout the entire church, engulfing it in fire, heading directly for the soldier who had tried to put his arm into the Tabernacle. He immediately jumped down from the Altar shouting: "Mon Dieu! Mon Dieu!" (My God! My God!). By now, the church was completely blanketed with smoke and flames, but nothing was burning. And then, I saw the soldier (who had kicked the door of the Tabernacle) run to the door of the church to leave, but his clothes were on fire. That was the only thing on fire in the whole church."* This was the sworn deposition of Mr. Bardovino Betlem to the Tribunal of the Holy Inquisition of Savigliano, on August 8, 1640.

The French soldiers ceased the massacre of innocent people in the church. With the same fury that they had climbed the mountain, they fled back down, to avoid what they knew to be the wrath of God. The Lord gave the little chapel a reminder of His glorious presence there during their time of need. Remembrances of the battle can be found all over the Church. Traces of the sacrilegious attack remained on the door of the Tabernacle, the frame broken at the top of the lock, the marble chipped from the iron and altered from the fire. Cardinal Maurice of Savoy gave the church a gift of a new Tabernacle, made of jewels and fine inlay work, rich in lapislazzuli and agates, work of the German Maestro Luca Longo.

Over the years, we have seen attacks on our Ministry. Penny always tells the community to pray for those who have come against us. She tells us, *"I really worry about those people who come up against this Ministry. I've seen it time and time again. The Lord deals harshly with those who come against His work."*

We see the same thing happening when the powers come up against anything that is of the Lord. The little band of Capuchins had no way of defending themselves against the crack French soldiers. They had no weapons; they had nothing. But they had the Lord on their side, and it was His Sanctuary which was being violated by these pawns of Satan. To top it off, the chapel was named after Our Lady, and the Lord doesn't like it when she's attacked.

Very often, we get mail and phone calls from our brothers and sisters out there in the front lines. They tell us of all the abuses, they're suffering at the hands of liberal pastors, and others in the Church who are not following the dictates of His Holiness, and the Magisterium. They ask us what they can do. It seems extremely frustrating. These pastors seem to have all the right people on their side, even though they're not following the dictates of Rome, or even the documents of Vatican Council II. "What should we do?" they ask us. We know it doesn't sound like enough, but the greatest weapon you have is Prayer. True, you must learn all you can about our Church, and about the rules of the Church,[4] but bottom line, you must pray for conversion of those in our church who would destroy it. They're going against the mandates of Jesus. They're trying to make it possible to open the gates of hell, and let all the evil come onto the earth. They're trying to keep Jesus from fulfilling His promise, *"I am with you always; the gates of Hell will not prevail against My church."* Keep praying; God is on our side.

---

[4] Every family should have a copy of the Pope's new *Catechism of the Catholic Church,* and use it.

Patierno - 1772

"I will not leave you orphans."[1]

Years ago, when we were researching Miracles of the Eucharist, we dreamed of the day, we would share these precious Gifts with others on Pilgrimage. That day finally came! Now, we had been to Shrines many times, but our pilgrims had never seen them. It was important, to us that the Miracle and Shrines be shown the respect they deserved, as *Miracles of the Eucharist*, Jesus in His Body and Blood, Soul and Divinity. We were not disappointed. The pilgrims showed great reverence to the Miracles and their Shrines.

We arrived in Orvieto, in the Cathedral where a miraculous Corporal was exposed for veneration. This Corporal is part of the Miracle of the Eucharist that brought about the *Feast of Corpus Christi*.[2] We were deep in awe before the Real Presence of Our Lord Jesus, miraculously with us. What a joy to be able to share Him with our brother and sister pilgrims.

So, when in the midst of all our reverence, we noticed a woman walking toward the Chapel of the Miracle of the Eucharist, *dragging her dog who knew better*, we were upset! First, we tried to reason with her, using our best Italian, and then when that failed, our pilgrims linked arms with us, blocking the entrance of the Chapel. Our grandson called the sacristan, who told her, she was not allowed to bring the dog into the church, much less the Chapel of the Miracle of the Eucharist. Then he left. She

---

[1]John 14:18

[2]the Miracle of Bolsena-Orvieto can be found in *This Is My Body, This Is My Blood, Miracles of the Eucharist - Book I*

looked at us, smiled, and said, *"How long will you be here? I have all the time in the world."*

We knew we had to leave, and that when we did, this woman would bring her dog into the Chapel. There was nothing we could do; we had to leave. Penny had a conversation with the Lord. *"Why do you allow people to do this to You, Lord? You know we have to leave. Why do you let people do these things?"* We left, judging sadly that the woman later entered the chapel with her dog.

We tell you this because we feel the same way about the Miracle of the Eucharist, we're about to share with you, one of the most unusual Miracles we have ever researched, one in which another illustrious Doctor of our Church[3] was involved, St. Alphonsus Liguori. The information, used for this chapter, comes from his writings. He was respected, well-balanced and prudent, not prone to folklore being passed off as miracle. We believe, this statement will validate the following Miracle, as it shows you where St. Alphonsus was in discerning the authenticity of an occurrence: *"There are many more false visions than those that are real."*

The Saint wrote: *"We have been informed from many who witnessed the Miraculous happenings, which we are now going to narrate; but wanting to make sure there was enough proof to make it known in print, not even satisfied with the testimony of the priests, I wanted to read with my own eyes, the conclusions arrived at by the Archepiscopal Curia of Naples and the decrees of Cardinal Sersale, archbishop of Naples."*

The Miracle

On the evening of **January 27, 1772**, thieves broke into the Church of St. Pietro[4] in Patierno, a small town on the outskirts of Naples. They stole the contents of the Tabernacle: part of which

---

[3]many other Doctors of the Church have been involved with Miracles of the Eucharist, to mention a few: St. Anthony and St. Thomas Aquinas

[4]Peter in English

Church of St. Pietro in Patierno, Italy

were two Pyxes[5] (one larger than the other), filled with *hundreds* of consecrated Hosts.

The following morning, **January 28th**, the priest went to open the church, as was his custom. You can just imagine the state of panic, when the pastor discovered the door unlocked, and upon investigating, the Tabernacle empty. He immediately sounded the alarm, to every church official in Naples. Immediately, a network of the Faithful began searching desperately for the missing Hosts. The pastor stressed they had to act quickly, as the thieves would throw away the Hosts, or sell them to satanic cults. The Faithful were mourning, weeping because there was no news of the Pyxes or the Sacred Hosts.

The search went on for weeks without any results. The church of Naples was greatly alarmed. The longer, the Hosts were missing, the more frightening became the possibilities, of what could have happened to them . Every promising clue led to a dead end. After weeks of frantic, vain searches, there was the first discovery.

On Thursday, **February 19th**, Joseph Orefice, a young man of about 18 years old, was walking near the Duke of Grottolelle's property, when he saw lights, resembling a sky full of stars. The next night, **the 20th**, he saw the same sight. He related what he had seen to his father, who shook his head incredulously, refusing to listen to him. The following day, **the 21st**, Joseph's father and

---

[5]Pyxes were larger than today, more like ciborium, capable of holding many Hosts.

11 year old brother John were walking past the spot where Joseph had spotted the lights. John turned to his father: *"Father, there are the lights which Joseph spoke of last night and you wouldn't believe him."* **Later that same evening**, the *two brothers* were passing by the Duke's land and *now, they both saw the lights!*

Sunday, the 22nd, Joseph sought out Father Girolamo Guarino and told him of the lights. Father Girolamo called his brother, Father Diego, and they along with Joseph, John and their friend Thomas Piccino, set out for the place of the lights. When they arrived, the priests saw nothing.

Monday evening, the 23rd, Joseph, his friend Thomas Piccino and another man, Charles Marotta, went to the spot where they had seen the lights. This time, they met up with two strangers, who asked them if they

Reliquary of the Miracle of the Eucharist of Patierno, Italy

knew what the lights were, that sparkled like stars. Another affirmation that something was going on! Joseph and his friends replied, they didn't know, excused themselves, and went to mark the spot where now they and the strangers had seen the lights. After having placed a marker on the spot (where there was a poplar much bigger than the others), they sought out the two priests, once again! They related to them what had happened, and then they *all* returned to the locale of the lights, now including the priests' nephew, a five year old boy. When they arrived, the child began to shout: *"Over there look at the lights; they look like two candles."* [Now, the lights did not appear the same, each time. Sometimes they looked like candles, sometimes as stars, and other times in other shapes.]

Word spread, and many people came to the area of the lights, swarming around the property, trying to make out the lights. Suddenly cries came from villagers, near a haystack in the middle of the property. They called the two priests to come and see what appeared to be a great light, like that of a flame, coming from the haystack. A woman, Lucy Marotta, was thrown down, as if by an invisible force, face down on the spot from where the light had emanated. They helped her up; and then, they all began to dig. They uncovered nothing! Joseph and John Orefice, along with Thomas Piccino and Charles Marotta, headed back toward town. Suddenly, they heard the shouts and cries of people who had remained behind. Upon returning to the location, *Thomas Piccino* fell face down in the dirt, followed by *Joseph Orefice*, who said it felt as if he had been pushed from behind. At the same time, the other two, *Charles Marotta* and Joseph's brother *John* stepped forward and fell alongside the other two. The four complained they felt as if someone had struck a heavy blow to the back of their heads with a cane. People helped them up, and advancing a few steps, they saw coming from under the poplar tree, *"a great splendor like a sun."* All four looked up; and in the midst of this brilliance, they saw a dove descending, as if following the light. When the dove reached the ground, it disappeared and the light with it.

What did the incident with the dove mean? No one knew, but those who witnessed it, testified under oath, before the Vicar of Naples, that it appeared supernatural. The luminous light returned to the area, where it had been. Everyone began shouting, *"There are the lights!"* Did the Faithful and the priests begin to realize that the dove and the lights were a sign the Sacred Hosts might be there, buried? In any event, they knelt and began to dig *feverishly*. As Thomas Piccino was digging, *someone spotted a Host.* It was as snowy white as a piece of white paper. There, from deep in the dirt, the Sacred Host was brilliant white! The Faithful ran to call the priests. Father Diego Guarino came, and knelt before the Host and lifted His Savior Truly Present; then placed Him in a white linen handkerchief. Everyone was shedding tears of joy and awe that the Lord "*Almighty had done great things for them. Holy is His Name.*"[6] Not satisfied that there might not be more Hosts, Father dug more. He found 40 Hosts; they had not lost their whiteness! Now, you have to remember that these Hosts were probably buried a month, before. Father Diego Guarino placed the 40 Hosts in the same handkerchief with the first Host, that had been found. He scooped up dirt, from where they had been buried. Priests came from far and near to see and upon seeing, venerate the Miracle of the Eucharist.

The Bishop was notified and he ordered the Hosts be brought, in solemn procession, to the church. The evening of **February 25th**, at 5:30, the Hosts were returned to the Tabernacle. The people were consoled, somewhat, that they had the return of these 41 Hosts, but were still disturbed and concerned for the fate of the still missing Hosts. Remember, there had been hundreds.

The next day **February the 26th**, they continued searching for the missing Hosts, to no avail. But that evening, the light appeared once again, in the same place as before. Everyone saw it. Father Diego Guarino cried out, "*Oh Jesus! Oh Jesus! You see a light? There, see it!*" A ray of light reached up to about 4 feet, and at the top of the light, it took on the shape of a rose. They were blinded by the brightness of the light.

Thursday evening **February the 27th**, still no Hosts, they were completely disheartened, until some soldiers who were riding by the property, stopped and told them that they had seen many lights, like stars, coming from the haystack. [They later testified the same recounting, of what they had witnessed, to the Bishop.] Joseph Orefice and Charles Marotta went to the property and when they arrived, they saw the haystack on fire, which had been set by the priests, so that they could search more thoroughly

---

[6]Luke 1:49

for the remaining Hosts. Nearby, men were prostrate, crying because they had seen the light several times, but it had disappeared. Joseph Orefice knelt and began reciting out loud the *Acts of Faith, Hope and Charity.*

When he finished, he and others saw a light, like a lit taper rise about four inches from the ground and then return there to hide, but not without leaving a sign on the ground where it had disappeared. Joseph Orefice and Charles Marotta ran to Father Girolamo Guarino who, upon arriving and finding the Faithful on their knees, immediately began to dig at the spot where the sign had been left. The people cried out that they could see the light, again. But although the priest saw nothing, he made the sign of the Cross on the ground. He ordered Joseph to dig the area left of the cross; he found nothing. But when they thought of digging elsewhere, Joseph (still on his knees), leaned on the ground and finding it soft, called out to Father Guarino, whereupon he used a knife to pierce the soft ground. He heard a noise like hosts breaking. Pulling out the knife, he saw a piece of sod attached to it, with a group of Hosts stuck to it. The priest fainted; the knife and the sod with the Hosts, dropped to the ground. When he had composed himself, he reverently picked up the Hosts, and placed Them in the same white handkerchief, he had placed the other Hosts. Father Guarino advised the parish priest who returned with a canopy, an umbrella, a pall, and a chalice into which the Hosts were all placed. He then set up a table covered with silk and when the pall and the umbrella were opened over the table, he set the chalice containing the Blessed Sacrament on it, and the Faithful all knelt around the table adoring their Lord, miraculously in their presence.

The priests informed the Bishop, who then ordered the Hosts be transferred solemnly to the church. The Faithful, bearing torches, joined the priests as they reverently processed, carrying all the Sacred Hosts back to the church under a canopy, accompanied by acolytes and an honor guard of people kneeling as their Lord passed by.

The various verbal and written testimonies, of the Diocesan process, date back to February 28th, 1772 and were concluded September 14, 1774. These are the conclusions of this ecclesiastical investigation:

1. It is understood that among the stolen things, were two Pyxes containing many Sacred Hosts.

2. The recognition of the Sacred Hosts by the Vicar General Bishop Onorati: The Hosts were placed in two ciboria made of silver, which were wrapped and secured by blue silk lace, imported from Spain, sealed by the red wax seal of Bishop Onorati.

The Archepiscopal Curia listened to the opinions of three theologians and three men of science. The scientific findings were: As the lights and the perfect, white, clean, incorrupt state of the Hosts were not explainable scientifically, they must be considered miraculous.

On August 29th, 1774, the Curia issued the following decree:

"We say, decree and declare that the mentioned apparition of lights and the intact conservation of the Sacred Hosts for so many days underground, has been and is an authentic and honorable miracle operated by almighty God, to illustrate more and more the truth of the Catholic Dogma and to increase all the more the worship and adoration toward the Real and True Presence of Our Lord Jesus Christ in the Holy Sacrament of the Eucharist."

Testimonies and Documentation of the Miracle

One of the respected witnesses was Mr. Haam, a gentleman from Prague, chancellor to the Embassy of the Imperial Majesty who had heard of the unexplained lights and the Hosts found unsoiled and intact, and had gone to investigate. He testified before the Archepiscopal Curia, what had transpired. It was about 9 o'clock in the evening when he had arrived. The crowd, gathered at the property, informed him of all the events, including the theft and the miraculous finding of the Hosts. Mr. Haam shared with them and, then later, the Curia, that eight or nine days before, around the 17th or 18th of February, he had seen what seemed like thousands of lights, and a great number of people gathered around the lights, silently and devoutly praying. He went on to say, he had become frightened and asked his coachman what he thought the lights were. The coachman ventured: *"Maybe a priest was carrying the Holy Viaticum to a dying person."* But Mr. Haam insisted this could not be; they would have heard bells tolling.[7] The horse would not move. No matter how much the coachman tried to coax the horse, to pull the carriage, he could not get him to budge. *"It must be the work of the devil, witchcraft,"* Mr. Haam said. After they arrived home, the coachman left the area and never returned.

This and other documentation of the facts, written depositions, and testimonies from qualified witnesses were submitted before the ecclesiastical tribunal court of the territory, and the findings were always the same, affirming the Miraculous happenings.

There have been Bulls issued, authenticating the Miracle as well as *plenary indulgences* granted for pilgrims visiting and venerating the Miracle on the anniversary of the Miracle. And on Holy Thursday of 1967, the church of St. Pietro of Patierno was raised to *"Eucharistic Diocesan Sanctuary."*

The miracle of the Sacred Hosts that occurred in 1772, was further diagnosed in 1972, by a Professor Peter De Franciscis, and the findings were that there was no scientific explanations of the happenings of the lights and the incorrupt Hosts.

The Miraculous Hosts are stolen

Great care was taken, over the years, to safeguard and protect the miraculous Hosts. But on 23rd and 24th of October, 1978, some thieves secretly entered the church of St. Pietro and stole various sacred objects including the Reliquary containing the Sacred Hosts. There have been many appeals, in the hope the

---

[7]This was the custom, to ring the bells, announcing the priest coming through, carrying the Viaticum, the Eucharist, to a dying person.

thieves would repent and at least return the Sacred Hosts, but till today, there is no trace of Them. The Sanctuary had taken such great care and the Faithful rendered such deep love and veneration, only for some predators to abduct Our dear Lord Jesus present in the Sacred Hosts.

Today, there are no Hosts, for those who need to see visible proof that our Lord truly brought about a Miracle, turning evil into good. But the documented testimony is *not* of myths passed on by natives of Patierno, but the sworn testimonies of priests, respected men of the community and the findings of a Church Tribunal. And as a Catholic, are you required to believe? No, but be sure that you are not pridefully placing yourself above Bulls issued by the Church, Bishops and Curias affirming it and Saints like Saint Alphonsus Liguori, *"fervent apostle of the Miracle."*

What won't Our Lord do for us? He gave us this Miracle and other Miracles of the Eucharist. The Faithful of Patierno saw and believed, and now do not see and yet believe. Is He telling them and us, as He did to Saint Thomas the Apostle, *"Have you come to believe because you have seen Me? Blessed are those who have not seen and have believed."*[8]

Why does the Lord allow His Eucharist to be desecrated? What is He trying to tell us?

In our former parish, the day after Thanksgiving, we spotted an unkempt young man in church. As was our custom, before Mass, we went around greeting everyone. John, a very special young man who was home for the holidays, introduced the stranger as his friend. [We later learned he had picked him up on the street.] I had a funny feeling about this young man, so I tried to be Eucharistic minister on the side of the church where he would come to receive Holy Communion. The other Eucharistic minister went to that side, forcing me to go to the other side.

---

[8]John 20:29

This is what transpired: When the young man was about to receive Communion, looking at the Host in his hand, he asked, *"What do you do with this thing?"* To which, John replied: *"Put it in your mouth and eat it."* After having placed the Eucharist in his mouth, he went outside, spit out the Host, onto the cement walk in front of the church, and stomped on the Host with the cleated heels of his heavy boots, saying *"I hate this thing."* After Mass was over, some women asked Bob to go outside with them. They told him what the young man had done and showed him the precious Host, profaned and desecrated by the heel of the sick young man. Bob reverently picked up the crushed Host, carried It lovingly into the church, and handed It over to our pastor. Bob's face was white! He and I were just beside ourselves. I began to cry. The woman said, "Oh God understands." Bob replied, "Sure, God understands. But He is no less desecrated. You run over someone and kill them, the family can understand, but the person is no less dead."

Did the people of St. Pietro of Patierno take the Miracle of the Eucharist for granted? Did they grow lax, leaving it up to the priest to safeguard the Miracle? Do we take Our Lord in the Blessed Sacrament for granted, that He will always be there, waiting? Do we take the Mass for granted, that we can go to Mass, each day, and there will always be a priest there to celebrate? Is this why we have a shortage of priests? Have we taken for granted, those specially anointed men who *"by virtue of the Sacrament of Holy Orders acts `in persona Christi in capitis'"*[9] victim-priest with *the* Victim-Priest Jesus Christ?

Will Jesus allow Himself to be taken away from us?

---

[9]in the person of Christ the Head - Catechism of the Catholic Church #1548

Pezilla-la-Rivière - 1793

Protect us, Lord, with your Eucharistic Presence

Treacherous times call for extraordinary courage. 1793 in France was just such a time. Satan had attacked the eldest daughter of the Church with the French Revolution in 1789, and the most ravaged, even worse than the nobility, was the Church. There are countless accounts of bishops and priests being *exiled*, and *executed* by the guillotine.[1] It was the worst ten years in the Church since the persecution of the Early Christians, worse than the early days of the Protestant Reformation. Satan was doing his best to deal a *death blow* to the Church in France.

French authors of that time describe the Revolution as follows: *"Death struggle between Christianity and a diabolical philosophy and as a trial permitted by Providence to revivify Catholicism."*[2] *"...the fruit of a plot hatched by philosophers, freemasons and fanatics to destroy the Church."*[3] It started as a means of wresting power from the Church in France, but more importantly, to seize her lands. This was methodically done by taking away all authority from the hierarchy of the church, and *seemingly* giving it to the common man, everyone doing their own thing. No rules, no sin, no direction, no conscience, no

---

[1]French method of execution, where the head is placed in a rack, and a razor-sharp blade comes down and decapitates the victim.

[2]*Considérations sur la France* - Joseph de Maistre - 1796

[3]*Mémoires pour l'histoire du Jacobinisme* - Abbé Augustin de Barruel - 1797

peace; the result, chaos and death. No one had the right to order anyone else to do anything, *except*, of course, the Legislative Assembly. They had lots of power, and they used it against the Church.

The rage of the common people that was aimed, at first at the royal family, missed its mark, and hit the clergy and the Catholic Church. Because the royalty and nobility had always linked themselves with the Church, when the peasants rose up against the king and his court, the Church got caught in the middle, a corridor filled with blood and tears. Between 1792 and 1794, an all-out attempt was made to *Dechristianize* the Church by the Legislative Assembly, and then when *they* were thrown out of power, by the National Convention. The persecution was wholesale:

† Deportation of bishops, priests and religious, with the condemnation of many of them to death;

† Closing down churches, indiscriminate destruction of shrines, smashing statues, stomping on crucifixes, burning relics, removing any and all traces of the Church and her family: Our Lord, Mother Mary, the Angels and the Saints;

† Prohibition of worship and all teaching of the Faith, punishable by death, if caught;

† Condemnation of all age-old traditions of the Church.

The *Dechristianization* of France went on a parallel course with the Reign of Terror. There were two stages: the *"little terror"* and the *"great terror"*. The "little terror" took place during the summer and fall of 1792, the "great terror" from September 1793 to August 1794. His children are running wild; others are being trampled underfoot; time for the Lord to act! In September 1793, He gave France, The Miracle of the Eucharist of Pezilla-la-Rivière.

The small village of Pezilla-la-Rivière was not near any big city. Perpignan, near the Spanish border, was the closest major city to Pezilla. Traditionally, movements, no matter what kind, usually begin in the big cities and work their way into the middle of a country. Example: The French Revolution began in Paris. Its tentacles stretched from Paris to Lyon to Dijon to Marseilles, strangling all the little villages in between. Its rage and rebellion exploded, traveling wildly along the coastal route by boat and throughout the countryside by stagecoach. It took a long time before the Revolution reached small towns like Pezilla-la-Rivière. Pezilla-la-Rivière's main industry was farming. Wine-making being the principal industry in the southeast of France, the farmers or grape-growers had their own set of problems, without being involved in all the politics of the big cities. They had to be concerned with feeding their families and making sure their crops did not spoil.

We're not going to attempt to say that everyone in this village was a church-going Catholic. But Pezilla-la-Rivière had a good priest, Jacques Perone. He was dedicated to his vocation and to his flock, the brothers and sisters of Pezilla-la-Rivière; and they loved him. There was a small group who prayed the Rosary, who adored Our Lord Jesus in the Eucharist, and were committed to Forty Hours Devotion. They were his people, and he was their priest.

The Revolution was fast spreading to the villages. Father argued heatedly with his superior, when he was ordered to leave Pezilla and head for the border of Spain, which was not a great distance. It was impossible! He couldn't leave his people. Fr. Jacques resisted to the very last minute. But by the time September 1793 arrived, word had spread around the countryside that all priests and religious were being hunted down by the police. They were to be turned over to the authorities, to be either exiled or guillotined. With these few options available, Fr. Jacques left for Gerona, a small town on the Spanish side.

But even with danger eminent, he couldn't bear to be away from his flock. He returned clandestinely, just when the persecution was reaching its peak, September 15, 1793. He celebrated Sunday Mass in the parish Church. He even officiated the Procession. He felt good, being back with his people; but it didn't take long for him to realize that he had better leave under his own power, rather than through death at the hands of the police,[4] as that wouldn't be of benefit to him or his parishioners. The *"great terror"* had arrived in Pezilla. In fact, it got so hot, and he had to leave so quickly, he was not able to consume the Hosts, left in the Tabernacle of the church. As he was heading south, at a village named Saint Feliu d'Avail, he said, almost to himself, *"What I wouldn't give to be able to return to Pezilla even for a quarter-hour only, to consume the Consecrated Hosts."*

He didn't realize it, but a local girl from Pezilla, Rose Llorens, who, with some others, was accompanying him part way, heard him say the words. She understood what he meant, and the danger that existed for the Consecrated Hosts. The church was officially closed. She knew that eventually, everything in the church would be inventoried and taken out to be sold, or disposed of as necessary. The Tabernacle would probably wind up at the metal shop, where it would be opened. When the Hosts in the Tabernacle were seen, They would either be desecrated by the shopkeeper or be sold to revolutionaries or satanists, of which there were many in France in 1793. In any event, the Lord in His Eucharistic Presence, would be profaned.

But how would she be able to save the Hosts? No one was allowed to enter, without authorization. The Mayor, Mark Estrade, was angry with all the Catholics in the town. He had been heavily chewed-out when it was learned that a priest had celebrated Mass in the church on the previous Sunday. How could he allow something like that to take place right under his nose? *And a procession?* He was not about to do any favors for Catholics. She wouldn't even consider asking him. She waited and prayed. The Lord was working. We can see the plan of the Lord starting to take shape. The first thing he had to do was to get rid of the Mayor, Mark Estrade. Impossible, you say? Possibly for man, but not for God.

---

[4]more like thugs than police

He chose the day after Christmas, 1793, when a new community council was elected. The new mayor of the town was Jean Bonafos, who was a good Catholic. *Yea God, Yea!* Rosa appealed to him as soon as she could after his election. On the morning of February 7, 1794, Rosa, the mayor Jean and Pierre Boyer, one of the members of the prayer group, opened the church. Inside the Tabernacle were five consecrated Hosts, four small ones in a pyx, and a large one in a lunette in the upper part of a Monstrance. They removed the consecrated Hosts from the Tabernacle.

Jean Bonafos decided to take the large Host in the Monstrance to his home. The others warned him that he was in danger, if he got caught with the Eucharist; he assured them he would be sure to hide the Host in a good place. Jean brought the Host home, and placed It in a wood chest, which he locked with a key, and hid under the floor of his house, close to the oven where bread was usually baked. No one knew where he hid the Eucharist, except his wife Tommasa, who vowed with her life that no one would ever learn from her. Jean sheltered the Consecrated Host in his home until after the hostilities had ended.

The other four Hosts in the pyx were wrapped in a purificator, and entrusted to Rosa Llorens. She brought them to her home, where her mother was waiting. At first, the mother put the Hosts into a built-in wardrobe, because she felt this would be the safest place. But then a nun, home from her convent (which had been closed down), told her it would be best to place the Hosts in a glass cup with a lid. Then it was all placed in a red silk purse.

Being a small town, word spread quickly that the Blessed Sacrament was being reserved in the house of Rosa Llorens. The whole town began coming to Rosa's house on a regular basis, to adore the Lord Present in the Hosts. They built a little canopy and on Thursday evenings, would take Our Lord in His Eucharistic Presence, out of his hideaway, still inside the little red purse, and have *Eucharistic Adoration*. There was a great deal of danger involved in Rosa and her mother opening their home to the people, any of whom could have innocently let it slip that the Eucharist was in their home, or others who might have informed the police. This went on for seven years, until 1800.

At one point, during the heat of the persecution in the village, *holocaust* better describes it, homes were burned; the church was attacked; people feared to walk on the streets; bishops, priests, nuns and religious hid out for the entire seven years. For those born in Pezilla-la-Rivière, whose family went back generations, such insanity could not be happening.

And yet, throughout, the little houses of Rosa Llorens, and Jean Bonafos were completely protected. It was as if Angels were sent to block those houses from attack by the enemies of God and the Church. A revolutionary once climbed up to the roof of Rosa's house while there were many people inside, adoring Our Lord Jesus in the Eucharist. He listened, at the chimney, to the conversations going on. Later, he told Rosa, *"I know that you are hiding the Blessed Sacrament in your house. I swear to you that I will not say anything to anyone." And he didn't!*

When the Revolution ended, many of the convicted revolutionaries declared about Pezilla-la-Rivière, in retrospect, *"That town was certainly protected either by God or the devil."* Naturally, we know *Who* was the power that saved the town from total destruction.

Double Miracle

Just prior to Napoleon Bonaparte's takeover, during the final days of the Revolution, called the Constitution of the VIII year, the priests were allowed to come out of hiding. Both the vicar of the parish and Fr. Perone worked their way back from Spain to their town. It had been seven years since they were forced to leave.

The Vicar, Fr. Siuroles, was the first of the two to return. He went immediately over to the house of Rosa Llorens to determine the condition of the consecrated Hosts which had been left there seven years ago. He didn't hold much hope, They would be anything but ochre-colored dust, if anything. When the red purse was opened, and the Hosts removed from the glass cup, everyone was in shock at what they beheld. Not only had the four Hosts not decomposed after seven years, but when the cover was taken off the glass jar, a dark brown band had formed around the outer edge of the jar; but inside the jar was white as snow, and the Hosts were as brilliant as the day, they had been placed in the jar. The Lord was telling the people in no uncertain terms that He had been with them, had protected them, and kept the promise, He made to us so long ago.[5]

Four days later, Fr. Perone returned to Pezilla-la-Rivière and went to the house of Jean Bonafos. He, together with Jean, took the wood chest from its hiding place under the floor of the house. They unlocked the wooden chest, and found the large consecrated Host still inside the Monstrance, as beautiful and white, as when It had been placed there, some seven years ago, right after the Mass and Procession on September 15, 1793.

The Hosts were arranged in a special Monstrance built for the Miracle of the Eucharist. The little town became a high point in the Diocese for priests and pilgrims. The local bishop of Saunhac-Belcastel instituted a Feast Day in honor of the Miracle of the Eucharist, the third Sunday of September, in honor of the Miracle given the town, during the *"grand terror"* of the French Revolution. The bishop of Carcassonne, Bishop de La Bouillerie, wrote a hymn in honor of the Miracle of the Eucharist, and a priest of the diocese, Fr. Hermann, composed the music. Much attention and honor was given to the Miracle of the Eucharist. God had protected His people through this Miracle; now the people were adoring and thanking their God.

In 1893, on the one hundredth anniversary of the Miracle of the Eucharist, a new church was built in Pezilla-la-Rivière. A new Monstrance was also designed, in which the large Host was placed in the center, with the four small Hosts placed around the

---

[5]Matthew 28:20 - *"And behold, I am with you always, until the end of time."*

*The Church built in 1893
for the Miracle
of the Eucharist*

large Host in the form of a Cross. The glass cup, in which the four small Hosts had rested in the home of Rosa Llorens for seven years, was placed in a special reliquary, and given to a Eucharistic Adoration Society in Paray-le-Monial.

Pezilla-la-Riviere has remained a Eucharistic village. The descendants of the courageous brothers and sisters who protected the Body and Blood of their Savior, and were in turn, protected by the Body and Blood of their Savior, have continued the tradition passed on to them by those who had come before.

The Hosts were left in their incorrupt state until 1930. Well-meaning villagers wanted to construct a more permanent Tabernacle behind the main Altar, which would better protect the Miracle of the Eucharist. The Miraculous Hosts were placed in their new home before the walls were dry. Because of the dampness, *the Hosts decomposed.* Our Lord in *that* Miracle of the Eucharist is no longer there. We have a hard time believing that the reason the Hosts decomposed was because construction was damp. Look at the history of this Miracle of the Eucharist, during the time of the French Revolution. Does it seem possible that a little thing like dampness would cause the Lord to leave the Miraculous Hosts? Or could it be that they lost faith in the

*The Miracle of the Eucharist
of Pezilla-la-Riviere*

Lord's willingness or ability to keep the Miraculous Hosts incorrupt? Did they think, they needed man's help to do something, only God could do? We have a short story to tell you by way of example. Our first miracle through the intercession of St. Thérèse happened in 1976. On our first pilgrimage, we were supposed to go to the Shrine of St. Thérèse in Lisieux, but didn't. When we got home, we were praying before a statue of the Little Flower in a mission church in San Diego, apologizing for not going to her Shrine, promising we would next year, when we found a novena to the Saint. We began petitioning her intercession, pleading for a miracle for a teenager in our parish who had Bone-Marrow Cancer. We received a rose[6] after the second day of the novena. We ran to tell the mother. She didn't believe us. She told us that she and her son were going to the doctor that very afternoon to ask for an amputation of the boy's kneecaps, because the pain was so terribly unbearable.

Later that afternoon, mother and son ran up to our house, with a rose. They kept shouting: *"It's a Miracle! It's a Miracle!"* The boy was completely cured of the Cancer. That rose stayed on our prayer table *for three years*, and never wilted; the water in the vase remained the level it was the day it was filled - *for three years*. We showed it to everyone who came to our home. Then our daughter and grandson came to live with us, with their little cat, who loved to eat plants. We feared, the cat would eat the rose which we now called our *Miraculous Rose*. We set the rose in the vase in our *open* breakfront. The air could enter the breakfront, but the wire grates on the doors, prevented the cat from getting in and eating the rose. However, within three days, *the rose withered and died*, and the water in the vase completely evaporated.

We didn't trust. Did the people of Pezilla-la-Riviere not trust the Lord? *Do we trust the Lord?*

---

[6]If the Lord is going to grant your petition, the novena said, St. Thérèse will send you a rose.

Réunion - 1902
A Miracle of the Eucharist no one could doubt

It is January 26 1902:
We are in a time of crisis.
It is the turn of the century.
The world is changing,
and with the world,
some within the Church
would have the Church change.
†

A holy priest once said, when we shared our hurts over some things that were being said and not said, done and not done in parishes around the United States, in our time:
"Bob and Penny, we have had strife and turmoil in our Church for 2000 years. The pendulum swings far to the left, then to the right, and then finally back to the center."

It was the beginning of the Twentieth Century. The pendulum had swung to the left. *Modernism* was attacking our Church deviously from within. You know you can fight heresy when it is coming from someone *outside* the Church; they have been attacking us from the very beginning. But when it comes from *within*, it is difficult for us to know what is the truth and what is a product of *the father of lies* - the devil.

When there is a crisis in the Church, we have a Miracle of the Eucharist, an Apparition of Our Lady, or God raises up Powerful men and women to defend Mother Church. This chapter is about a Miracle of the Eucharist and a powerful man who was raised up - a Pope and Saint - Saint Pope Pius X - to defend the Church.

The Miracle

Our Miracle takes place in 1905, in **Saint Andrew's Roman Catholic Church**, a parish church on an island in the Indian Ocean. Réunion Island was a possession of France, at that time. St. Andrew's is a parish 27 kilometers (approximately 18 miles) from the village of Saint Dionysius.

Our Lord chose to bring about this Miracle of the Eucharist, and to allow It to remain throughout Perpetual Adoration.

On a day that started out no different than any other day, our Lord chose a special parish, with special people - no, a *holy* parish with *holy* people, to appear to them on the Host in the Monstrance throughout exposition of the Blessed Sacrament. The Vision manifested Itself, right after morning Mass at eight o'clock and remained throughout the day, right up to Benediction with the Blessed Sacrament, at three in the afternoon.

The Apparition

It was the Seventh Sunday in ordinary time. Father Lacombe had the Blessed Sacrament exposed, before beginning the Mass. [*This must have occurred during Forty Hours Devotion* which *"is a continuous period of prayer before the Blessed Sacrament, begun and terminated with a Solemn High Mass, procession where possible, Litany of the Saints, and special prayers.*]*[1]

During the Mass, at the time of Consecration, when Father looked up to the Host in the Monstrance, instead of the Host, he beheld the Face of a Man stricken with sadness, His Eyes closed, His Head bowed wearily to the right, tears running down His Cheeks. [It reminds us of the Vision, Saint Teresa of Avila had of Our Lord at the Pillar that changed her life.] Father Lacombe was afraid, he was suffering from an optical illusion, that he was seeing things, so he said nothing.

---

[1]There is uninterrupted exposition of the Blessed Sacrament in a Monstrance for forty hours, signifying the approximate number of hours, Our Lord's Body lay in the tomb between His death and His resurrection on the third day. From New Catholic Encyclopedia - Catholic University of America.

But, he had difficulty getting it out of his thoughts. When Mass was over, Father Lacombe went into the Sacristy and began to remove his vestments. As he was in the process of hanging them up, a man came in and asked him to bless a religious medal. Father told him to first go before the Most Blessed Sacrament and pray. Father directed the man to closely observe the Host. The man returned, soon after, clearly shaken, and declared, he had seen the Face of a Man in the Monstrance!

The Priest then asked the Altar boys to go kneel before the Blessed Sacrament and tell him what they saw. They returned and reported that they had seen the Holy Face!

Then two elderly women, who lived nearby, came into the church, knelt before the Blessed Sacrament and concurred, they too had seen the Face of a Man in the Host. Father then asked their niece, little Maria Le Vaillant to climb up the steps of the staircase behind the Altar. Maria also beheld the Face of Our Lord Jesus Christ, and later said: *"I cannot forget what I have seen, I will always remember the Face of our Lord. His Face will always be before me. It has made an indelible mark on my life."* [Miss (little) Maria Le Vaillant of Hautecourt, whose ancestors had emigrated to the Island of Réunion during the French Revolution, was 9 years old at the time. She would later hand over her documented recollections of what happened and what she had personally witnessed to Mr. Felice Philibert, of the village of Puy.]

News of the miracle spread quickly throughout the village, and people began flocking to the church to view the Miracle. They all wanted to draw close to the Altar; some even went behind the Altar. And those who went behind the Altar saw the same Vision, as those in front of the Altar. At first, they could not believe their eyes; there must be some sort of explanation. They thought, perhaps they were seeing a reflection from the candles or from the outside; maybe the light was casting a shadow on the Host which made it appear to have a Face upon It. They extinguished the candles. They closed the shutters of the windows, blocking out most of the light in the church; but the Holy Face was more radiant than before, flooding the Altar with Its light. They could see the Image even more clearly!

Almost every one saw the Holy Face. Our Lord shared Himself with everyone, sinner and Saint alike. He allowed all to see His Holy Face: the Faithful as well as the infidels of the island, upright citizens along with members of the underworld. Again, as when He preached and walked among us, He called the children unto Him; they came, they saw and all adored the Face of Christ on the Host.

All the Nuns of Saint Joseph of Cluny beheld their Bridegroom's Face, all but the Mother Superior - Mother Edouard. She was the only one who did not see anything. [But the following year, when the Blessed Sacrament was exposed, she was the *only one* who saw the Face of Our Jesus.]

The word spread and they came from far and near, all seeking the Face of their Lord. But not all saw! Some did not see the Holy Face, even after having prayed for a long time. Others, in an attempt to see more clearly, brought binoculars; but the Vision was clearer and more distinct to the naked eye. Even unbelievers, who came to the church out of curiosity, saw the Holy Face as had the believers.

Now, the Masons have always tried to wipe Our Lord from the face of the earth. A Mason from the area, Lewis Defeuille, begin to spread a false rumor around town that the priest had fabricated the story of the Host with a Face on it, that somehow he had placed the Image on the Host, himself. No one paid any attention to his ravings. They insisted: *"If this was true, how come so many people attested privately to having seen the Vision?"*

Around two in the afternoon, the Apparition started to change. In place of the Holy Face, a crucifix slowly appeared. It grew and grew until it loomed larger than the Host, towering above and below It. The Host, with our Lord Crucified on the Cross, remained visible, glowing white and shimmering, white like snow.

Needless to say, that day, an immense crowd came to Vespers, to adore the Lord in His Blessed Sacrament and to participate in Benediction with the Blessed Sacrament. As they were singing the hymn *"Tantum Ergo,"* the Vision disappeared.

The bishop of Saint Dionysius ordered, the Miraculous Host be preserved. All were questioned as to what they believed the meaning of the Miracle to be. Some wondered if this was a prophecy or forewarning of a disastrous calamity that would befall them. Others, wiser, saw in this Miracle of the Eucharist, the desire of God, in this supernatural manifestation, to touch the hearts, in particular, of unbelievers and of sinners.

Several thousand people witnessed the Miracle. Immediately, people stepped forward, declaring what they had seen. Hundreds of signatures were collected, attesting to the authenticity of the Vision.

In 1904, Father Lacombe, pastor of Saint Andrew's stood up before the **Eucharistic Congress at Angouleme** and testified as to the supernatural happenings at his parish church.

Then at a Priest Retreat, at Périgueux, he recounted *again* all that had transpired that special day, in January, when the world stood still, and Our Lord chose to prove through his parish that He was really, truly present, in *His Body, Blood, Soul and Divinity*, not only during the Sacrifice of the Mass but forever as long as the Consecrated Host is present in the church.

Now, as we said, many heresies were being insidiously spread, in an endeavor to draw the priesthood away from the Truth, all in the name of *Modernism* (even the title sounds prideful and pompous). Although many of his brother priests were probably exposed to this new package of heresies, which in reality were many old heresies previously condemned by Councils (now conveniently wrapped together under one name), they were spellbound as he recounted the Miracle of the Eucharist. Is this not what they had believed when they were ordained? Is this not what had burned in their hearts, the first day they entered the

Seminary? Is this not the reason, they were born? They were not only hanging on to his every word, they were truly touched. *They were on fire!*

It was not only Father Lacombe who gave witness to this supernatural occurrence. *Many* eye witnesses testified what they had seen, and it was always the same: They had seen the Holy Face of Jesus!

All the evidence was overwhelmingly in affirmation of the Miracle; but we know that wherever Our Lord is about proving He is here among us, the enemy lies in wait to attack. There were many who *rejoiced* that Our Lord had so generously chosen their parish to show His Miraculous Image. And then, there were those who had left the Church, who could not stand the Lord being glorified through a Miracle of the Eucharist. After all, had they not been trying to persuade the Faithful that the Lord was not present in the Holy Eucharist? This Miracle was not cooperating with their proselytizing, their focus to draw as many away from the Church as they could. *"Misery needs company."* It's like an alcoholic, an adulterer, a drug addict, who cannot be alone in their sin or in their misery; they need company, and so they take many innocent, unaware souls down with them. How will they lure innocent souls? Discredit the Miracle; discredit the priest; discredit the Church.

Some of these poor, wretched malcontents didn't know *why* they were outside the Church; their ancestors had fallen prey to the snares of heresies and schisms that had separated them from Mother Church, centuries before. And then there were those who had fallen for the *new* heresies and schisms that threatened to split the Church, at this time. Oh, if they had been as zealous in defending the Church as they were in attempting to destroy her.

Hard as they tried, although the enemies of Christ, and the Church that He founded, did everything they could to discredit the Miracle, no one could refute that it had taken place, since there had been such a large crowd present in the church, who saw It with their own eyes. *First*, It was seen by the Faithful inside the church, *then* by persons outside. Villagers from Saint Dionysius, 18 miles away, came and declared, they had beheld the Face of a Man in the Monstrance.

The Lord chooses whom He wills, to manifest Himself. Just as He sat and dined with sinners as well as Saints, He did not *now* discriminate, and reveal Himself only to those Faithful who believed, but sometimes to the most unlikely. Those who never went to church, as well as those who did not believe that Our Lord was Really present in the Eucharist, came; they saw and they could not deny what they saw. *They believed!*

Even the mayor of the village, Mr. Duménil, who was a good man but not a practicing Catholic, was touched. He had not seen the Miracle with his own eyes, as he had come to the church after the Holy Image of Our Lord had left. But he sent two young girls into the church, hoping the Lord would make Himself present to them, as he felt he had not seen the Miracle because he was not worthy. He believed, although he had not seen. This reminds us of Jesus' words to Thomas the Apostle *"Blessed are those who have not seen and believe."* Would you not say, he also benefited from the Vision?

✝

Was this Miracle of the Eucharist, a reward Our Lord was bestowing upon Father Lacombe and his parishioners, for having Perpetual Adoration, for spending time with Him at Mass and before His Blessed Sacrament? If you recall, Our Lord said to His three specially chosen Apostles in the Garden of Gethsemane: *"'My Soul is sorrowful even unto death: stay here and watch with Me.'*[2]*...He fell upon His Face, praying, saying: 'My Father, if it be possible, let this chalice pass from Me.'"*[3] When He came upon His Disciples, fast asleep, He said: *"Could you not stay awake and watch with Me?"*[4] Then knowing how powerful are the temptations of this world, He warned them to *pray!* *"The*

---

[2]Matt 26:38
[3]Matt 26:39
[4]Matt 26:40

spirit indeed is willing, but the flesh is weak. "[5]

Had these parishioners and their holy priest kept the Lord company in His time of deep pain? Some say that Our Lord's suffering ended on the Cross. They do not want to look upon Him on the Cross, so they remove our Crucifixes and even in some churches the Cross altogether. Do you believe, Our Lord is *not* suffering when He witnesses some of His beloved bishops, priests and brides of Christ denying Him and His Church? Was He seeing the many apostasies and heresies that would separate His children from His Church?

Why did Our Lord cry out to the Father: *"My Father, if it is possible, let this chalice pass from Me?"* What had Our Lord seen that caused Him so much agony? What was Our Lord's pain? Did He see the many innocent souls, who, for the last 2000 years have been led astray? Did He see those who would deny Him out of fear or ignorance, as they had denied Him when Pontius Pilate gave them an opportunity to choose Him between Him and a murderer? Are we choosing murderers, today, over Jesus when we just stand by and do nothing, as we lose all we hold dear?

What was Our Lord's pain, at the time of this Miracle, that caused Him to weep? Was his anguish for all His priests who no longer believed? Is it for His Priests, today? Is Our Lord bringing this Miracle to them, so that their hearts burn as they place their holy, consecrated hands over the bread and wine, and remember that it is through those hands and the power of the Holy Spirit that Jesus comes to life on the Altar? Was it, then, and is it *now*, to *strengthen* them that they not run away, as the original Apostles did;[6] or deny Him, as their first Pope - St. Peter did? Does Jesus love our priests and bishops, our religious - enough to die for them, even as they are denying Him? Does He love them? Yes, to the point of opening His Arms on the Cross to embrace them, to hold them, to console them. *Did He come for them?*

---

[5]Matt 26:41
[6]with the exception of St. John

Was and is Our Lord's Heart bleeding because He has been witnessing those, He so carefully created, being annihilated by greed and selfishness? Do we think, He looks down upon us, uninvolved, an apathetic bystander, while man commits one genocide after another? Does He need you and me to spend one hour with Him in His Garden of Gethsemane of today - before the Blessed Sacrament? That night, when He was so horribly wounded, betrayed and denied, what was His pain? Did He weep, did He sweat blood and tears, because He could see children turning against parents and parents killing their own flesh and blood?

Who will sooth His Wounds, wipe His Brow, tell Him they *love* Him, tell Him they would *die* for Him, tell Him they will *live* for Him? With this Miracle, did the Lord multiply the blessings and His Graces, as He did at Capharnaum with the little boy's gift of five loaves and two fish? Will He, through you, today? See how the Lord responds to the smallest gift, we give to Him, as He did, in this Miracle of the Eucharist.

At the beginning of the 20th Century, Jesus sent us Saint Pope Pius X

Can you just imagine how furious the devil was! He was out to destroy the Church, and so the father of lies went after those who could best help him do it - bishops and priests. Our Lord sent us this Miracle, in a time of crisis for the Church, when the Church was being *bombarded* by series of attacks. *Modernism*[7] had been slowly infecting the priesthood for years and through them the laity.

In this time of crisis, Our Lord, ever Faithful to His promise: *"Hell will not prevail against My Church"* gave us Saint Pope Pius X, a powerful man who became a Saint.

He was a reluctant Pope, in that he pleaded, he not be elected. But once having accepted the Keys of the Kingdom, he became one of the most important Popes of our Church. He actively

---
[7] Modernism - Read about this Heresy in Bob and Penny Lord's book: *"Scandal of the Cross, and its Triumph"*

battled *Modernism*, a malignant apostasy that was eating away at the Church.

August 4, 1903, white smoke came from the chimney of the Vatican, and the Church had a new Pontiff. One of the Pope's first acts was to put an end, for all time, to any civil interference with the election of a Pope. [Much of the scandal that has been spread about our Popes is a result of the *few* Popes who were elected through the influence and interference of heads of state of powerful nations.] When bishops complained that by alienating countries, especially France, the Pope had lost much church property, he declared: *"They are too concerned about material goods, and not about spiritual."* The Bishop of Nevers (where the incorrupt body of St. Bernadette lies in a glass sarcophagus) said in rebuttal to his brother Bishops: *"at the cost of sacrificing our property (he) emancipated us from slavery"*. [This is a lesson to all in the Church who would compromise our Church and our beliefs in exchange for financial aid from any government.]

The reluctant Pope became a powerful warrior, a staunch Defender of the Church, daring to be unpopular, but always loving. Sound like any Pope you know? July 3, 1907 *Lamentabili sane exetu* was issued by the Holy Office with the Pope's approval. It outlined and repudiated 65 areas of Modernism that were filled with serious errors.

That same year, on the Feast of Our Lady's Birth, September the 8th, the Pope issued an encyclical: *"Pascendi dominici gregis"* which was to unequivocally condemn what it termed: *"the resumé of all the heresies"* (Modernism). Saint Pope Pius X did not stop with this encyclical; he decreed many measures formulated to protect the faith of the laity and most especially that of his beloved priests.

Things were so serious that he issued the *motu propio "Praestantia"*[8] on November 18th of the same year requiring obedience of his Bishops and priests to both *"Lamentabili sane exetu"* and *"Pascendi dominici gregis"*. To those theologians

---

[8]this term refers to papal documents.

who wrote and advocated Modernism, he warned that they would be gravely censured should they continue to espouse these heresies. Despite these stern warnings, despite excommunications of those refusing to obey, despite books promoting these heresies being added to the List of Forbidden Books, Modernism did not cease to spread its poison. The Pope had no recourse but to issue a directive requiring Priests to take an oath denouncing Modernism. To the end of his Pontificate, Pope Pius fought against the evils of Modernism.

This is one of the ways, the Pope attempted to save the innocent lambs entrusted to him. This attack on the Church could leave the Church much wounded. How would he provide his children with *ammunition* to fight? On April 15, 1905, he issued an encyclical *"Acerbo nimis"* emphasizing the need of the Faithful to receive instruction - to learn the true Faith. Has not our present Pope John Paul II done the same with the encyclical *"Veritatis Splendor"* and the new *Universal Catholic Catechism* (which should be in every Catholic home in the world)?

Saint Pope Pius X handed down encyclicals and decrees that he urged his priests to obey. He provided the laity with knowledge of Who their Lord is, as our present Pope is doing, today. He knew that there can be only one Truth - one universal catechesis - one instruction on our Catholic Faith, and that is the Magisterium, the teaching that has been passed down by the Apostles.

Now, how could he *best strengthen* his children for the battle? The Eucharist! He had fed them through Our Lord in His Word; now he would feed them through Our Lord in His Eucharist. In the decree *"Sacra Tridentina Synodus"*, he encouraged greater devotion to the Eucharist, urging the Faithful to receive Holy Communion more frequently. So, we owe our gift of receiving Our Lord every day at daily Mass, and each Sunday (or, with the absence of a priest to celebrate the Sacrifice of the Mass, when attending a Communion Service). This, he did December 20, 1905.

August 8, 1910, the Pope issued a decree allowing and encouraging children to receive First Holy Communion at an early age (at the age of reason - the only requirement, they know and understand *Who* the Eucharist is).

The motto of our Ministry is: *The Body of Christ - the Eucharist, The Mother of Christ - Mary Most Holy, and the Church of Christ through his Vicar on earth - the Pope.* We have said, over and over again, you can not have one without the other; if you do, you will lose your faith, you will lose your Jesus. You cannot know Jesus without His Mother. Who knows Jesus better than His Heavenly Mother? And you cannot truly know Jesus and Mary, without the guidance of the father that Jesus left us to guide and protect us - the Pope.

Having provided encyclicals and decrees *protecting* the Faithful, having equipped them with true knowledge of the Faith through Catechism Instruction, having fed them with the gift of frequent reception of the *True Bread* Which comes down from Heaven, our Pope, Saint Pius X, by his example, his great devotion to Mother Mary, gave us, once more, our Heavenly Mother as our own to know and to love, to turn to, to listen to, as she teaches us how to know and love her Son Jesus Christ. Our Pope Pius X, like Pope John Paul II was known for his deep devotion to Mother Mary. [Again, does someone attack the Pope? Just wait, they will attack Mother Mary, dispute the Word, belittle the Eucharist, leave the Church. They all go together.]

There are so many great legacies, our Pope, Saint Pius X left us. So much was accomplished during his Pontificate. We are only outlining that which we feel pertain, most especially, to the *Miracle of the Eucharist* that we have shared with you, in this chapter. But, we would be remiss if we did not end this chapter and this brief insight into a Defender of the Faith by telling all our Priests, Saint Pope Pius X loved you deeply; he respected you and he always bestowed honor upon you. That did not mean that he allowed you to fall into error and to bring the Faithful, entrusted to you, down with you through the heresy of Modernism.

Love is not always giving us our way.

Even Martin Luther said, shortly before he led so many unsuspecting Catholics away from their Church: *"Thank God, that God in His wisdom gave us a father - our Pope."* And then, he disobeyed him. We are a family and a family cannot function in peace and harmony without a head, without a father. Our Pope is our father on earth, standing in for Jesus Christ. Our Popes down through the centuries, left to us by Jesus Christ, know that without the Eucharist there is no life in the Church; without the Sacrifice of the Mass, there is no Eucharist; without the Priest, there is no Mass, there is no Eucharist - the Church is dead, we are dead! We dedicate this chapter to all our priests that we need so badly. We love you! Jesus and Mary love you! Your Pope loves you!

We have said, over and over again, that Our Lord will always bring about Miracles of the Eucharist, *the Body of Christ*, Mother Mary will appear, *the Mother of Christ* or/and He will raise up a powerful man to save His Church when She is in danger, *the Vicar of Christ*. If ever there was a time, the beginning of the 20th Century *was* that time. If ever there was a time, this, the end of the 20th century *is* that time. And once more, Our Lord has sent us a Pope who will bring the ship of the Church safely into harbor.

Will you spend one hour with Jesus, adoring Him in the Blessed Sacrament? Will you wipe away some of the tears caused by so much abuse and neglect? Who will keep Our Willing Prisoner of Love, company, He Who waits for someone to visit Him? During this Miracle, as in the Garden of Gethsemane, Jesus cried; Jesus was weary and hurt. He only asked the Disciples, He trusted, to stay awake and watch with Him. Will you say yes?

Saints and Lovers of the Eucharist

It is so exciting to be able to look through the pages of history, and see how the Lord has given us unbelievably powerful *Lovers of the Eucharist* in the brothers and sisters who have gone before us. St. Teresa of Avila, or as she is more accurately known, Teresa la Grande, was called *"Loca de la Eucaristía"*, which translates to *"Crazy over the Eucharist"*. St. Thérèse the Little Flower, called her First Holy Communion, *"...that first sweet kiss of Jesus."* In our time, Mother Teresa of Calcutta attributes the growth in her vocations to the Real Presence of Jesus in the Eucharist. *Three* brilliant Teresa's, *three* different periods in history, *one* bold attitude towards Jesus in the Eucharist.

The people we're going to share with you in this chapter are all considered profound people in the church. We love and respect them for their holiness, their spirituality, their infused knowledge, their obedience, their faithfulness to Mother Church and their love for Our Lord and his Mother. They all speak of the Eucharist as if It were the very essence of their existence or as the Angel said to Elijah, *"food for the journey"*. Why then, do we doubt, ask questions, look for proof? Why can't we accept the strength of Jesus in the Eucharist, if not because of His words, because of His *Words in action* by those who followed?

We want to share with you now just a *few* of those thousands and millions of Saints, who were washed clean by the blood of the Lamb.[1] Let us take to our hearts and minds their wisdom, their discernment, their special closeness with the Lord in the Eucharist.

---

[1]Rev 7:14

Mother Mary - #1 Lover of the Eucharist

"My Soul proclaims the greatness of the Lord, and my Spirit rejoices in God my Savior. For He has done great things for me, and Holy is His Name."

We celebrated the Mass of the *Feast of the Assumption*, and our priest in his homily, invited all of us to say the prayer of Mary's Magnificat, because every time we receive the Eucharist, our souls proclaim the greatness of the Lord. He is inside of us. That gave us food for thought. We are like Mary when we receive the Eucharist! We carry Jesus in our hearts, as she did. We actually

Mother Mary
Our Lady of the Eucharist

bring the Body, Blood, Soul and Divinity of our Savior with us, to others, as His Mother did for those nine months. She gave thanks for the Gift, she was given, of her God within her. We must give thanks also for the Gift of our God within us. Mary was a living Tabernacle, a living Ciborium. When we receive the Eucharist, we are also, like Mary, a living Tabernacle, a living Ciborium. As her Son, Mother Mary loved Jesus; and as her Lord, she adored Him. It only stands to reason, she would be a lover of the Eucharist.

The Gospel of St. Luke tells us that Joseph and Mary went to Jerusalem every Passover. Although it doesn't specify it, in Scripture, we believe that Mary followed Jesus and His apostles throughout His entire public Ministry. We most assuredly believe she was with her Son at *The Last Supper*. Even if she didn't know it was to be His last meal, it was the Passover Seder, which was very important to the Jewish people; it was the time when the family got together to remember the Passover, their exodus from slavery. Now, the solemn blessing of the lamp was an important rite of the evening meal of sabbath or festivals. *It was the privilege of the mother of the family to light the sabbath lamps.*[2]

Would not Mary have been there with her Son on this their last Passover together, the Passover before His death? Would He not have wanted her to be there, when He instituted the Eucharist? We know that Jesus loved and revered His Mother Mary more than any other living creature. We know that Mary was with the Apostles in the Upper Room, when the Holy Spirit descended upon them. Why wouldn't she have been there for this last meal with her Son?

And if she was at the Passover meal with Jesus, did she not receive His Body, and drink His Blood? Would she not have been the first to eat His Body, Body from her body, and drink His Blood, Blood from her blood? Would anyone have had more right than she? I don't think so.

St. Ambrose, in speaking on the Eucharist and the Virgin Birth, says, *"The body which we make (by the Sacramental rite) has a Virgin as Its origin. Why do you seek the laws of nature in the Body of Christ, since it was by an exemption of the natural order that the Lord Jesus Himself was given birth by the Virgin?"*

Vatican Council II[3] says of Mother Mary,

"Thus the Blessed Virgin advanced in her pilgrimage of Faith, and faithfully persevered in her union with her Son unto the Cross, where she stood, in keeping with the divine plan enduring with her only-begotten Son the intensity of His suffering, associated herself with His sacrifice in her mother's heart, and lovingly consenting to the immolation of This Victim which was born of her."

We are told by the Council of Trent that the Sacrifice of the Mass is a continuation of the Sacrifice of the Cross. We believe that Mary took part in everything that had to do with her Son. Thomas Aquinas tells us, and very logically, that when we eat

---

[2]Corpus Christi - Fr. Michael O'Carroll p.134
[3]Constitution on the Church, 58

the Flesh of Jesus and drink His Blood, we're also eating and drinking the body and blood of Mary.[4]

"The Holy Eucharist is the Bread that comes from our Heavenly Mother. It is Bread produced by Mary from the flour of Her Immaculate flesh, kneaded into dough from Her virginal milk. St. Augustine wrote, 'Jesus took His Flesh from the flesh of Mary.'

"We know, too, that united to the Divinity in the Eucharist there is Jesus' Body and Blood taken from the body and blood of the Blessed Virgin. Therefore, at every Eucharist we receive, it would be quite correct, and a very beautiful thing, to take notice of our Holy Mother's sweet and mysterious presence, inseparably united with Jesus in the Host. Jesus is always the Son, She adores. He is Flesh of Her flesh and Blood of Her blood. If Adam could call Eve when she had been taken from his rib; 'bone of my bone and flesh of my flesh,'[5] cannot the holy Virgin Mary even more rightly call Jesus 'Flesh of my flesh and Blood of my blood?' St. Thomas Aquinas said:[6] The Flesh of Jesus is the maternal flesh of Mary, the Blood of Jesus is the maternal blood of Mary. Therefore, it will never be possible to separate Jesus from Mary.

"For this reason at every Holy Mass which is celebrated, the Blessed Virgin can repeat with truth to Jesus in the Host and in the Chalice, 'You are My Son, today I have generated you.'[7] And justly St. Augustine teaches us that in the Eucharist 'Mary extends and perpetuates Her Divine Maternity,' while St. Albert the Great exhorts with love, 'My Soul, if you wish to experience intimacy with Mary, let yourself be carried between Her arms and nourished with Her blood'.... Go with this ineffable chaste thought to the banquet of God and you will find in the Blood of the Son the nourishment of the Mother."[8]

---

[4]From *"Jesus Our Eucharistic Love"* by Father Stefano Maneiii, O.F.M., S.T.D.

[5]Gen 2:23

[6]Taken from the *"Intact Virgin"*

[7]Psalm 2:7

[8]From *"Jesus Our Eucharistic Love"* by Father Stefano Maneiii, O.F.M., S.T.D.

And so during the Consecration, when you look upon Her Son's Real Presence in the Eucharist, remember she was at the foot of the Cross when He died for us, and she is present now, still at the foot of the Cross, the Altar, saying yes! There is a tradition that the Way of the Cross was instituted by Our Lady as she walked the path that Jesus took to Calvary, every day for the rest of her life. She stopped every place where He fell. She wept as she recalled His suffering on the way to the Crucifixion.

St. Thomas Aquinas - Angelic Doctor

St. Thomas Aquinas is considered one of the foremost defenders of the Eucharist in the History of the Church. He is given the title, **"Angelic Doctor"** because of his writings on the Angels, and their role in the Church, but he is equally noted for his brilliant writings on, and defense of, Our Lord Jesus in the Eucharist. He had always been known for his piety, but after his ordination, his love of the Eucharist took on greater dimensions. When we think of the intimacy of the Priest and the Eucharist, at the moment of Consecration, that unity that takes place; when we think of the fact that the Priest is victim-priest with Jesus, *the Victim-Priest*, we can just begin to feel the emotion, the relationship between disciple (Thomas Aquinas) and Lord. His biographer, William da Tocco wrote *"when consecrating (the bread and wine) at Mass, he would be overcome by such intensity of devotion as to be dissolved in tears, utterly absorbed in its mysteries and nourished with its fruits."*[9]

Thomas Aquinas was given one of the most brilliant minds the world has ever known;[10] but everything he wrote and did revolved around his Love, the Eucharist. St. Thomas Aquinas was drafted to be a part of the Miracle of the Eucharist that would

---

[9]Butler's Lives of the Saints

[10]The writings of Thomas Aquinas have been required learning in all the seminaries of the world from his time up until the last ten or twenty years, and even then only in some seminaries has Thomas Aquinas been replaced. But another interesting thing, the writings of St. Thomas Aquinas have been embraced by Astronomers of the world, and that is just in the last five years.

dispel the deadly heresy of Berengarianism,[11] saying yes, through his Pope, to the compelling mandate of the Lord to have a Feast Day instituted, honoring the Blessed Sacrament.

When the Pope, Urban IV, could not deny the persuasive message of the Lord, through the pleadings of followers of a simple Belgian nun, Blessed Juliana of Liege, then through the undeniable Miracle of the Eucharist in Bolsena/Orvieto,[12] and the Miracle of Daroca, both of which happened at the same time, he issued the Papal Bull, *Il Transiturus*, in 1264, in which he instituted the *Feast of Corpus Christi,* the Body of Christ. He immediately called on Thomas Aquinas to write the Liturgy for that most glorious Feast. He knew the Lord had placedThomas in this world, at this time, for the purpose of glorifying His Blessed Sacrament through the splendid Liturgy he would write. Among the beautiful hymns in honor of the Blessed Sacrament that St. Thomas wrote, are the memorable *"Tantum Ergo" and "O Salutaris".*

The way that the Lord works in the lives of His Powerful Men and Women is, he doesn't just use them once, and hide them under a bushel basket,[13] but having molded and formed them into vessels to do His Will on earth, He uses them over and over again. St. Thomas is a perfect example of this. He became so well-known, especially in his knowledge of the Eucharist, that St. Louis, King of France, in 1269, called on the Saint to come to Paris, to speak to the students of the University of Paris. There was a question on which they were totally divided: Did the Presence of Jesus *really* remain in the Eucharist, or only in appearance? The King entrusted Thomas Aquinas with the mission to enlighten these young minds as to the Truth, the foundation of our belief in the Real Presence of Jesus in the Eucharist.

---

[11]more on this heresy and others that have attacked the Church over the centuries: *"Scandal of the Cross, and Its Triumph"*

[12]chapter on the Miracle of Bolsena and Orvieto can be found in Bob and Penny Lord's book: *"This is My Body, This is My Blood, Miracles of the Eucharist - Book I*

[13]Matt. 5:15; Luke 11:33

Now, Thomas Aquinas was not only a brilliant man, but a very humble man. As well known as he was, he knew that nothing he could say to these young minds, astute in their own rights, could convince them of the Real Presence of Jesus in the Eucharist. Knowing that all wisdom comes from Wisdom Himself, he did the most intelligent thing he possibly could have done - *he prayed and fasted!* Does that sound familiar? Our Lady has been asking us to do that since the Wedding Feast at Cana. Well, St. Thomas Aquinas prayed and fasted for three days. During that time, he wrote a treatise, which he placed before *Our Lord* on the Altar, *before* he presented it to the students. When he finally delivered his arguments, supporting the *Real Presence* of Jesus in the Blessed Sacrament, it was not only accepted unanimously by the students, but by the entire Church. Thomas, as all the greats before and after him, gave all credit to Jesus in the Eucharist.

After his brilliant dissertation on the Blessed Sacrament, he had a vision of Our Lord Jesus, in which the Lord said to Thomas, *"Thou hast written well of the Sacrament of My Body."* St. Thomas Aquinas went into ecstasy, and levitated. His entire body floated into the air and hovered over the chapel, for such a long time, the brothers in the convent were called. Upon entering the chapel, they beheld Thomas suspended in the air.

There was another instant when the Lord would speak these words to Thomas. Towards the end of his life, he had another apparition of Our Lord Jesus. Thomas was in the process of writing the third part of his Summa, which deals with Christ's Passion and Resurrection. A sacristan saw him kneeling before the Altar, in ecstasy. St. Thomas Aquinas' eyes were riveted on the Crucifix. The sacristan testified that he heard a voice, as if coming from the Crucifix, say aloud, *"You have written well of Me, Thomas. What would you desire as a reward?"* Thomas broke into tears, as he replied, *"Nothing, Lord. I'm doing it all for you."* This word from the Lord has become the motto of our ministry, repeating over and over again, *"We are doing it all for You, Lord."* Keeping our eyes and hearts on Jesus Crucified, how can we complain! The sign of a man's true imitation of God is *humility*. Thomas, in his brilliance, knew he was nothing and the Lord all. There is an episode in the life of St. Thomas that some authors might find difficult to accept. Once again, Thomas had a revelation from Heaven. He had been laboring on his *Summa Theologiae,* one of the most famous treatises on the existence of God which has ever been written. He was celebrating Holy Mass. At the moment of Consecration, as he lifted His Lord high, Thomas had a revelation of Heaven. We don't know what he beheld, or what the Lord said to him, but after this Divine sign, he never did any more work on his Summa Theologiae. He stopped writing altogether. The brother who had been working feverishly with him, trying desperately to get the Summa Theologiae finished, could not understand this sudden about-face. He asked St. Thomas what had persuaded him to change his mind. St. Thomas said to him, *"The end of my labors has come. All that I have written appears to be as so much straw after the things that have been revealed to me."*

Not that we can even be mentioned in the same breath as St. Thomas Aquinas, (all we have in common is our love for the Lord, His Eucharist and His Church) but we must admit that the more that we get to know the Lord and through that knowing, love Him, we find ourselves, with St. Thomas Aquinas, proclaiming that *everything we have ever written "is just so much straw!"* compared to Our Lord in the Word and in the Eucharist. We, as with St. Thomas Aquinas, taste the goodness of the Lord and we are hopelessly in love with God, Our Savior. His precious Hands, always filled with surprises, we feel at times, our hearts will burst. We have to believe that St. Thomas had such a special relationship with Jesus, and such assurance of how much the Lord loved Him, and yes, knowledge of what Heaven was like, that after that glimpse into the celestial, anything that had to do with things below were, even good things, in fact, just so much ....*straw.*

St. Ignatius of Antioch - Martyred for the Faith

"I have no pleasure in the food of corruption or in the delights of this life. I desire 'Bread of God' which is the Flesh of Jesus Christ, who was the 'Seed of David' and for drink I desire His Blood, which is incorruptible love".[14]

St. Ignatius was the holy fiery bishop of Antioch in the late First, and early Second Centuries. It is believed, he had a personal relationship with Sts. Peter and Paul; it has been written it was Peter who recommended Ignatius to be the second Bishop of Antioch, a post which he held for 40 years. There are also narratives about his knowing and visiting Our Lady. Well, think about it; he was part of that time, just after the Crucifixion of Our Lord Jesus; he was part of that great rush of excitement of the early community of believers.

He was a powerful disciple, although he never took credit for it. He is considered the most important pastor in the post-Apostolic era. He was the first and strongest Defender of the Real Presence of Jesus in the Eucharist against heretics, of that very early time in the church, who denied that Jesus had both a physical *Body* and Spirit *(Docetism)*, and that, therefore, we do not receive the Body and Blood of Jesus in the Eucharist, because He never had a Body. St. Ignatius battled against these heretics throughout his entire ministry, even as he was being carted off to Rome to be thrown to the wild beasts in the Amphitheater. He wrote letters defending the Real Presence of Jesus to various Bishops of the Church in Asia, condemning the heretics and the errors they were spreading about the Real Presence of Jesus in the Eucharist.

Now, what happened next is something only the Lord could do. You know the saying, *"God works in mysterious ways"*? Well, this is a perfect example. In Antioch, Ignatius was condemned to be sent to Rome, where he was to be thrown to the wild ferocious animals, to be devoured by them in the Coliseum or Amphitheaters. They also hoped that he could be used as a

---

[14]Butler's Lives of the Saints

powerful example to the Christians about what happens to anyone defying the Emperor, no matter how important he is. As an important member of the Christians, if they could persuade him to save his life by hailing the Emperor instead of Christ, they would be able to control them and kill this movement that they could not squash, even by the threat of the Coliseum.

He was a big figure in the church. So you would think they would send him on an express boat directly to Rome. Right? *Wrong!* They sent him on the equivalent of what we would call today a "cattle car" or "banana boat", or a local train. It made every stop possible all over Asia on the way from Antioch to Rome. News of his arrival at various cities got to the various cities before he did. As his ship docked each time, at the various cities, the Faithful came to meet and listen to him preach on the Reality of the Eucharist, of the Lord Who is with us. It was as if, the Emperor sent him on a final missionary journey at the expense of the state, on his way to Rome.

His writings have always been considered important and authentic, because they were actually taken from the time of Jesus. Ignatius lived in that period of the Infant Church, during the Acts of the Apostles, and the missionary journeys of Sts. Peter and Paul, Barnabas and Luke, Mark, St. John and all the early evangelists. What we receive from the writings of St. Ignatius of Antioch about the Eucharist, are not teachings which were handed down to him. *He got on-hands training. He was there when they were being taught for the first time.* We've only picked out a few of his teachings about the Eucharist. They are powerful:

"Make an effort, then to meet more frequently to celebrate our Lord's Eucharist and to offer praise. For when you meet frequently in the same place, the forces of Satan are overthrown, and his baneful influence is neutralized by the unanimity of your faith. Peace is a precious thing; it puts an end to every war waged by fallen angels or earthly enemies."

"Take care, then to partake of one Eucharist; for one is the Flesh of our Lord Jesus Christ, and one the cup to unite us with

His Blood, and one Altar, just as there is one bishop assisted by the presbyters and the deacons, my fellow servants."

When St. Ignatius was on his way to be martyred, he begged his followers not to interfere. His only request was:

"Only pray for me that God may give me grace within as well as without, not only to say it but to desire it, that I may not only be called, but be found a Christian. Suffer me to be the food of wild beasts through whom I may attain unto God. I am God's grain and I am to be ground by the teeth of wild beasts that I may be found the pure bread of Christ."[15]

St. Peter Julian Eymard, Eucharistic Adorer

St. Peter Julian Eymard

Peter Julian Eymard is called, among other things, "Champion *of the Blessed Sacrament"*. He had such a singleness of purpose, in his great devotion to the Blessed Sacrament that he would Found an Order devoted solely to adoration of the *Blessed Sacrament* and the spread of that devotion. That Religious Order is called *"Priests of the Blessed Sacrament."* There's a teaching here, which we don't want to miss. He went from Diocesan *priest*, to the Order of *Mary*, to founding an Order in honor of the *Blessed Sacrament.* Wherever you find the Mother, you will find the Son; wherever you find the Son, you will find the Mother. Wherever you find the Mother and the Son in the Eucharist, you will find the priesthood. We have never researched or written about any Saint who has not had a great devotion to the Eucharist, coupled with

---

[15]A soldier, seeing the valiant way St. Ignatius of Antioch died, placed his body on the fire and had it burned to ashes. After which the ashes were scooped up and sent to Antioch - from Butler's Lives of the Saints

a great love for Our Lady. Peter Julian Eymard confirms this in his choice of ministries.

At the beginning of his priestly ministry, he devoted his time to normal parish activities, but he felt a powerful draw to the Blessed Sacrament. The Eucharist was always the Center around which his life revolved. He proclaimed more than once, *"Without it, I would have been lost."*

One time, while carrying the Consecrated Host in procession on Corpus Christi Sunday, he had a religious experience: *"My soul was flooded with faith and love for Jesus in the Blessed Sacrament. Those two hours seemed but a moment. I laid, at the Feet of our Lord, the Church in France, myself, and everybody throughout the world. My eyes were filled with tears: it was as though my heart were under the wine-press. I longed, at that moment, for all hearts to have been within my own and to have been fired with the zeal of St. Paul."*

Even during his time with the Marists, he couldn't help pondering and meditating on the Eucharist. A pivotal point in his life occurred on a pilgrimage to a local Marian shrine in 1851. The Lord put a thought into his head, and he could not get it out of his mind. *There was no Order devoted to the Blessed Sacrament!* In his own words,

"One idea haunted me, and it was this; that Jesus in the Blessed Sacrament had no Religious Institute to glorify His mystery of love, whose only object was entire consecration to Its service. There ought to be one....I promised Mary to devote myself to this end. It was still all very vague and I had no idea of leaving the Order (Marists)."

[Author's Note: When you hear the words, haunted, or *"I couldn't get it out of my mind"*, you know it's the Lord. Blessed Juliana of Liege, whom the Lord used, to institute a Feast Day in honor of the Blessed Sacrament, expressed her feelings in the same way. She had a vision which haunted her day and night. Everywhere she went, every day, it was there. So, my brothers and sisters, if you feel an overpowering feeling that has to do with the Eucharist, in particular, you can be pretty sure it's the Lord hounding you *(like the hounds of Heaven which St. Augustine speaks of).* And He won't let you live until you do what He wants.]

He felt he couldn't hold back any longer. The burning inside of him to protect, adore and give honor to his God, Jesus in the Eucharist, took over his life. He presented his idea for a new Order of the Blessed Sacrament to his Superior General, who told him to *wait*. Obedience, being at the zenith of his vows, he waited. He was still chomping at the bit, but because his Superior asked him to wait until his plan had more substance to it, he obeyed; something we seem to have lost the meaning of, in today's world. For *five years*, he waited, and then in 1856, with the approval of his Superior, he presented his proposal to the Archbishop of Paris, *who approved it in twelve days!* He not only approved it, he gave St. Peter Julian his first house in Paris; and on January 6, 1857, the Blessed Sacrament was exposed in his chapel for the first time.

They had to change houses in 1858, and they moved into a small chapel in Paris. St. Peter Julian called this his *"miracle chapel"*, due to all the graces and miracles obtained through the adoration of the Blessed Sacrament, in that location. In 1859, Pope Pius IX greatly praised the movement. Spurred on by that endorsement, the Order grew in leaps and bounds. More houses were opened in France. Vocations, which had been slow in coming at first, grew in extraordinary proportions, and before long, the Order of the Blessed Sacrament became a full-blown congregation of priests and lay brothers. They were available for any and all kinds of tasks within the Church, but everything had to take second place to their adoration of the Blessed Sacrament.

In researching the life of St. Peter Julian Eymard, we found that he truly put everything into the Hands of the Lord through the Blessed Sacrament. An example of this was when he wanted to go to Rome to get Papal approval of the Community, and obtain a Plenary Indulgence for adoration before the Blessed Sacrament, even if the Tabernacle is closed. He picked the worst possible time. The Archbishop of Paris, whose recommendation he needed, had just died. Now, St. Peter Julian wanted to wait for a new Archbishop to be appointed, but as the Pope, Pius IX, who had been extremely supportive to St. Peter Julian's Order, was very ill, it would not be wise to wait to go to Rome. However, the week, he and his two companions went to Rome was *Holy Week*; Rome was extremely busy, as was His Holiness. But St. Peter Julian placed everything in the Hands of Our Lord Jesus in the Blessed Sacrament. His philosophy was, if the Lord wanted it, He'd have to make it happen. Apparently the Lord wanted it; because St. Peter Julian Eymard *got everything he asked for.*

Mother Angelica - Defender of the Faith

Mother Angelica

We have found the same parallel with many religious communities who have as their charism, *Adoration of the Blessed Sacrament.* There is an *anawim*, abandonment, in the face of what at times seem like impossible odds, an attitude of complete faith in the Lord. Our Mother Angelica and her community are perfect examples of this.

In the eyes of the world, the power behind Eternal Word Television Network in Birmingham, Alabama, is a huge white satellite dish in back of the studios. Large white pipes contain the cables which send the message from the studio to the satellite dish, beaming it up into the sky, to a satellite in space, spreading the Word of God all over the world. It has an awesome look of power about it.

But the energy force which feeds life into the studio, the cables, indeed, into everything that lives and breathes at EWTN is another White Sphere, much smaller in size, but much more powerful, located inside the Chapel. *It is Our Lord Jesus in the Eucharist.*

Mother Angelica maintains that the driving force that has made things happen in Birmingham since 1962, in Our Lady of the Angels Monastery, with the tremendous growth of this Community of cloistered Nuns, with the printing press operation, and on a much grander scale, *Eternal Word Television Network,* and now *Eternal Word Radio Network,* the only Catholic Cable Television and Shortwave Radio Networks in the world, is the *Eucharist,* the Lifeblood of everything.

While the world knows this woman as a down-home, straight-shooting, tell it like it is, caring but outspoken television personality, who bucked all the odds to create a Catholic television Network in the suburbs of Baptist Belt Birmingham, her Nuns, the *Poor Clare Nuns of Perpetual Adoration,* know her as their spiritual mother, their teacher, their friend, their *role model.* And although Convents are closing up all over America, the *cloistered* Nuns of Our Lady of the Angels Monastery, and the priests and brothers of the *Missionaries of the Eternal Word*[16] are alive and well and growing under the tutelage of this powerful woman in our Church.

At one point, when we were interviewing Mother Angelica for our chapter on her, she shared:

"Every morning, after Communion, I pray, 'Let everyone who passes this Chapel on the highway, feel Your Presence.' Well, one day, two women came down and asked my mother, Sister David, who was an extern Sister by this time, 'What kind of place is this?' She replied, 'It's a Monastery.'

"They said, 'The funniest thing happened when our car got to the driveway; we felt, well, just a feeling, and when we passed the driveway, it went away. And so, we've been going back and forth for about an hour. When we pass the driveway on this side, it leaves. When we return (to the driveway), it comes back. When

---

[16]An Order founded by Mother Angelica of priests and brothers.

we go, it leaves again.'"

Mother Angelica continued, *"Sister David brought them into the Chapel and said, 'This is our Chapel and that's Jesus.'*

The women asked, 'Where?'

Sister David went up and showed them the Monstrance where Jesus was. The women knelt down and said, 'We feel the same Presence!'"

Who is Mother Angelica?

Mother Angelica is a Nun, a Foundress, a Mother Superior, an adorer of the Blessed Sacrament, a Defender of the Faith, a loyal daughter of the Church. This is her mission and *everything* stems from that love she has for our Lord Jesus in His Body, Blood, Soul and Divinity, the Holy Eucharist. We remember, the first time we heard that Mother Angelica and her Nuns spent *hours* each day in prayer. Looking about this huge complex, this Network that brings the Good News to millions of the Faithful of the Catholic Church, we foolishly inquired, *"Then how does this all come about?"* only to be countered with, *"Mother and the Nuns pray, and Jesus in the Blessed Sacrament does the rest."*

We asked Mother Angelica did she ever feel just plain scared!

"No, I don't think that anything ever scared me. I think I always thought, from the time I knew there was a God, that He loved me. I figured He always did and He would take care of everything now. Because, see, I've never known the end of the tunnel; I've never seen the end of the tunnel. I just see God wants me to do something, or God permits something in my life, and it doesn't enter my mind to say, 'Why did You do this?' Only one time I did that, and I never did it again. It was here at the Network and everything was going wrong. We were very low on money; banks were after us, creditors; I had a lot of pain. We were just having problems every which way. It seemed everyone was against us, the Church, bankers, lay people, everybody saying we can't do it; this is foolish!"

"So, I went before the Blessed Sacrament; I was very

angry, and I said, 'Lord, I told You, I'm not the one for the job. Why me?' And suddenly, as I felt this so deeply, I heard the Lord say very distinctly, 'Yes, and why Me?' I never asked again."

So, now we know the secret of the success of EWTN. Plug into the Power Source, which is the Eucharist, and all things will flow. The Healing Power that went out of Jesus, as the woman with the hemorrhage touched His cloak, is the same Power, He gives us through the Eucharist. It surges through our souls to our veins and arteries, and continues out of our bodies into everything we touch. The Power of the Eucharist is what makes it all happen.

Saint John Vianney, Patron of Parish Priests

We cannot speak of the Eucharist and Its Miracles, Jesus' Real Presence on the Altar, and in the Tabernacle, without paying homage to the Priesthood. And in speaking of the Priesthood, who better to represent them, but the Patron Saint of all Parish Priests, St. John Vianney.

How did John Vianney, now Curé Vianney, feel about the priesthood? Let him speak for himself:

"Oh! How great a person is the priest! The priest will truly

St. John Vianney

understand himself only when he gets to Heaven... If we understood what the priesthood means, we would die, not from fright, but from love!"

How did the Curé feel about the Blessed Sacrament in the Tabernacle? When he gave instructions in the church, he was acutely aware of the Lord in the Blessed Sacrament. He could never preach with his back to the Tabernacle. Although he had a pulpit placed on the right side of the sanctuary, so his back was not to the Tabernacle, Christ was so present to him in the Blessed Sacrament, that his voice would tremble with emotion as he spoke.

His greatest Joy - the Holy Eucharist! We have spoken of pain and trials. Like with the other Saints, the Curé embraced his daily cross because of the *joys* in his life; the greatest of which was the Holy Eucharist. For the Curé, the greatest sign of the Lord's triumph in his parish, was the effort the people of Ars put into making the procession of the Blessed Sacrament, on the Feast day of Corpus Christi, so extraordinarily magnificent.

These celebrations later were called the *"pilgrimage of Ars."* Ranking with the Shrines of the Blessed Mother at Lourdes and La Salette, this pilgrimage to Ars, in the nineteenth century, drew Frenchmen from all parts of France to this formerly unknown and remote village. It is important to stress, without devotion to the Holy Eucharist which originated on the Altar, as the Curé celebrated Mass, none of this would have come to pass. They had come to know their Lord and Savior in the Eucharist and it was to Him and His faithful priest they were doing homage.

An anonymous writer described his experience during a *pilgrimage of Ars* celebration. He said he came *by chance* to Ars. He was not ready for what he saw before him. There was a procession advancing, a canopy of gold cloth sheltering a gilded Monstrance. An old man, the Curé, walked slowly and solemnly, carrying the *God* of all! The voices of the pilgrims, accompanied by Angels, filled the air, singing hymns in praise of this God alive in their presence. The canopy stopped! Over two thousand people dropped to their knees in adoration of their Lord. The priest, hands trembling with emotion, raised the Monstrance and blessed everyone in the Name of the Father, and of the Son, and of the Holy Spirit!

These were the days our priest lived for. His face was almost transfigured, as he looked upon his Lord and the people this Lord so loved, He left them His Body and Blood. The Curé was to them what every priest is called to be, another Jesus Christ, a mirror of Jesus with them. How he reflected this Lord he so adored! People gravitated toward the light that emanated from his face. They saw Jesus in him, and they had come to trust this representative of His, as they had Christ, in Galilee, when He had walked the earth.

St. John Vianney could *feel* his Savior's presence in the Tabernacle, so he took every opportunity to adore Him in the Blessed Sacrament. His Presence brought tears to the Curé's eyes. This passion he felt for the Lord was no on-again off-again affair. Speaking of the Lord Really Present in the Holy Eucharist, he said:

"If we had a lively faith, we would certainly be able to see Him in the Blessed Sacrament. There are priests who see Him every day during the Holy Sacrifice of the Mass."

Many who saw the Curé during the Mass, believed he was speaking of himself as one of those priests, but the Curé would never have admitted that, never wanting attention brought to himself.

The Curé goes Home to his Lord! The Curé asked for his confessor. He reached out hungrily for the last Sacraments. He began to cry. When asked why the tears, he replied, *"Ah! When I think I am about to receive the Lord for the last time!"*

And then, touched by the generosity of his King, he whispered, *"How good God is! When we cannot go and see Him, He comes to us!"*

He kissed the Crucifix and as his confessor came to the words, *"May God's Holy Angels come to meet him and bring him into the heavenly Jerusalem."* the Curé fell into the sweet sleep of eternity. Without struggle, he gave up his spirit to the Angels who surely had come to bring him Home.[17]

---

[17]excerpts from chapter: St. John Vianney - Bob and Penny Lord,s book: *"Saints and other Powerful Men in the Church."*

St. Thérèse of the Child Jesus of the Holy Face

St. Thérèse of Lisieux

The Little Flower of Jesus had such a strong love relationship with Jesus in the Blessed Sacrament, we cannot possibly speak of Saints and the Eucharist without mentioning this powerful Saint. We want to quote from her Autobiography of a Soul, with regard to her First Holy Communion:

"At last the day came, that greatest of days for me; even the tiniest details of that visit to Heaven have left their imprint on my memory, not to be described.

"There are scents which you can't expose to the air without their losing their fragrance; and there are experiences of the soul which you can't express in human language without losing their inner meaning, their heavenly meaning...

"What comfort It brought to me, that first kiss Our Lord imprinted on my soul! A Lover's kiss; I knew that I was loved, and I, in return, told Him that I loved Him, and was giving myself to Him for all eternity.

"And now, ...something had melted away, and there were no longer two of us - Thérèse had simply disappeared, like a drop lost in the ocean; Jesus only was left, my Master, my King."[18]

In looking through the writings of St. Thérèse, whether it be her Autobiography, or the collected letters of St. Thérèse, both of which we recommend you read, we can't help but see the importance and stress she put on the Eucharist. In response to a letter she received from her cousin, Marie Guerin, on the 30th of May, 1889, Thérèse wrote:

---

[18]*Autobiography of a Soul* pg 232 - written by the Saint

"I think I must tell you something that has caused me great pain. It is that my little Marie is not receiving Communion...on Ascension Day or on the last day of Mary's month....Oh! What pain that gives to Jesus!

"The devil must indeed be clever to deceive a soul like that! ....But surely you know, darling that that is the one goal of his desires. He realizes, treacherous creature that he is, that he cannot get a soul to sin if that soul wants to belong wholly to Jesus, so he only tries to make it think it is in sin....When the devil has succeeded in keeping a soul away from Holy Communion, he has gained all...and Jesus weeps!

"Yes, your poor little Thérèse does know. She has also passed through the martyrdom of scruples; but Jesus gave her the grace to receive Communion all the same, even at the time when she thought she had committed grave sins...

"No, it is not possible that a heart 'that finds no rest save in the sight of the Tabernacle' should offend Jesus enough to be unfit to receive Him. What offends Jesus, what wounds His heart, is lack of trust.

"Dear little Sister, receive Communion often, very often... there you have the sole remedy if you want to be cured (of scrupulosity)."[19]

When we wrote the biography of St. Thérèse of Lisieux for our book, **"Saints and Other Powerful Women in our Church"**, we opened with a statement by Pope St. Pius X with regard to the Little Flower. He stated, on March 15, 1907, in a private conversation, that St. Thérèse was *"The greatest Saint of modern times"*. This was before the Cause for her Canonization was opened. Now, in reading the footnote to the letter the little saint sent to her cousin Marie Guerin, it states:

"This letter, with its accurate Eucharistic teaching, a teaching largely forgotten at the time when it was written, was to win the admiration of Pius X. 'Opportunismo! Opportunismo!'

[19]Collected Letters of St. Thérèse of Lisieux - Sheed and Ward London 1949 Pg. 94-95

he cried out, as the opening lines were read; then, addressing Msgr. de Teil, Vice-Postulator of her cause: 'Oh! this is a great joy to me...we must hasten the process (of beatification) quickly!'"

The above footnote came at a time of danger for the Church when the plague of Modernism was spreading, killing the faith of Bishops, Priests and soon the laity. This authentically theological teaching on the Eucharist, was written by a *sixteen year old girl,* who, with it, was defending the Real Presence of the Lord in His Eucharist. We have always believed that someday the Little Flower of Jesus would be raised to the title of Doctor of the Church, for the wisdom and spirituality found in her autobiography. We are, once more, in danger! The world is on a collision course of destruction and death. All the heresies of the past have erupted into one curse, New Age. Is it time, for the Church, to proclaim St. Thérèse, Doctor of the Church, so that our seminarians, preparing for the Priesthood, can learn from this little Carmelite whose autobiography, written out of obedience, has been read by millions? Could this happen during the reign of our current Pope, John Paul II, who has visited the shrine of St. Thérèse in Lisieux and paid tribute to her? Let's pray!

St. Margaret Mary Alacoque

St. Margaret Mary Alacoque

St. Margaret Mary Alacoque is a perfect example of the *longing* our brothers and sisters, before us, suffered by not being able to receive the Eucharist daily or sometimes, weekly. It's really ironic that we have been given this gift, through the actions of our saintly Pope St. Pius X, in the early years of the twentieth century, and we take them for granted. The dear saints, who preceded us, *longed* for Jesus in the Eucharist, and out of obedience, had to be content with the once a month, or once every few weeks, they were allowed to receive. Margaret Mary Alacoque was to say:

"I could have passed whole days and nights there, (in front of the Blessed Sacrament) *without eating or drinking, or knowing what I was doing, except that I was being consumed in His Presence like a burning taper, in order to return to Him love for love....*

*"...I never failed to go as near as I could to the Blessed Sacrament. I envied and counted those alone happy (*only happy those*) who were able to communicate often and who were at liberty to remain before the Most Holy Sacrament ...*

*"It happened that once before Christmas, the parish priest gave out (*said*) from the pulpit that whoever should not have slept on Christmas Eve could not go to Communion;*[20] *as in punishment for my sins I was never able to sleep on the vigil of Christmas, I did not dare communicate* (receive Communion). *That day of rejoicing was consequently for me a day of tears which took the place of food and pleasure."*

"My greatest joy (in becoming a religious) *in the prospect of leaving the world was the thought that I should be able to receive Holy Communion frequently, which up to then I had not been permitted to do. I would have thought myself the happiest person on earth, had I been allowed to do so often and pass the nights alone before the Blessed Sacrament...*

"On the eves of Communion I found myself rapt in so profound a silence, on account of the greatness of the action, I was about to perform, that I could not speak without great effort; and afterwards I would have wished neither to eat nor drink, to see nor speak, owing to the greatness, consolation and peace which I then felt."

The following are words spoken to Margaret Mary *by our Lord Jesus* during an apparition to her, as the Most Sacred Heart.

---

[20]It was an unusual but widely-held and popular belief held in that time that if you did not sleep on Christmas Eve, you were not allowed to receive the Eucharist on Christmas Day.

"In the first place, thou shalt receive Me in Holy Communion as often as obedience will permit thee ...

"Thou shalt, moreover, communicate on the first Friday of each month, - Every night between Thursday and Friday I will make thee share in the mortal sadness which I was pleased to feel in the Garden of Olives..."

The greatest gifts, the Lord could give St. Margaret Mary came, during the Sacrifice of the Mass, usually during or right after the Consecration. He gave her the image of His Sacred Heart during this time.

"One day when he (St. Claude Colombiere, Margaret Mary's Spiritual Director and confessor) *came to say Mass in our church, the Lord granted signal graces both to him and to me. As I went up to receive Him in Holy Communion, He showed me His Sacred Heart as a burning furnace, and two other hearts were on the point of uniting themselves to It, and of being absorbed therein. At the same time He said to me: 'It is thus My pure love unites these three hearts for ever.'*

"He afterwards gave me to understand that this union was all for the glory of His Sacred Heart, the treasures of Which He wished me to reveal to him (Colombiere) *that he might spread*

St. Paschal Baylon

them abroad, and make known to others their value and utility."

St. Margaret Mary Alacoque is best known for the Apparitions of our Lord Jesus in His Sacred Heart. Through the work of St. Margaret Mary, in obedience to Jesus in the Sacred Heart, Devotion to the Sacred Heart is very popular throughout the World.

St. Paschal Baylon

St. Paschal Baylon is a contradictory sign in the Church. He was never a priest, and yet his name is synonymous with the Eucharist. For a Lay person to be given the official title of *Patron of all Eucharistic Congresses and Confraternities of the Blessed Sacrament*, how could this be? When we wrote of other Saints and powerful Men and Women in the Church, you complained we had not written enough about lay persons who had become Saints. Well, here we have not only a lay person who became a Saint, but he is Saint of the Eucharist, Patron to *Eucharistic Congresses and Confraternities of the Blessed Sacrament.* Our last two Popes, in particular, have been turning to the laity to evangelize, telling us by virtue of our Baptism, we are mandated to evangelize. It is not only *their* Church, as we so conveniently used to pass the buck. We are part of them. It is our Church, and we can lose her or save her. It is up to us.

When a Eucharistic Minister asked a priest: What should we do if we see someone leaving the Altar with the Eucharist in his hand? And he replied, *"Nothing, it is between that person and the Lord."* What do you think St. Paschal Baylon would have done? So do we visit Our Lord in the Blessed Sacrament? Do we sign up for only one hour per month to spend with the Lord, so that our church can have Perpetual Eucharistic Adoration? What do you think St. Paschal would have done?

He never had as close a relationship with the Eucharist as a priest would have. And while we were surprised to hear it, we have been saying for years that the laity is the strength behind the Church. And while we don't put ourselves in the same category as St. Paschal Baylon, in the Catholic world, our name is synonymous with the Eucharist also. Another interesting thing about Paschal Baylon is that outside his little town in Spain, his name is virtually unknown.

We first heard the name Paschal Baylon when we lived in Westlake Village in California. Our parish church was St. Jude's. But the neighboring town, Thousand Oaks, has as their parish church, St. Paschal Baylon. So we knew there was a Paschal Baylon, and that he was a Saint. We must say, after having read about him, he is a most fascinating Saint, and truly a Powerful Man in our Church.

He was born in a very small village in between Castille and Aragon in Spain. He lived a very simple, very focused life. He always knew what he wanted, to be with his Lord Jesus in His Eucharistic Presence. That was it; that was his total goal in life. But he was an obedient member of his family. As long as they needed him, he was there for them. As a young man, actually until he was twenty-four years old, he was a shepherd for his poor family. In this job, he couldn't always get to Mass. On these occasions, he would put his flock away for a short time, kneel in the fields, facing in the direction of the chapel where he knew the Mass was being offered, and stare at the sanctuary. Shortly after Paschal's death, an old shepherd who had known him in those young days, testified that more than one time, *he saw Angels flying gently from the Chapel to where Paschal was kneeling*, and brought the young man the Blessed Sacrament suspended in air above a chalice, not for Paschal to receive the Lord, but that he might gaze on his Lord and Savior, and venerate Him in the Blessed Sacrament.

He joined the Franciscan Order as a lay brother. He became part of the community of St. Peter of Alcantara, who was very instrumental in the life and spirituality of St. Teresa of Avila, who was living at that time. Paschal longed to spend all his time in front of the Blessed Sacrament. His biographer tells us that whenever he was not required to be somewhere else, Paschal was in the chapel, on his knees, before the Blessed Sacrament. He spent long hours in front of the Tabernacle, kneeling without support, his clasped hands held up in front of, or higher than his face. Whenever he had time free from his duties, he always made his way to the Church to spend time in the Presence of Our Lord. It was his delight to serve Mass after Mass in succession, just to be there. He would pass whatever time he could, starting early in the morning, and ending late at night, after everyone had gone off to bed. While he was never disobedient to the rules of the community, he always just managed to be the *first* one at the chapel in the morning, and the *last* one to leave the chapel at night. As much as he loved Jesus in His Eucharistic Presence, he never would have disobeyed a legal order to be with His Lord.

He was a Saint; he was always a Saint even while he was alive. Everyone in his community, indeed everyone he had ever met, agreed that he was a Saint. During his lifetime, miracles took place, especially where the sick and poor were concerned. However, the miracles accelerated to gigantic dimensions as he lay on his funeral bier. He died at age 52 in the year 1592, on the same Feast day of the year that he was born, Whitsunday, or Pentecost Sunday. He was beatified in 1618, which is some kind of a miracle, because it was before his founder, Peter of Alcantara's beatification, and Peter died thirty years before Paschal.

There was an unusual happening which may have had some effect on how swiftly Paschal was canonized. There are reports that the sounds of someone knocking from his tomb went on for hundreds of years. We know that would get anyone's attention. When the Lord wants to get your attention, He's not beyond using a baton, or a 4 x 4, or having strange sounds coming from your tomb. Whatever the case with St. Paschal Baylon, he is one of the understated, powerful men in our Church, who loved His Lord in the Eucharist.

We are all called to be Saints and Lovers of the Eucharist. St. Teresa of Avila was called *"Daughter of the Eucharist"* We have been chosen to be *Sons and Daughters of the Eucharist.* Let the Lord take over in your life; allow yourself to be *"consumed by the Eucharist,"* as St. Augustine tells us, and be changed. Take *"food for the journey"* as the Angel told Elijah, "else the journey will be too long for you.[21]

---

[21] 1 Kings 19:7

St. Louis Marie de Montfort, regarding Saints of these last days:

"....towards the end of the world, ...Almighty God and His holy Mother are to raise up saints who will surpass in holiness most other saints as much as the cedars of Lebanon tower above little shrubs."

*"These great souls filled with grace and zeal will be chosen to oppose the enemies of God who are raging on all sides. They will be exceptionally devoted to the Blessed Virgin. Illumined by her light, strengthened by her spirit, supported by her arms, sheltered under her protection, they will fight with one hand and build with the other. With one hand they will give battle, **overthrowing and crushing heretics and their heresies, schismatics and their schisms, idolaters and their idolatries, sinners and their wickedness.** With the other hand they will build the temple of the true Solomon and the mystical city of God, namely, the Blessed Virgin..."*

"They will be like thunder-clouds flying through the air at the slightest breath of the Holy Spirit. Attached to nothing, surprised at nothing, they will shower down the rain of God's word and of eternal life. They will thunder against sin; they will storm against the world; they will strike down the devil and his followers and for life and for death, they will pierce through and through with the two-edged sword of God's word all those against whom they are sent by Almighty God."

"They will be true apostles of the latter times to whom the Lord of Hosts will give eloquence and strength to work wonders and carry off glorious spoils from His enemies. They will sleep without gold or silver and, more important still, without concern in the midst of other priests, ecclesiastics and clerics. Yet they will have the silver wings of the dove enabling them to go wherever the Holy Spirit calls them, filled as they are, with the resolve to seek the glory of God and the salvation of souls. Wherever they preach, they will leave behind them nothing but the gold of love, which is the fulfillment of the whole law."[22]

---

[22]True Devotion to Mary #47 - 59

Part II

The Sacrifice of the Mass

The Ongoing Sacrifice of the Cross

The Dispute on the Blessed Sacrament
from the Raphael Stanzas - Vatican Collection

Who is this Jesus...*Who comes to us under the appearance of bread and wine?*

Whenever we talk to someone who has left the Church and returned, their song is always the same. *"If they put lighted matches under my fingernails, I would not deny my Lord and His Church."* How well we can relate to that outcry of the heart. It is as if the Spirit Himself is speaking; as in Holy Scripture, where we are told that the Spirit prays for us, when we do not know how to pray. Our mouths open and our hearts, not our minds, cry out: *"I love Him! I cannot live without Him! There is no life without Him!"*

When we were writing about the Martyrs,[1] and interviewing eyewitnesses who knew them, the thought kept running through our minds and hearts, *could we die* rather than deny our Faith? But you know, the closer you walk toward Jesus, the more you get to know Him, you find yourself deeper and deeper in love with Him and there is no other answer; there is no other way. When you discover Whom it is Who dwells inside your Church, Whom you have to deny when you deny your Church, the Roman Catholic Church, your eyes and the eyes of your heart and soul find their way to Jesus on the Cross, and you are ready to die for the Church.

As those of you know, who have read our book: *"We came back to Jesus",* it wasn't always so for us. We were *"Sunday go to church Catholics."* Penny knew very little; Bob knew too much. Penny *emotionally* felt my Jesus, but didn't know why she felt Him *only* in the Catholic Church. Bob had gone through twelve years of Catholic schooling; he went to Mass because Penny felt Jesus there, and he wanted to please her. When we lost our son to an overdose of drugs, we blamed Jesus; we

---

[1]Bob and Penny Lord's book: *"Martyrs, They died for Christ"*

punished Him; we left the Church. And we will scream from the mountain tops, "There is no pain, no emptiness as intense as the loss of our sweet, most precious Lord Jesus." We have known people who have lost loved ones say that our pain, that of losing a child, is one they could not bear. We agree: *"Yes, it is a part of your very self that is cut out of you; your heart bleeds from the wound that will not heal; but it cannot compare with the unequaled sorrow, the nothingness, the death that overtakes you when you have cut Jesus out of your life."*

Do you ever think about those who have left the Church? Do you notice how they go from one church to another? *Their hearts are restless.* For you see, the Lord, before sending us down from Heaven, takes a piece of our heart and keeps it for Himself. We, on earth, are seeking that missing part of our heart. No one on earth can fill that void. There is only One Who can, and He is our Lord, the same Lord Who comes to us during the Sacrifice of the Mass, the Same Lord Who is a willing prisoner of Love in the Tabernacle. And though those who have left Mother Church do not realize it, they are hungering for the Only One Who can satisfy their hungry heart, a hunger that cannot be fulfilled by man or manna.

Jesus said at Capernaum: *"Your fathers hungered and they were fed with manna from Heaven and they hungered still. The bread that I will give, you will never hunger. I am the Bread of life. He who eats of this Bread will never die."*[2] Jesus is talking of eternal life, life that includes this world; and when He speaks of death, it is everlasting death that begins in this world. Jesus said: *"Unless you eat My Body, you have no life in you."*[3] To those who will eat His Body and drink His Blood - the Eucharist, He promised life, eternal life - Resurrection: *"And I will raise you up in the last day."*[4] Now, suppose, as some twentieth century heretics

---

[2]John 6:31-33
[3]John 6:53
[4]John 6:54

love to prosyletize,[5] Jesus never said those words? Suppose, the bad news that there is no Heaven, no everlasting life is true, and when you die, there is nothing? What have you lost by believing there is a Heaven and everlasting life? In believing Jesus' words, you have at least had peace on earth. But suppose the Church is right, and the words of Jesus are true? What will you have lost by not believing? *Eternal life!*

Those who have left the Church and returned, remind us of the disciples who met Jesus on the road to Emmaus. They are grieving for the Messiah Who is no longer in their lives. They feel lost and helpless, alone, empty. Then when they hear Holy Scripture, explained, their hearts burn. Searching, they go from preacher to preacher and good sounding sermons, seeking Him; but there is something missing. What they come to realize is, it is the Lord in His Body, Blood, Soul and Divinity, the One Who is waiting for them in the Roman Catholic Church. They, like the disciples, only recognize Jesus in the breaking of the bread - the Sacrifice of the Mass. We are not saying that the Lord is not present in His Word and in the people, in the churches of our brothers and sisters in Christ, but as the hearts of the disciples burned when Jesus explained the Scriptures, yet they did not recognize Him in the Word, only in the breaking of the bread, the Mass, so it is with the Lord's children, still till today.

We need the Lord in His *entirety* - in His Word and in His Body and Blood. We need the Lord in His Priests because out of Divine humility and love, He chooses vessels through which His Love, His Grace can flow. We find the Lord in His people, because He has made us one, *"one in Him as He is one in the Father"*. But it is by partaking of the one Bread, when we share in the Eucharist during the Mass, we become One Body,[6] we become one in Him as He is one in the Father. It is by communing with Him, in Holy Communion that we become community; we become

[5]proselytize - to exert undue pressure, to a point of being unscrupulous in bringing one to another's viewpoint. The Catholic Encyclopedia by Broderick
[6]1Cor 10:17

Church. When we receive the Eucharist, we do not consume Jesus, we are consumed by Him (St. Augustine), and we are no longer the same.

This is what Holy Scripture is saying when we read: *"They will know us by how we love one another."*[7] What do you think is the motivating force which makes us love one another? The Lord Who is Almighty in all that is Good, with Love that is overflowing, fills us through His Body, Blood, Soul and Divinity with a super human capacity to love. It is not we who love, but the Lord Who loves through us, for we are no longer ourselves but are transformed into His Instrument, using His Heart to love, His Eyes to see, His Arms to open wide and embrace our brothers and sisters.

A priest once said, when Catholics realize what happens on the Altar during each and every Mass, when they recognize Who it is Who comes to us at the moment of Consecration, Who remains with us in the Holy Tabernacle, we will have to come to church two or three hours early; it will be Christmas and Easter every Mass, the churches will be filled to capacity spilling out into the street. Walk with us, now, as we share in the Paschal Mystery.

✝

With our return to the Church, was our return to Our Lord and to the Mass. Since that first day, since that first Mass when we heard the readings and the Gospel, we knew we had found our Lord; He had waited for us; He still loved us. *We were home!* We found ourselves growing closer and closer to the Lord through His Word, to what He was saying to *us* during the Mass; the Mass became *personal* to us. But the high point was the Eucharist! Although we did not quite understand the fullness of His action on the Altar of Sacrifice, in our small church in California, we knew He was there! We knew in an unexplainable way, the way a blind man knows his loved one has entered a room. We could see Him through the windows of our hearts, and we were in love.

---

[7]John 13:35

But as one Mass followed another, six Daily Masses each week culminating into one glorious Sunday Mass, one year into another until nineteen years flew by as if overnight, we found ourselves discovering more and more about our Lord, just as one finds out more about a loved one, the more we are with our beloved.

As we began to learn more and more what is really happening during the Mass, we found ourselves coming to terms with the price our Lord paid for us, we found ourselves staring at *the Cross*. He loved us so very much, His Heart was pierced out of love for us. He loved us so passionately; He carried that love on the Cross and that love ripped through His bruised and beaten Body. That love was nailed along with Him on that Cross. Love hung on that Cross and was raised on high with the Spotless Lamb Who offered Himself to the Father out of love for us. The Cross! That's what we discovered, as one Mass became another for us. We found a Jesus Who loved us to the point of death on the Cross. We found a Jesus Who loved us with so much fire, at the Last Supper His thoughts were of *us*. He so longed to continue loving us, Jesus commissioned His first Priests to bring Him to us during Mass. Not satisfied with that short time with us, He remains in the Monstrance and is a willing Prisoner of love in the Tabernacle.

Just as we think we know all there is to know, another awesome truth of this great Mystery unfolds before our eyes. As we are pounding these words on our word processor, we find ourselves being blinded by tears. Our emotions always run high when we write about our Church, our Lord and His Mother, His Angels and the Saints, but nothing compares with when we write of the Eucharist. We start to see the words come to life; we are in Bethlehem, and Jesus is coming to life before our eyes. We feel the presence of The Holy Spirit Who descended upon the Blessed Mother and the Apostles in the upper room on Pentecost, now reaching out to us, now pouring out His Love on us, now infusing strength into us as He did to the Apostles, giving them the courage to become Martyrs.

Jesus is revealing Himself so intimately, in the Holy

Eucharist, so passionately, and why? So we can begin to know how very much He loves us.

The Sacrifice of the Mass -
in the Father's Mind and Heart, right from the beginning.

We know that from the very beginning, when our first parents Adam and Eve were betraying the trust that God the Father had placed in them, He was already planning the Redemption of *their* children, the Redemption of the world, through the great Sacrifice of His Only Beloved Son Jesus, His Son Who would be the new Adam, Who by His *obedience* would pay for what Adam by his *disobedience* had brought about.

We travel through the Bible and we find Abraham.

The Lord our God is asking him to sacrifice his only son. Although Abraham did not understand the Lord's command, he said *yes*. That *yes*, like the *yes* of Mother Mary could not have been an easy *yes*! But he said *yes*.

The Lord put Abraham to the test:

"Take your son, your only child Isaac, whom you love, and go to the land of Moriah. There you shall offer him as a burnt offering, on a mountain I will point out to you.'...He (Abraham) chopped wood for the burnt offering and started on his journey to the place God pointed out to him.

"Abraham took the wood for the burnt offering, loaded it on Isaac, and carried in his own hands the fire and the knife. Then the two set out together. Isaac spoke to his father Abraham, 'Father...Look here are the fire and the wood, but where is the lamb for the burnt offering?' Abraham answered, 'God Himself will provide the lamb for the burnt offering.' Then the two of them went on together.

"When they arrived at the place, God had pointed out to him, Abraham built an Altar there, and arranged the wood. Abraham stretched out his hand and seized the knife to kill his son.

"But the Angel of the Lord God called to him from Heaven. 'Abraham, do not raise your hand against the boy...Do not harm him, for now I know you fear God. You have not refused me your son, your only son.'...Abraham saw a ram caught by its horns in a bush. Abraham took the ram and offered it as a burnt offering in place of his son.'"[8]

As we dig deeper into the circumstances surrounding Abraham's *yes*, we see the prefigurement of God the Father doing what He did not finally ask Abraham to do - sacrificing *His* Son! The world was not redeemed of the sin of Adam and Eve by Abraham's *yes*. No, a sacrifice was necessary. Adam had broken the covenant; and a new Adam would have to pay. As with Abraham, once again a human would be called to say *yes* to the sacrifice of a Child. But the Sacrifice would have to be of a Spotless Lamb, a Victim without blemish. God sent His perfect, beloved Son to the earth through the Womb of a human - Mary, an extraordinary human born without the stain of sin, a woman, the one that God spoke of in the Garden of Eden, who would crush the head of the enemy. She said *yes* to bearing a Son Who would be the Messiah, the God-man Who would be the spotless sacrificial Lamb. As with Abraham before her, Mary said *yes*. But unlike with Abraham, God accepted *her* Son as the final Sacrifice.

The *wood* that was to be used for the sacrifice was placed on Abraham's son Isaac's shoulders. And then *unknowingly*, Issac carried the wood upon which he was to be sacrificed. Jesus carried the wood, the Cross He was to be sacrificed upon. Only with Jesus, He *knew* and said *Yes*.

Abraham's son was to be sacrificed on an Altar on top of a mountain. Jesus died on the Cross on a mountain top - Calvary.

God the Father, along with His Son Jesus, paid the price for our sins, the price He did not exact from Abraham.

---

[8]Gen 22:2-13

†

Who is this Jesus Who comes to us
under the appearance of bread and wine?

Recently a teacher of Scripture, in a Catholic High School, said "They have to *know* Jesus before I can teach them about the Holy Eucharist." At first, we felt offended. Then it hit us, how can you revere, adore, worship a Lord you do not know? The question and answer we memorized in our youth comes to us, once more: *"Why did God make us? He made us to know Him, to love Him and to serve Him."* What better way, what more personal way than through the Cross, the Sacrifice of the Cross, and now the Sacrifice of the Mass, the ongoing Sacrifice of the Cross.[9]

Before we can adore our Jesus, hidden under the appearance of a piece of bread and a cup of wine, we have to travel with Him and the Apostles to the upper room, to the evening of Passover when they celebrated the Last Supper, together. You have to know how Jesus carefully planned, so that we could have Him with us till the end of time. You have to look inside the moment: What was Jesus thinking? Who was He thinking of? What were His feelings, as He prepared for His horrible Passion? Was His Heart breaking for His Mother who would share in His pain? Had His bleeding begun for those who would betray Him, run away from Him, deny Him, ignore Him, who would stand by and do nothing? Before we can feel passionately involved with what is happening on the Altar, we have to first know what happened to Jesus those last days and hours of His Life.

We go to Jerusalem. Jesus had entered triumphantly on Palm Sunday. Here it was Thursday, the first night of the Passover. Jesus was in the upper room. Below, there was the tomb of David, the king from whose lineage, it had been foretold the Messiah would come. Jesus sat with His trusted Apostles. Before Him were the bitter herbs, the wine and the unleavened bread that the

---

[9]Council of Trent

Jews would partake of at this time, each year, in commemoration of the Passover of the Jews from captivity.

✝

We must go back in time to the Israelites and their liberation from Egypt. The Pharaoh of Egypt had enslaved the Jews. The Lord God commanded Moses to go to the Pharaoh and tell him that unless he let His people go, He would send down many plagues upon him and his people. Moses protested: His fellow Israelites (the Jews) had not listened to him; why would the Pharaoh listen to him. The Lord promised Moses that after He was finished with the Pharaoh, not only would *he* obey the Lord God's commands but the hard-hearted Israelites who had refused to heed Moses, would know the power of the Lord, and obey.[10] Even after nine plagues, the Pharaoh, whom the Lord God had made stubborn for His purpose[11] did not get the message. He refused to allow the Israelites to leave Egypt.

The Lord God told Moses He would send a tenth plague - the death of the first born of every Egyptian household, including that of the Pharaoh. The Lord God told Moses to have the Israelites, on the tenth of the month,[12] take an animal from the flock, an animal without blemish, a male one year old which could be from the sheep or the goats. They were to keep the animal until the fourteenth day of the month, when it was to be slaughtered; the blood of the animal to be placed on the doorway and lintels of the house where it was eaten. The Lord God went on to say, that very night the animal must be roasted on an open fire and then eaten with bitter herbs and unleavened bread. No part of the animal was to be left over till the morning; but should any be left over, it was to be burned. He further instructed Moses to tell the Israelites they were to eat hastily, their loins girded ready for departure.

He also told Moses that He would, that night, strike down

---

[10]Exodus 5:11

[11]Exodus 7:3

[12] Lord God declared to Moses that this was, from this day forward, to be the first month of the year of the Israelites.

every first-born of the land, man and beast alike. The Lord God said that the blood on their lintels would be a sign they were His people; He would *pass over* their home, and they would escape the punishment He would inflict on the land of Egypt. The Lord God said: *"This day is to be a day of remembrance for you, and you must celebrate it as a feast in the Lord God's honor...for all generations."* For seven days you must eat unleavened bread...On the first day you are to hold a sacred gathering... *"*[13]

At midnight, the Lord God struck down the first-born of every household, man and beast alike, including that of the Pharaoh. The Pharaoh called Moses, along with his brother Aaron, and pleaded with him to have the Israelites leave their land. And they did so, carrying with them, their unleavened dough.

But after the Pharaoh ordered safe passage for the Israelites, he changed his mind and sent his armies after them. The Lord God opened the Red Sea for the Israelites that they might pass through unharmed. But when the Egyptians in hot pursuit, entered the Sea, it closed in on them, drowning every one of them. Moses told the people of Israel that they were to keep this day in remembrance of the day they were released from slavery, and when they celebrated this favor, granted to them by the Lord God, they were to eat only unleavened bread. They had been told by the Lord God that through His power, they would flee from Egypt. He directed them not to use leavened bread. Therefore they did not use yeast. In the Old Testament, one of the prayers said during this special feast of Passover is: *"What makes this night different from other nights?"*

†

This night, Passover, centuries later, Jesus, the Bread of Life would leave His Body under the appearance of a piece of *unleavened bread*, a Host, and His Blood in a chalice under the appearance of wine, so that all His children would, through His Body and Blood be freed from *eternal captivity.*

---

[13]Exodus 12:14-17

How much did Jesus love us? He knew what was ahead for Him. He had told the Apostles, He would be betrayed and that He would have to suffer the Passion. He knew the pain His Mother would share with Him, not only this night but for all the nights and days she would remain on earth, without Him. And who was He thinking of, that night? Us! He would free us from captivity. He would once more open the Red Sea by His Blood on the Cross, and free us from the sin that separates us from Him, and continue to free us through the unbloody Sacrifice of the Mass. This is one of the few times Scripture speaks of Jesus singing. He is going to His death, a horrible death on the Cross and He is singing[14]! Is it possibly because He knows that He is not really leaving us? Is it because He will be a part of us every time we receive Him in Holy Communion? Is it because He can speak to our hearts, as we keep Him company in the Blessed Sacrament?

God the Father spoke to Moses and commanded that the Feast of Passover be celebrated as a commemoration of the time that He, by His power, released the Israelites from captivity.

God once again is reaching out to His people, only now it is Jesus, His Son, the Second Person of the Holy Trinity:

"When the hour came He took His place at table, and the apostles with Him, and He said to them, 'I have longed to eat this Passover with you before I suffer; because I tell you, I shall not eat it again until it is fulfilled in the kingdom of God.'

"Then taking a cup, He gave thanks and said, 'Take this and share it among you, because from now on, I shall not drink wine until the kingdom of God comes.'

"Then He took some bread and when He had given thanks, He broke it and gave it to them saying, 'This is My Body which will be given up for you; do this as a memorial of Me.'"[15]

Jesus said *"Do this as a memorial of Me."*[16] in commemoration of this time that He, by His power, was releasing the new Jerusalem,

---

[14]Matt 26:30
[15]Luke 22:14-19
[16]Luke 22:17-19

the new Israelites, the Catholic Church from the slavery of sin.

And His faithful priests are remembering Him and his Gift to us at an ongoing Last Supper, the Sacrifice of the Mass. Long before God the Father sent His Son to the earth to be the final Spotless Lamb offered to Him for the redemption of man's sins, He, through His prophets and priests of the Old Covenant, was paving the way for Jesus'ongoing offering of Himself to the Father through the Sacrifice of the Mass.

It is our Lord Who is speaking to us through the readings and the homily, teaching us once again, preaching as He did when He walked the earth. During the Offertory, it is He Who is receiving the offerings. As the Holy Spirit prepares to descend upon the Altar, it is Jesus Who is praying the Eucharistic Prayer. We see a priest or bishop but they are representing *visibly* the One Who is *invisibly* present. Whenever we have shared this truth with priests, a truth they knew and maybe have forgotten, or painfully put away with the prayer card of their ordinations, they protest at first and then say it is a *humbling* thing to accept. And we reply "It is an awesome responsibility, a call to holiness, to sainthood and to martyrdom, if need be. It is the Sacrifice of the Cross, only now on the Altar of Sacrifice."

Our Lord has called us to be One with Him, as He is One with the Father. He desires we *all* be part of this Passover when He comes to us in His Word and in His Eucharist. Our Lord knows that only through His Body and His Blood can we become one body, can we be in communion with Him and the Father. He chooses man in his weakness, granting him the grace to participate in this most monumental time when Jesus offers His Heart, whether he calls him as a priest who will bring the Lord in His Word and in His Eucharist - His Body, Blood, Soul and Divinity to the Faithful; whether as a Deacon; whether as a Lector proclaiming the Readings of the Mass; or as a Minister of the Eucharist; or as one of the Faithful who exclaim with their Amen *"I believe - I agree - I say Yes!"*

Jesus fulfills the Old Law

"You took no pleasure in holocausts
or sacrifices for sin."[1]

The imperfect Sacrifices offered under the Old Law were prefigurements of the One Perfect Sacrifice of Jesus Christ in the ongoing Sacrifice of the Cross - the Sacrifice of the Mass.

Why do we speak of the Old Law? Our Faith goes back to before the beginning of time. In order to understand Jesus' Sacrifice, in order to fully understand His ongoing love for us through the Sacrifice of the Mass, we must know what God's plan has been for us from the very beginning. So many people have a false, sometimes childish concept of God the Father. I know, I did. I would always say: "I love Jesus because He came to heal, to forgive; He died for us. God the Father is always punishing. He seems so angry." That was before we came back to Jesus and His Church, and I started to study about God the Father.

God, our Father has had infinite patience with His children, a Faithful God to an unfaithful people. He never gave up on us. As we were complaining (as in the desert), as we were worshiping false idols, as we allowed the slightest wind to blow us away

---

[1]Hebrews 10:6

The Last Supper by Leonardo da Vinci
Convent wall of Santa Maria delle Grazie, Milan, Italy

from Him, He was putting the plan of our salvation into the works. Even knowing how we would treat His precious Son Jesus, He never went back on His promise. Even as He could see his Son being rejected, spit upon, scourged and mocked, He still went ahead with his plan for our salvation. How Loving our Father is! How *unconditionally* loving our Heavenly Father is!

Understanding the Mass in light of the Old Law[2] and its Sacrifices

Under the Old Law there were four kinds of Sacrifices: of peace, of thanksgiving, of atonement, and of petition.

(1) Sacrifice of Peace - Old Covenant

The Priests of the Hebrews (or Jews) offered up to God these Sacrifices with the focus of rendering unto God the worship and adoration due Him as our Creator, King of the Universe.

In the world, we have no problem understanding the paying of homage to sinful man in the personhood of a President of a country who may disappoint us, to a King or Queen who will, in

---

[2]Old Covenant

his or her humanness, betray us. Why do we not recognize the *privilege* it is to have a King, such as our God, to adore, to worship, to follow! We should be honored to have such a King! The citizens of Great Britain have paid high taxes gladly to have their royal family. **New Covenant** - Unlike earthly rulers, our King exacts no payment for His precious gifts. We are not His subjects; we are not His slaves. He has, through His Son Jesus, raised us up to be His children, no longer as we are but changed by the Body, Blood, Soul and Divinity of His Son in the Eucharist, inheriting a share in His Kingdom. Do we go to Mass to worship Him as our King, to adore Him as our Creator, to love Him as our Heavenly Father? That constitutes taking part in the Mass.

(2) Sacrifice of Thanksgiving - Old Covenant
They offered these Sacrifices to give thanks to the Lord for all His generosity, His untiring faithful support and involvement in their lives, His overflowing, never-ending, infinite, ongoing gifts. **New Covenant** - Do we take time to thank our Lord? A very holy Bishop in the United States, once told us: *"I appreciate the gift, you bring to the Faithful of my Diocese, of the Reality of our Lord present in the Eucharist. This is definitely true and that realization is so needed; but when you preach, please add, they should be at Mass to give thanks to our Lord for the breath they just took, and the breath they are about to take; because without Him, they would not have the power to live no less breathe their next breath."*

Do we give Him thanks for life? Do we look at our spouse beside us, our children and grandchildren, our brothers and sisters, our parents, our friends and give Him thanks? Or do we bolt out of church after having received Communion, never pausing to give our Lord even a moment of praise and thanksgiving? Are we aware that Jesus is still very present on the Altar, that He has become part of us and we a part of Him, that we have been consumed by Him,[3] that He is still inside us, inside those around us, possibly those we step over to get out, those we cut off in the parking lot in our rush to get somewhere else? Do we know that Jesus remains physically inside us for at least fifteen minutes? Do we give Him thanks for the Gift, He has just given us of Himself? As we become aware of what happens during the Mass, maybe we will pause and take time to give Him proper thanks.

(3) Sacrifice of Atonement - Old Covenant
This Sacrifice was initiated to obtain the pardon of sin.

[Till today, Jewish people fast and abstain from working on the Day of Atonement, Yom Kippur]

This was the prefigurement of our Lord Jesus entering Heaven; therefore, leaving us the promise that through His Sacrifice on the Cross, we too would rise from the dead.

During the Feast of Atonement, the *emissary goat*[4] was laden down with all the sins of the people, led out of the camp of the Hebrews, and abandoned in the desert, left to be devoured by wild blood-thirsty beasts.

New Covenant - Jesus was loaded down by the sins of men. He was contemptuously led out of Jerusalem, the Jerusalem, He had entered just days before triumphantly, only now *"to be deserted and abandoned to ferocious beasts, the Gentiles who crucified Him."*[5]

Jesus fell three times under the weight of the Cross, the Cross heavy with our sins. This was foretold in Isaiah: *"The Lord hath laid on him the iniquity of us all."*[6]

As the words scream out from the page, our minds and hearts go back to the Passion of our Lord Jesus. Did we not, *do we not* share in the abandonment of Jesus when we look the other way,

---

[3]St. Augustine tells us that when we receive the Eucharist, we do not consume Him; He consumes us.

[4]emissary-a person or agent, a secret agent, sent on a specific mission or serving as an emissary (Webster's Dictionary) as in the case of the emissary goat who was used by the Jews of the Old Law for this type of sacrifice.

[5]St. Alphonsus Liguori - The Holy Eucharist

[6]Isaiah 53:6

as He is once again being mocked, spit upon, crucified? Did only the Gentiles crucify Jesus? When Pilate asked them who they wished released, Barrabas, the insurrectionist or Jesus, their King, were we among those who responded, *"Away with this man, and give us Barabbas?"*[7] Did we choose an insurrectionist, thief and murderer over our Jesus?

When Pilate called Jesus their king, did we join those who cried out against Him, and exclaim, as we do on Passion Sunday and Good Friday, *"We have no king but Caesar?"*[8] And is Pilate once again asking us, *"What am I to do with the man you call king of the Jews?"*[9] Is he today asking: "What shall I do with your Jesus on the Altar, in the Tabernacle?" Do we not shout *"Crucify Him! Crucify Him!"*[10] when we go along with the crowd and keep silent as our Lord in the Eucharist is maligned and mocked, defamed and desecrated? If we consider what is taking place during the Sacrifice of the Mass, we experience, in a most poignant and painful way, the Sacrifice of Jesus on the Cross.

(4) The Sacrifice of Petition - Old Covenant
a means of petitioning or pleading to God for His help in time of need, and asking Him for the Grace to accept His will.
New Covenant - Do we not have an opportunity to bring our petitions, our loved ones, to our God so present on the Altar and in the Tabernacle, to our Jesus so ready to hear us, as God the Father heard His children and granted *their* petitions? Do we *first* go to our Lord when we are in a crisis, or is it a last-resort measure when all else fails?

---

[7]Luke 23:19
[8]John 19:16
[9]Mark 15:12
[10]Mark 15:14

There were five necessary conditions for Sacrifice - under the Old Law:

The victims being offered to God, as sacrifices, in order to be pleasing and acceptable to Him:
(1) had to be holy, consecrated (or sanctified);
(2) had to be offered up to God, an oblation (as in the Offertory of the Mass);
(3) had to be immolated (or put to death);
(4) had to be consumed by fire, (called holocaust, at that time) or by the heat of the mouth (as we consume the Host, today).
(5) and it had to be a joint participation of Priest, people and fire (as today in the Mass).

(1) The victim had to be consecrated to God.
Old Covenant - As God was, is and always will be the Divine Majesty of the whole world, the offering had to be holy and worthy of the greatest of all Kings. The animal to be offered, and then sacrificed, had to be without blemish, or stain, or defect of any kind.[11]
New Covenant - The Lamb of God, the new and final Sacrifice, had to be holy and free from sin, in order to be a worthy Victim to satisfy God. Only Jesus, the Son of God (with the exception of His Mother Mary), was born without blemish, without sin, spotless. And only Jesus could continue to offer Himself to the Father on our behalf, for the redemption of our sins, in the ongoing Sacrifice, the Sacrifice of the Mass.
Under the **Old Law**, once the animal had been sanctified, it could not be used for any purpose other than as a Sacrifice to God, and because it was considered holy, it was only to be touched by a Priest.
Under the **New Law** - St. Thomas Aquinas said that only the consecrated hands of the Priest were to touch the Eucharist.

---

[11]Deuteronomy

(2) The Victim had to be offered to God.
In the **Old Covenant,** this was done by the Priest using words that the Lord Himself gave to the Priests of the Old Law, prayers we have heard intoned during the Offertory of the Mass for almost 2000 years.

(3) The Victim had to be immolated or put to death.
The victim was not necessarily put to death; instead, at times, *bread* was used for the Sacrifice. The Sacrifice of the *Loaves* was accomplished not by fire, but by the natural heat produced within the mouths of those who ate the Holy Bread.

(4) The Victim had to be consumed.
Old Covenant - The Victim had to be consumed by fire. This part of the Sacrifice was called *Holocaust.* The Victim had to be completely destroyed, not a trace left. This was to show the omnipotent power of God over all His creation; to show that He Who brings life into the world out of nothing, can reduce that life to nothing. This Sacrifice was an acknowledgment of God's Supremacy over all His Creation, a solemn proclamation that everything before God is nothing. The smoke that came from the sacrifice rose into the air toward Heaven, to be received by God as pleasant aroma as we read in Noah: *"Noah...offered holocausts upon the Altar; and the Lord smelled a sweet savor."*[12]
New Covenant - As we receive Our Lord in the Eucharist, we are consuming the final Victim, our Lord Jesus in His Body, Blood, Soul and Divinity, not by fire but by the heat of our mouth. *The Council of Trent* states that the Sacrifice of the Altar is the same as that of the Cross. It further proclaims that the Sacrifice of the Mass, instituted by our Lord Jesus at the Last Supper, the night before He died, is a *continuation* of the Sacrifice of the Cross. Do we, after having received Him, meditate on the reality of having received the King of the Universe Who is offering Himself in Heaven to the Father, as He is offering Himself on the

---

[12]Gen 8:20

Altar to His Father through His priest?[13]

(5) All present had to participate in the consummation of the Sacrifice.

Old Covenant - The Priest and all the assembly present, had to consume the Victim, except in the case of a Victim of Holocaust.[14] The Sacrifice was divided into three parts: one part for the Priest, one for the people and one for the fire. By the fire, the pleasing fragrance or incense of the Victim could rise to God in Heaven Who would then be sharing with the people and the Priest, thus communicating (or in communion) with His creation.

New Covenant - During the Sacrifice of the Mass, we all participate in the consummation of the Sacrifice; only now the Altar of Sacrifice is the Altar of the Cross. *This is why a Cross, has always been required on or above the Altar.*[15] A holy priest once told us that because his back is to the Crucifix, he places a Crucifix on the Altar, so that during the Mass, unifying himself with the Sacrifice of Calvary, he can look upon His Lord, the One he is standing in for, and say yes to being victim-priest with Him.

Jesus fulfilled all the conditions of the Old Law.

The first condition, that of *sanctification* or *consecration* of the victim, was fulfilled by God the Father, in the Incarnation of the Word Himself: *"Whom God the Father has sanctified and sent into the world."*[16]

St. Alphonsus Liguori writes that this salutation by the Angel Gabriel *"The Holy One that shall be born of thee shall be called the Son of God."*[17] affirms that the Divine Victim, God's own Son Who was to be sacrificed for the salvation of the world, had

---

[13]Council of Trent Sess. 22, c.2 - from *"The Holy Eucharist"* by St. Alphonsus De Liguori

[14]See (4) where the victim is completely consumed by fire.

[15]Sacramentary - #270 - The Cross is to be easily seen by the Congregation, either above the Altar, or near it

[16]John 10:36

[17]Luke 1:35

already been sanctified when He was born of the Virgin Mary. Our Lord at the moment of taking on a human Body, was consecrated to God to be the Victim of the great and final sacrifice that would be completed on the Cross. Mary gave birth to a Baby born to be crucified for the salvation of sinful man. And this is what we are called to remember every time we participate in the Sacrifice of the Cross.

The second condition, that of *oblation,* was fulfilled, as well, at the moment of *Incarnation* when our most precious Lord Jesus willingly *"offered Himself as Victim to atone for the sins of men."*[18] He knew that He was the only One Whom God the Father would accept as a suitable Sacrifice. Man, because of his sinfulness, was not worthy to be used as an offering to God, and subsequently, unacceptable to God for the redemption of sin in the world. Jesus knew that only through *His* Sacrifice could He make *us* holy, and through His Grace, acceptable to God.

But this offering of Jesus to the Father was not just for *that* time, but for *all* time. It was not a one-time offering but an *ongoing* offering to the Father.[19] It was not just for that moment; it was at that moment that it *began!* And what was begun, has continued and will continue until the time of the Antichrist where it has been prophesied that there will be **no** Sacrifice of the Mass for twelve hundred and ninety days (3 years and 6 1/2 months). *"And from the time that the continual sacrifice shall be taken away, and abomination unto desolation shall be set up, there shall be one thousand two hundred and ninety days."*[20]

But the Sacrifice of Jesus Christ will never cease, since the Son of God will always continue to offer Himself to His Father by an *eternal* Sacrifice. Jesus Himself is not only *the Priest,* and *the Victim,* He is an *eternal* Victim and an *eternal* Priest. He is not a priest and a victim according to the order of Aaron, where the priesthood and the sacrifice were temporary and imperfect,

---

[18]Hebrews 10:8 - *"The Holy Eucharist"* by St. Alphonsus De Liguori
[19]The Sacrifice of the Mass
[20]Daniel 12:11

rendering it inadequate to appease the anger of God against rebellious man. Jesus is a Priest *forever* according to the order of Melchizedek, as David foretold: *"Thou art a priest forever, according to the order of Melchizedek."*[21] The Priesthood of our Lord Jesus Christ is *eternal*; it will never end. Jesus will be offering, even after the end of the world, that same Victim Who was offered on the Cross at Calvary. As long as we need Him to, Jesus will be offering Himself to His Father for the glory of God and the salvation of our souls.[22]

Do you hear what our Church Fathers have been teaching for centuries, right from the beginning? It is that during Mass the priest, in the Person of Jesus Christ the Head, is offering himself in communion with our Lord to the Father for the salvation of the Church, for us, the Body of Christ. That is what is happening at Mass. Should we want to go to Mass? Is it the most important thing we do in our life? Well, if we believe there is life after death, then it is. All that we have, our bodies, our clothes, our homes will disappear. But our souls are eternal. When you think how very temporary our time on earth is, and how eternal our time is afterward, I would think we would want to spend most of our time preparing for our eternity. When our Lord left us His Body, Blood, Soul and Divine Self in the Holy Eucharist, He was thinking of our *eternity*!

The third condition of the sacrifice - the immolation of the victim - was finally, for all time, accomplished by the death of Our Lord Jesus on the Cross, the Perfect Victim. His was the last Sacrifice. By His willing immolation on the Cross, He, once and for all, ended the need for all other bloody sacrifices to appease God the Father.

The fourth condition of the sacrifice - "There remains for us to verify, in the Sacrifice of Jesus Christ, the two other conditions requisite to render a sacrifice perfect - that is, the consumption of the victim and the partaking of it.

---

[21]Psalms 110:4; Hebrews 7:17
[22]Hebrews 7:15-19

"It is then asked, What was this consumption of the victim in the Sacrifice of Jesus Christ? For although His Body was by death separated from His Holy Soul, yet It was not consumed, nor destroyed.

"....this fourth condition was fulfilled by the Resurrection of Our Lord; for then His Adorable Body was divested of all that is terrestrial and mortal, and was clothed in Divine Glory....it is this glory that Jesus Christ asked of His Father before His death: *"And now glorify Thou Me, O Father, with Thyself, with the glory which I had, before the world was, with Thee."*[23] Our Lord did not ask for this glory for His Divinity, since He possessed it from all eternity, as being the Word equal to the Father; but He asked it for His humanity and He obtained it at His Resurrection, by which He entered in a certain manner into His Divine Glory."[24]

The fifth condition of the Sacrifice was called the *partaking or Communion*. This condition is fulfilled in Heaven, as Jesus is *eternally* offering Himself to the Father, and the Saints in Heaven are partaking of this Sacrifice. [This is what is called the Communion of Saints.] As we are receiving the Body, Blood, Soul and Divinity of our Lord's resurrected Self, the Saints in Heaven, in *Communion* with Him, and us, are partaking of the Lord.

During the Sacrifice of the Mass, on earth, the consumption and Communion are accomplished, when we receive the Holy Eucharist or Holy Communion. *The Council of Trent* tells us that the Sacrifice of the Mass, instituted by the Lord at the Last Supper, is the *continuation* of the Sacrifice of the Cross. When Jesus left us his Body and Blood, to be shared by us through His priests, He desired that in and through this unbloody Sacrifice, we might receive the redemption of our sins.

Although the redemption of our sins was fully accomplished by Jesus on the Altar of the Cross, Jesus desired to leave us a *visible* Sacrifice, an *unbloody* Sacrifice, through His priests, which

---

[23]John 17:5
[24]The Holy Eucharist - St. Alphonsus De Ligouri - Pg. 23

would represent visibly the *bloody* Sacrifice fulfilled on the Cross. In this way, we could be part of His Sacrifice; we could be present when He, out of such powerful, passionate Love, died for our sins. Knowing this was paramount for the salvation of His Church, Jesus, at the Last Supper, instituted the eternal Priesthood (according to Melchizedek). He offered Himself, His Body and Blood under the appearance of bread and wine, to the Father in Heaven, and commissioned His Priests to do the same on earth, until He comes again.

The Same One, our Jesus, Who offered Himself to the Father during His Sacrifice on the Cross, is the Same One Who is continually offering Himself to the Father during the Sacrifice of the Mass through His Priests, and all for *our* salvation. He is the Same Victim Who willingly offered Himself on the Cross, Who is the Victim Who offers Himself, with His Body and Blood, in company with His victim-priest, during the Mass. Do we know this? Do we fully realize what is happening? At each Mass, are we filled with the awesome reality that Jesus is truly present, in our midst, in love with us His children, offering Himself over and over again for us and our salvation?

At each Mass, we not only receive the Sacrament of the Holy Eucharist Who is Food for our souls, Food for our journey here on earth, we receive the Eucharist Who is the healing, forgiving Lord among us, the Lord Who, suffering our neglect and apathy, continues to come to us, vulnerably, under the appearance of humble bread and wine. Jesus left us the Sacrifice of the Mass because He desires that we receive the same fruits of those who were present at the Sacrifice of the Cross on Calvary, the fruits that sprung forth because of His Sacrifice. He wants us to be part of the Church which sprung from His Heart, pierced for our sake and salvation. He wants us to be healed by His Blood and purified by His Water which gushed forth from His Heart.[25]

---

[25]Jesus' message of Mercy to Bl. Sister Faustina

Who among us would not have wanted to have been there, at the foot of the Cross, beside Jesus' Mother? Who among us would not desire to have taken His place, to have suffered in His place, to have died in His place, sorrowing like His Mother that we cannot. Jesus desires, with all His Sacred Heart, to cleanse us of our sins with the Blood, He shed from His Five Wounds. In the Miracle of the Eucharist of Lanciano, the wine visibly turned into human blood; the blood petrified into five pellets.[26] The custodian asked us "Why *five* pellets?" He answered his own question: "They represent the five Wounds of Jesus on the Cross." The Lord manifested this Miracle of the Eucharist to speak to us, to tell us of the *Real* presence of Himself in our midst, in His Body, Blood, Soul and Divinity. When we receive the Eucharist, we receive the *Real* Body of Jesus in His Flesh, the Real Blood of Jesus; we are united with the Real Divine Jesus! We are at the Cross of Calvary. The Lord has died for our sins. He has left us His Mother. We are His family. We are His Church. He is with us. No more lambs to be sacrificed. He died once and for all. So that He could remain with us, to be part of us, to lead us, to help us, to forgive us when we fall, to listen to us, to love us, He left us Himself in the Eucharist. And every moment of every day, in every corner of the world, Jesus comes to life on the Altar of Sacrifice during Holy Mass, and we are not alone!

And so, the plan of the Father has been completed and is being completed through Jesus Christ, His Son. Long live Christ the King!

---

[26]read more about The Miracle of the Eucharist of Lanciano in Bob and Penny Lord's best selling book: *"This is My Body, This is My Blood, Miracles of the Eucharist - Book I"*

The Liturgy of theWord

We know *now* why we wrote our first book: *"This is My Body, this is My Blood, Miracles of the Eucharist* - Book I. We know *now* why the Lord has placed it on our hearts to write this sequel. This is why! **It's the Mass!** All we have written *"is so much straw compared to the Eucharist"*, to the Mass, to quote St. Thomas Aquinas when he saw a vision of Heaven. For to us, the Mass is an earthly vision of what Heaven must be like. Over the last eight

Jesus on the Cross

years, as we dug deeper and deeper into the Miracles of the Eucharist, we discovered, more and more, they all came about to bring to the Lord's entire family the Truth that *Jesus is alive and well, and He is in our Church.*

Jesus, High Priest presiding on the Altar of Sacrifice

As Roman Catholic Christians, **we all gather together** in one place for the Eucharistic celebration, for the Mass. *Jesus Christ is the Head of the celebration, the High Priest forever*, according to the order of Melchizedek, presiding through a bishop or priest who is acting in the person of Christ the Head (*in persona Christi capitis*).[1] Our Lord Jesus Christ is presiding, offering

---

[1]Catechism of the Catholic Church

Himself to the Father, just as He did on the night of the Last Supper; except now He cannot be seen with the eyes of the head but by those (of faith) of the heart. He is invisible to the naked eye, but as with a blind man who cannot see, if you are quiet and you are listening with your heart, you *know* it is He!

Where does the Mass come from?

In the *"Catechism of the Catholic Church"*, our Pope and his Bishops have stated that *"the basic lines of the order of the Eucharistic celebration have stayed the same since the Second Century till the present time"*. As far back as 155 AD, Saint Justin wrote to the Emperor Antonius explaining what Christians did during the Holy Mass.[2] We never lose the awe and wonder, every time we return to the Vatican and stand in front of St. Peter's Basilica. We are 2000 years old, 2000 years of unbroken succession, unbroken promise. The Lord promised us, He would not allow hell to prevail against His Church. And we are still here. And we will be here when He returns!

The Mass is the ongoing Sacrifice on the Cross

What is the Mass called?

The Mass is called a *celebration*, and it is. But if we lose touch with the *reason* it is a celebration, we have lost the point, we may have lost the Lord. The Mass is a celebration *because* of the Sacrifice of the Cross, just as there would not be the

---

[2]Catechism of the Catholic Church - p. 339, Sec. 1345

Resurrection without the Crucifixion. Without Good Friday, we would have no reason to celebrate Easter. The celebration is the *Resurrection* of the Mass while the *Crucifixion* is the Sacrifice of the Mass. Sure, we are called to be an Easter people. But we must remember why, and at what cost to Our Lord. And that's why it is said that more touches the Heart of God toward our salvation through one Holy Mass, reverently celebrated, than is accomplished through all the acts of mercy put together. What do we celebrate? The Mass, the ongoing Sacrifice of the Cross.

The Mass is called the *Lord's Supper*. It is the reenactment of that night when the Apostles thought their hearts would break, as the Lord told them that He was to die. Not thinking of Himself and the price He was about to pay, nor the pain His Mother would have to endure, seeing her Beloved Son suffer the Crucifixion, the Lord left us His Body, Blood, Soul and Divinity. He thought of us. He left us not only the Eucharist, He left us the *means* through which we could receive Him. He taught His Apostles right up to the very end. First, He gave them the example of washing their feet that they might understand the direction their lives were to take, and then He commissioned them to feed His lambs with the Food of Life, the Eucharist. He left us the Mass.

The Sacrament of the Eucharist is sometimes called **the breaking of the Bread**.[3] Our Lord presided at table that Last Supper, the Seder of the Jewish people that commemorates the Jews flight from slavery. At *this* Last Supper, the Mass, once again Jesus presides at table, and once again God's people have reason to celebrate the breaking of bread, the *total* flight from the slavery of *sin*. The breaking of bread is a way for us to recognize Our Lord with us, just as at Emmaus when the disciples recognized Jesus in the breaking of the bread. It is by this eating of the one Bread that we are in communion with Him and become one body in Christ. *"Because there is one bread, we who are many are one body, for we all partake of the one bread."*[4]

---

[3] Catechism of the Catholic Church
[4] 1Cor 10:17

The Sacrament of the Eucharist is known as an action of **thanksgiving to God.**[5] Eucharist means thanksgiving in Greek. It is fitting that we give thanks during the Mass and recognize it as a time of thanksgiving. The Incarnate Word became man and through His death and Resurrection, we were redeemed of our sins. *"It is right to give Him thanks and praise"*, we proclaim at Mass. We praise and offer thanks to Our Lord for the living Word that comes to us during the Mass; because through His Word, we begin to know Our Lord and His plan for us, better. We should thank Our Lord during the Mass for the grace to belong to the family of Christ and have the privilege to receive the Eucharist, Our Lord in His Body, Blood, Soul and Divinity. Yes, the Mass is a time to give thanks to the Father for all He has done for us, especially the gift of our redemption through His Beloved Son.

The Mass is the **memorial of the Lord's Passion and Resurrection.** *The Sacrifice of the Mass is the ongoing Sacrifice of the Cross.* At Mass, we are called to remember the price He paid for us at the Sacrifice of the Cross. If we take this time to recall His pain, His rejection, His Passion, His Love, His unconditional obedience to the Father, it will give us the strength to follow Him, if need be, to our Way of the Cross to Crucifixion and Resurrection.

The Mass is known as **The Holy Sacrifice of the Mass** because on this Altar, the final sacrifice, that of the spotless Lamb, Our Lord Jesus Christ, is made present on this Altar of Sacrifice. This *"sacrifice of praise, spiritual sacrifice, pure and holy sacrifice"*[6] is used to describe the Sacrifice of the Mass because this Sacrifice *"surpasses and completes all the sacrifices of the Old Covenant."*[7]

---

[5]Catechism of the Catholic Church - p.335 (1328)
[6]Catechism of the Catholic Church
[7]Catechism of the Catholic Church

When we receive Holy Communion, with this Sacrament of the Eucharist, we will be **united with Jesus Christ,** Who through this unity with His Body, Blood, Soul and Divinity forms us into one body. We will be in communion with the Saints who are partaking of the *bread of Angels, the bread from Heaven, the medicine of immortality,*[8] *viaticum."*[9]

The Holy Mass is so called because it calls us to holiness, to go forth because of the metanoia[10] that has taken place, to go forth and complete God's plan for us in our daily lives, to be one in Him through obedience to His Church. The Mass is called *Holy* because the Holy One Who comes to life, dies (sacramentally) and is resurrected during this ongoing Sacrifice of the Cross and Resurrection.

The Mass is about to begin

We hear the music begin! We all stand, and **our priest processes in,** accompanied by Altar servers (who also have been called acolytes). One acolyte leads the procession, carrying the processional cross. Two Altar servers, bearing candles, flank him and the cross. And we are reminded of the Way of the Cross when in Jerusalem, our Lord carried the Cross weighed down by our sins. As we look upon the processional cross, we are transported to that time when the world stood still, when our Savior processed to His death, flanked by Roman soldiers. As our eyes glance upon the processional cross that the Altar server is carrying, we are reminded that the Sacrifice of the Mass, the

---

[8]St. Ignatius of Antioch - Catechism of the Catholic Church - Pg. 336 # 1331

[9]viaticum is the name of Holy Communion when it is given in a public place of private manner to someone in danger of death, during an illness, or to soldiers going into battle. It may be given without Communion fasting at that time and may be repeated as often as required. When the Sacrament of Anointing of the Sick is administered at the same time, Viaticum precedes it. ref. The Catholic Encyclopedia - Broderick

[10]means conversion in Greek

re-presentation,[11] the ongoing Sacrifice of the Cross is about to begin, once more. Are we part of those who accompanied Mother Mary and St. John the Apostle, as they walked beside Jesus? Or are we part of the apathetic, uninvolved, *business as usual* bystanders?

Our celebrant and his ministers bow before the Altar

Mother Church desires that all the Faithful take an active part of the Liturgy of the Mass, according to their particular ministries. But the members do not all have the same function. The priest or bishop, by virtue of his Sacrament of Holy Orders, is the only one empowered by the Holy Spirit to act in the Person of Christ the Head, "as it were an 'icon' of Christ the Priest."[12]

The priest and all in the procession bow or genuflect, before ascending the steps to the Altar, to the *"sacrificial Altar."*[13] Once there, the priest and the deacon kiss the Altar which *"is the Lord's Cross."*[14]

In the Early Church, the emphasis was placed on Eucharist as a *"meal"*. With this focus, a table was used as one would use for a meal. In the second century *the agape* (or meal concept) and the Eucharistic Rites were separated. This is when the Church placed her emphasis on the *Sacrifice* of the Mass. With the Eucharistic Rite, stressing the *death of our Lord Jesus Christ on Calvary and His Resurrection,* an Altar became important, to represent the Cross. It was used by the Priest to re-present (makes present) the Sacrifice of the Cross and Christ's victory over death.

Again with the use of an Altar, we see our links with our foundation - the Old Testament, the Old Law. The Altar of the Old Testament was used to sacrifice lambs (without blemish) to the Father in Sacrifice. Our Lord Jesus fulfilled the Prophets by

---

[11]Catholic Answers - May/June 1994 "The Real Presence" by M. Mazza
[12]Catechism of the Catholic Church
[13]Catechism of the Catholic Church p. 305, sec. 1180
[14]Catechism of the Catholic Church p. 306, sec. 1182

offering Himself to the Father as the Final Sacrifice:

"For You are not pleased with sacrifices
should I offer a holocaust, You would not accept it.
My Sacrifice, O God, is a contrite spirit;
a heart contrite and humbled, O God, You will not spurn.[15]

In the Early Church, wooden Altars were used because of their mobility. With the threat of being discovered, the early Christians had to be able to move their Altars quickly. With the danger of persecution no longer present, our churches, wanting to give greater honor to the Altar, began creating them out of marble and stone.

In certain Eastern liturgies, the Altar is also the symbol of *the tomb* (Christ truly died and is truly risen)[16] In the early Church, Mass was celebrated on the tombs of the Martyrs. It was not celebrated to the Martyrs but to God the Father through their intercession.

It was an ancient custom to honor deceased heroes. To the Christians, the **Martyrs** were the greatest of all heroes, and Mother Church has always honored them in a special way for the selfless sacrifices they made for her, to the point of martyrdom. As far back as St. Cyprian, we see the Sacrifice of the Mass being celebrated at the grave sites of the Martyrs. When you visit the Catacombs in Rome, you will see Altars surrounded by tombs chiseled out of the walls where the early Christians were buried. As almost everyone who became a Christian knew that he would die a Martyr's death, you can safely say that Mass was celebrated in communion with the Martyrs, asking for their intercession. As the Sacrifice of the Mass was, from the beginning, considered the ongoing Sacrifice of the Cross, by celebrating the Lord's Last Supper there at their tombs, the Christians were paying homage to their dead Martyrs, linking their death and sacrifice with that of Our Lord on the Cross. On the walls you see drawings or

---

[15]Psalms 51:18-19
[16]Catechism of the Catholic Church p. 306, sec.1182

graffiti of Christians symbols depicting the Eucharist and the Sacrifice of the Mass.

There are three **relics** of Saints, imbedded inside the Altar stone or *mensa*[17] of the Altar. *The Faithful for almost two thousand years have been venerating* the Saints through their relics in the Altar, and as our ancestors did with the Martyrs, praying for their intercessory protection.[18] The Church has honored the Saints and prayed for their intercession because of their virtue and obedience while they were on earth. We turn to them, as intercessors, because they have been redeemed and are in the Kingdom with Our Lord.

The priest and his ministers do not bow to the Saints nor to the Martyrs but to our God to Whom the Altar has been erected. Every Altar in a Catholic Church is an *Altar of Sacrifice* where Jesus, through His priest, will offer Himself to the Father in the continuation of the *Sacrifice of the Cross*.

The priest will incense the Altar

We have been at Mass, many times, and witnessed priests and bishops incensing the Altar.[19] Whenever we have been at Mass with His Holiness, he has always incensed the Altar . **Incense is a sign of prayer and petition.** Its tradition dates back to the Old Testament (the fragrance and the smoke rising, from the sacrifice of the sacrificial lamb, to God the Father), when David said: *"Let my prayer come like incense before You."*[20] Then in the New Testament, at the very beginning, when incense is offered by the Magi to the Christ Child in the manger.[21] And then, where it is most graphically revealed in the Book of Revelation:

"Another Angel came and stood at the Altar, holding a gold censer. He was given a great quantity of incense to offer, along with the prayers of all the holy ones, on

---

[17]mensa - either the flat-top of a fixed Altar or the Altar stone of a portable Altar

[18]New Catholic Encyclopedia-Catholic University of America

[19]Incense may be used at anytime to solemnize the celebration.

[20]Psalm 141:2

[21]manger means eating place

*the gold Altar that was before the throne. The smoke of
the incense along with the prayers of the holy ones went
up before God from the land of the Angels."* [22]

We are told by the early Church Fathers that the Angels accompany the Holy Spirit as He comes down upon the Altar during the Eucharistic Prayer.[23] We are also told that there is an Angel of the Mass who is present on the Altar. This is fully understandable, since the Angels never left Jesus from the moment of Incarnation till He died on the Cross and then were present when He rose from the dead. Therefore, it is quite fitting that our priest incense the Altar , along with the Angels on earth and in Heaven, offering up to God the Father a fragrance pleasing to Him. As your priest incenses the Altar, join with him offering thanksgiving to our Lord for His Sacrifice that we might be part of the family of God and its redemption.

The priest makes the sign of the Cross.

When the congregation has finished singing the entrance hymn, the priest makes the sign of the Cross and greets the Faithful. **He makes the sign of the Cross!** This clearly signifies that the Sacrifice of the Mass is the continuation of the Sacrifice of the Cross. The sign of the Cross[24] - the means used to bring about degrading death, became the instrument which helped to bring about glorious eternal life. The cross, used to crucify the worst of criminals, became the sign which gave Christians the courage to gladly give up their lives for their Lord and Savior. Through the Cross, despair turned into hope! Satan knew the power of the Cross. He shouted to Jesus: *"Get down from the cross!"*

The Cross has always been an enemy of Satan. He hates it!

---

[22]Rev 8:3-4

[23]St. John Chrysostom - chapter: *"Attacks From Within"* from the Lords' book: *"Scandal of the Cross and Its Triumph"*

[24]The sign of the Cross has been part of the Mass since the early days of the Church

George Bernard Shaw said *"It is the Cross which bars the way."* Archbishop Fulton J. Sheen said: *"Sure it bars the way; it bars the way to hell!"* The North American Martyrs were killed for making the sign of the Cross. Blessed Father Miguel Pro, a Twentieth Century Martyr, standing before a firing squad, held high the cross he had received on the day of his ordination in one hand and a rosary in his other hand, as he cried out: *"Viva Cristo Rey"* - Long live Christ the King.[25] The Cross!

The sign of the Cross represents **the Holy Trinity**. The priest makes the sign of the Cross, saying *"In the Name of the Father, and of the Son, and of the Holy Spirit"*. In the Name of the Father, and of the Son, and of the Holy Spirit - the *outer sign* of the Holy Trinity reflects the *inner truth* of Their Presence on the Altar and in our midst, just as They were there at the Sacrifice of the Cross. For just as They are three distinct Persons, They are One God, equal and *consubstantial.*[26] Each of the Three Persons in the One God are distinct and yet of the same substance, same nature[27] as of the Other Two. As He did at the Sacrifice of the Cross, now at the Sacrifice of the Mass Our Lord Jesus is offering Himself through His priest to the Father. We believe our Lord Jesus, the second Person of the Trinity, did not die alone. Although *He* was the One to die on the Cross, the Sacrificial Lamb, He was not alone. [We know that He was doing the Will of the Father. Remember when He spoke to the Father in the Garden of Gethsemane and said *"If it be Thy Will, let this cup pass from Me. But Thy Will, not Mine."*[28]] We believe that the Father was there on Calvary with His Son to accept His Sacrifice for the

---

[25]from the chapter on Bl. Miguel Pro in the Lords' book: *"Martyrs, They Died for Christ"*

[26]consubstantial - being of one and the same substance, as the three Divine Persons are of but one substance as set forth by the first ecumenical council of Nicea in 325 A.D.

[27]Catechism of the Catholic Church

[28]Matt 26:39

redemption of our sins. He asked God the Father to forgive us: *"Father forgive them, for they know not what they do."*[29] We believe that God His Father was there when, as His last act of love and obedience, our Jesus commended His Spirit to the Father. The sign of the Cross[30] represents our **Baptism**, which initiates us into the family of God, the Holy Trinity. It is a reminder that we were not only washed by the Blood of the Lamb, we were baptized into His Family by His death.[31] When our Lord died for us, we were "washed in His Blood, Baptized into His death and given life in Him."[32]

The celebrant greets the people.

Here we again become aware of the Holy Trinity's presence, in our midst, as the celebrant greets the people: *"The grace of our Lord Jesus Christ and the love of God and the fellowship of the Holy Spirit be with you all."* This has been passed down to us by Saint Paul in his Second Letter to the Corinthians.[33] Our response: *"And also with you."* has replaced *"And with your spirit."*[34] St. Paul used the latter, several times in his letters to the Galatians, to the Philippians, and to Timothy.

With these words, we, the Body of Christ, unite ourselves with one another, we the Faithful and our priest, one in our professed belief in Jesus Christ.

When we hear those words from our priest that we, in the company of the Saints are receiving the grace of our Lord Jesus Christ, the love of God the Father and the holy guidance and companionship of the Holy Spirit, our hearts have to almost crack our ribs, as we feel them expanding with the love we feel filling us.[35]

---

[29]Luke 23:34
[30]the sign of the Cross is the oldest gesture of our Faith
[31]from "The Mass" - Father Guy Oury
[32]from "The Mass" - Father Guy Oury - p.48
[33]2Cor 13:13
[34]the Hebrew expression meaning *and with you.*
[35]When they examined some of the Saints after they had died, they discovered their hearts were so enlarged, they broke the ribs of the Saint.

The Penitential Rite

At this point in the Mass, the priest invites us to examine our consciences and to express sorrow for our sins. The sinner remains dead in sin[36] unless God, through His infinite goodness and mercy, restores him to life in Him.

When Jesus walked the earth, the lame pleaded with Him: "Master, that I might walk", and the blind: "Teacher that I might see." They asked Him to heal them of their physical afflictions; He forgave them their sins, and then He healed them of their physical infirmities. He knew that without the cleansing of the soul, without true repentance, there can be no lasting healing. And so, before we can be open to the redemptive healing of our Lord Jesus Christ in the Holy Eucharist, we need to recall and repent of our sins.

In the past, our priest or the bishop and his ministers would prostrate themselves, face down, as they do today on Good Friday, before ascending the Altar, silently pleading with the Lord for forgiveness of their sins.

In the first half of the Twentieth century, the Church began introducing more participation of the Faithful. The Congregation began to join in, saying the prayers formerly only said by the priest and his Altar servers. Seeing the merits of a communal petitioning of forgiveness, Vatican Council II introduced a penitential rite which included all the people.[37]

As we read in the chapter on the Old Testament roots of the Mass, the one offering the Sacrifice should be holy; therefore, as we are in communion with the priest as he offers the Sacrifice, we are asking the Lord to cleanse us of our sins that we might be worthy to offer this Sacrifice in company with the celebrant. We ask our Lord at this time to pardon us of any sin, we may have unintentionally forgotten to confess, praying that our soul be

---

[36]only if mortal sin is present, in which case the *Sacrament of Penance* is necessary.

[37]from "The Mass" - Father Guy Oury p.50

spotlessly clean as we welcome our Lord in His Eucharist - His Body, Blood, Soul and Divinity to be one with us.

As our Lord Jesus, as He was drawing His last breath on the Cross, asked God the Father to forgive us, now our priest intercedes for us, as he closes the Penitential Rite with *"May almighty God have mercy on us, forgive us our sins, and bring us to everlasting life."* To which we respond *"Amen."*

Blessing with the Holy Water

At some Sunday Masses or special Holy Days, the celebrant may include the **blessing of the water and the sprinkling of holy water**. The holy water is our Link with our Baptism, a Sacramental which reminds us, we have been baptized and cleansed by the Holy Trinity. This tradition of blessing and sprinkling holy water dates back to the days of the Apostles.

As we are blessed with holy water, we call to mind our Baptism. The only way we can explain it is the feeling we have after we have come out of the baths at Lourdes. We do not want to talk. We want to go off by ourselves and drink in the Lord, to be silent and hear Him, to be alone with Him like St. Catherine of Siena. There is a cleansing of the spirit that is unexplainable. You cannot remember any hurts you have suffered. You feel clean, holy! That's the way we feel at Mass when we are blessed to have holy water fall on us. We do not think about the silk dress or suit we are wearing. Will it spot? You almost wish it would, so that every time you look at the spot, you will remember you have been called to holiness, first by the waters of Baptism and then by the cleansing water at Mass. The devil hates holy water. At the ministry, in addition to a crucifix in every room, we have holy water fonts, as well as a huge rosary hanging on the wall of the staircase leading to the upper floor. If Satan hates the Cross, and the Rosary and holy water, then that's good enough reason for us to be armed with these sacramentals.

If the blessing and the sprinkling of holy water takes place during this time in the Mass then the Penitential Rite as well as the Kyrie (Lord have mercy) is eliminated.

The Kyrie

Again, we cannot explain it but when the Kyrie is said or especially when it is sung in the original Greek, it brings tears to our eyes. It is so beautiful. Our invocation, our pleading with the Lord:

Kyrie, eleison   Lord, have mercy
Christe, eleison   Christ, have mercy
Kyrie, eleison   Lord, have mercy

At this point in the Mass, this prayer used to be offered up to the Father three times, the Faithful reciting *"Kyrie, eleison"* three times. Then three times to Jesus His Son, reciting *"Christe, eleison"* three times. And then three times to the Holy Ghost, reciting *"Kyrie, eleison"* three times.

Although this prayer originated in the Church in the East, the Mass being celebrated in Greek, it was during the Pontificate of Pope St. Sylvester that the Kyrie was adopted in the **Latin Church**. It may be recited or sung as a part of the New Order of the Mass. We do have the privilege of hearing it sung at the Latin Mass.[38]

We recite *"Lord have mercy; Christ have mercy; Lord have mercy"*, the echoing cries of our ancestors, the Jews. But the most poignant references are to be found in the Gospels when the needy cried out to Jesus: *"Son of David have pity on* us."[39] We read of the woman who thought *"If only I can touch the tassel of His cloak I shall get well."*[40] Such was the faith that Jesus inspired in all whom His shadow fell upon. Do we ask the Lord for His mercy, believing as they did that He hears, and sees, and will answer us?

---

[38] The Latin Mass is allowed to be celebrated with special permission from the local bishop.
[39] Matt 9:27
[40] Matt 9:22

The Kyrie in the vernacular[41] is sometimes used as another form of the Penitential Rite at Mass.[42] It not only expresses true sorrow for our sins, but also praises Jesus for His mercy which is everlasting.

The celebrant, along with the Faithful sings or prays the Gloria - *Gloria in Excelsis*

As we proclaim God our King, our hearts swell and we join Saint Polycarp who, as he was being martyred at the stake, gave thanks to God for His great glory.[43]

Knowing that God loves us and, never giving up on us, He has heard our pleas and answered them, we turn to Him in thanksgiving for all He has done, is doing and will do, proclaiming Him to the mountaintops.

It is such a joyful, exciting part of the Mass. You can feel the happiness of God, as He hears us lifting our voices in praise and worship of Him.[44] As our Jewish brothers and sisters did before us, it is only fitting that we, the *New Jerusalem*, give thanks to God the Father for all He has done for us, extolling in a loud voice He is our King, our Almighty God and *Father*! Imagine, God is our Father!

Having given due praise to our Father, then we give praise and honor to his Son, our Lord, the Lamb of God Who takes away the sins of the world, while at the same time pleading with Him to have mercy on us, to receive our prayer and to give it to the Father.

We then proclaim Jesus *"the Holy One, the Lord, the Most High **with the Holy Spirit**"*, recognizing the Third Person of the

---

[41]the language of the country

[42]At some Masses, both the Confiteor and the vernacular of the Kyrie are recited.

[43]*The Mass* by Father Guy Oury - pg.55 - Chap. 4

[44]Although we often read the words of this beautiful prayer, it is really a song of praise, a "canticle." The earliest Christians carried on the Jewish practice of singing canticles based on Holy Scripture during their liturgy. The Gloria, in the very words we use today, was found in Christian prayer books, as early as the year 380.

Holy Trinity, our Comforter and Guide. We give glory to the Holy Spirit Who is *God personified.*[45]

We acknowledge They are One, as then we cry out *"in the glory of God the Father."* This is the Faith for which our Saints lived; this is the Faith for which our Martyrs died, and we acclaim that belief and the Profession of that belief that Jesus and the Holy Spirit are One with God the Father, as we say a heartfelt: *Amen!*

The Opening Prayer

This Prayer used to be called the *Collect* as it was a collection of prayers the priest said for the Faithful around him. In the Early Church of the Second Century, there is no mention of an Opening Prayer. It would appear they went right to the Readings. But in the Church of the Middle Ages, these prayers became beautifully elaborate, including petitions to different Saints. Today, the priest solely addresses a simple prayer to the Father, in Jesus' Name.

At this time in the Mass, the priest encourages us to pray silently, sharing with our Lord our smallest as well as our largest cares. It is also a time to soulfully prepare ourselves, contemplating on the great gift we are about to receive - our Lord in the Word and in the Eucharist.

The Liturgy of the Word

The Mass is composed of the *Liturgy of the Word* which includes the teachings passed down through the centuries by the prophets in the Old Testament, by the Apostles in the Acts of the Apostles, by the letters of Saints Peter, Paul, James, Jude and John, the Book of Revelation and by the accounts of Jesus' Life in the Gospel.

One Jewish custom which found its way into Christianity was the respect given to the physical presence of the Scriptures. Just as the Hebrew Torah, or scroll of God's Word, was lavishly decorated and carried around the temple in procession, so the Christian Book of the Gospels was bound in leather trimmed

---

[45]Holy Spirit - p.269, The Catholic Encyclopedia by Broderick

with gold.

The Lectionary is carried to the Altar, in solemn procession. Two acolytes or Altar servers flank the lectern with candles, paying respect to God Who is present in His Word. The Book is then incensed before the priest or deacon begins to read the Gospel. After he finishes reading, the priest kisses the Book, paying homage to His Lord present in the Word. When we were Lectors, I would always kiss the Lectionary before processing in with the priest. I could feel the presence of God in His Word.

The Homily

The priest now, in his Homily, will preach to the Faithful, using the Readings and the Gospel as his base; the Lord, through His priest, once again speaking to His people. The priest will enjoin the congregation to accept the Readings and the Gospel as the Word of God, the Word Who is God - to accept with the head and act through the heart - to allow the words to come to life, to burn in their hearts, to set them afire.

In the Middle Ages, the Homily was an essential part of the Liturgy of the Word. Most of the Faithful did not know Latin and therefore much of the Mass, and the Scripture readings were not understandable to everyday Faithful. Most of those who attended Mass, received much of their education of the Faith and the life of Jesus and Mary from the Homily and from the *"sermons in stone and stained glass"*. This is why there can be found, till today, in some of our older churches in Europe, so many fine paintings, murals and stained glass windows recounting the stories of our Church, of our Saints, of our Jesus and His Mother Mary. Because so few knew how to read, and there were so few books, most received their instruction through these works of art. This form of learning is still the most dynamic. Do we not say that one picture is worth a thousand words?

In our Sanctuary, there is an *Altar of Sacrifice* upon which the bread and wine will change into the Precious Body, Blood, Soul and Divinity of Our Lord Jesus Christ, and a *Lectern* upon which, through the Prophets of the Old Testament and the Good

News of the New Testament, we will be nourished by the Word of God.

Let us speak of the Word of God. The Word of God is important in our lives because it reveals to us *Who* Our Lord is and the *price* He paid for our salvation. You hear people say, they do not have to go to Mass, that they have an ongoing dialogue with the Lord: He understands them. Sure God understands them and us; but how do *we* love someone we do not know? People often ask: *"In Heaven, is everyone close to God, or are some closer to God than others?"*

Who is your God? Who have you spent your whole life getting to know? Who has been your priority, the main one in your life? That's the one you will know; that's the one you will go to, after you die. The Saints spent the major part of their lives getting to know the Lord, and in the knowing, their love for Him grew and grew to the point of exclusion of most of the world, with its lures and entrapment. Where do you think they are in the Kingdom?

Mother Mary knew God the Father and obeyed Him. She had learned about Him through the inspired Word of the Prophets. And through that knowledge and obedience to the Father she gave us the Incarnate Word, the Second Person of the Holy Trinity, our Lord Jesus. Without her knowledge of the Lord and His plan of salvation, how would she have known who the Angel Gabriel was and Who had sent him? She knew and she said yes to the point of giving up her Son to the Cross. She most perfectly did the Will of the Father. Where do you think she is in the Kingdom? She was full of Grace, you say. God's Grace is showered upon *us* through the Sacraments. Mary cooperated with God! He wants to bestow graces on us; we need only to cooperate!

The Profession of Faith

Part I of the Catechism of the Catholic Church is dedicated to **The Profession of Faith**.[46] The Pope felt this was so important, he committed *one of four parts, covering no less than 265 pages*!

When we stand together, as a community of believers, and proclaim our Faith, we are agreeing with the teaching imparted to us in and through God's Word. *The Apostles Creed* is the oldest Profession of that which we, as Christians have believed and proclaimed down through the ages. It is a faith statement declaring our allegiance to the teachings of Mother Church. As we say the Creed, we are in communion with our Lord, His Mother, and our entire Heavenly Family.

"I believe!" Having written last year about the Martyrs who died rather than deny this Faith, this Profession of what we believe, and have believed from the very beginning, this Creed or *Credo* takes on deeper meaning. Meditating on the brothers and sisters who went before us, it is difficult to just say the words. The Martyrs, the Early Christians, the Catholics today who are being martyred just because they are Catholic, march before you, and you stand convicted. That's when the words take on their *real* meaning! Our Pope said it is not sufficient to know the relationship between Sacred Scripture and that which we believe, we must, in believing, *obey* this Faith we have professed.[47]

"I believe in God the Father Almighty, Creator of Heaven and Earth." Here we are professing that God is the Creator of all that is, ever was or will be, in Heaven and on earth, so we are pledging ourselves to His Will in our lives. Whenever we say these words, our minds and hearts go back to that moment in the Garden of Eden when God could have given up on us, but didn't. So unconditional was His Love that as one man and woman were disobeying and hurting Him, He was already planning for Our

---

[46]There are only four parts
[47]Catechism of the Catholic Church

Lady to be the bearer of His only Son Who would by His Sacrifice, redeem the world. What is about to happen at the Mass is, *"a visible Sacrifice (as the nature of man demands) by which the Bloody Sacrifice which He was to accomplish once for all on the Cross, would be re-presented, its memory perpetuated until the end of the world, and its salutary power be applied to the forgiveness of the sins we daily commit, "*[48] that act of love by the Father and the Son. Remembering all He has done for us, we address Him as our Father and as our Father, we obey Him and defend Him. It is not enough to believe, we must act on that belief.

The Creed goes on to extol that we are called to believe in *Jesus Christ, God's only begotten Son,* the Son Who died for us, that we might know eternal life with His Father in Heaven, the Son Whose last thoughts were of us. On the night before He died, He loved us so very much He knew we would not survive as a Church or as a people of God, should we be left orphans, and so, He left us Himself at that Last Supper which was the first Mass with Jesus the High Priest presiding. As we slowly repeat the words in the Creed that have come down to us through the ages, our hearts have to start beating wildly, pounding with an anticipation, an eagerness, an excitement, as we feel ourselves coming close to that time in the Mass when our Lord will come to life on the Altar and offer Himself to the Father for us. This Lord Jesus Christ, Whom we profess to believe in, will share Himself with us during the Liturgy of the Eucharist, in His Body, Blood, Soul and Divinity.

We acknowledge that *"We believe in the Holy Spirit, the Lord, the giver of life, Who proceeds from the Father and the Son."* As we prepare for the Mass, it is only fitting we recognize the Holy Spirit in our lives, for He is about to descend upon the Altar accompanied by myriads of Angels. The Holy Spirit is present in the Creed, not only during the Liturgy of the Eucharist,

---

[48]Catholic Catechism - Pg 344; Council of Trent(1562); 1Cor 11:23; Heb 7:24,27

but during the Liturgy of the Word when *"He has spoken through the Prophets"*. Is it any wonder why Faithful have died rather than deny this or any of the truths proclaimed in the *Credo*? Do our hearts burn, as we pledge that we will worship and glorify Him?

We could write a book on the *Credo* itself, but the Pope has done it so simply, so eloquently, so thoroughly, it would be presumptuous for us to add anything to his teachings. But let us stress, in these times of confusion and division, where everyone seems to be doing their own thing, it is more imperative than ever to say the Profession of Faith, listening to the words and then living them. Our Pope has faced much persecution, as the Martyrs before him to bring us this truth. And when we take this truth to heart, the Mass becomes the most important part of our life, the Eucharist the only real nourishment we need - our Food for the journey to Heaven.

We believe in One, Holy, Catholic and Apostolic Church, and all its teachings! The Lord had three short years to prepare His chosen ones to pass on the Truth, to guide and safeguard His Church. He walked with them. He ate with them. He taught them. He knew them. Recall when they turned to Him and questioned Him: why He spoke to the people in Parables and to them differently, specially. He told them, He knew He could trust them. He said that, knowing one would deny him three times and one would betray Him. He was pouring His *Signal Grace*[49] upon them. And those who cooperated, though falling at times but rising again to serve Him, He made future shepherds of His Church. He so loved us, He died for us. He left us His Body and Blood in the Eucharist, knowing His Church would not survive

---

[49]Signal Grace is that Grace from God that allows men to become Martyrs; it fills one with the strength to do His Will against tremendous odds. It is the Grace, God poured upon St. Maxmilian Kolbe which gave him the courage to stand up and give his life for another prisoner of Auschwitz, proclaiming he was a Catholic Priest.

100 years without the Eucharist. He gave the Keys to His Church to our first Pope, St. Peter. And He made a promise that hell would not prevail against His Church, and He is keeping that promise. He told us He would not leave us orphans, and He is with us, alive, in our Church. This is what we believe. We believe in His Church and all it teaches. We are obedient to His Church and all it teaches. This is what we profess and this is what makes us Catholic!

General Intercessions

Our Profession having been proclaimed, we, having been reminded who we are and why we are here, Mother Church in her wisdom, calls us, the Faithful as one, to petition the Lord for ourselves, for our loved ones, for those who have left the Church and those who have remained, for our priests and religious, our Pope, our Bishops, the heads of State, and to offer to God praise and thanksgiving for what He has done, for what we understand and what we fail to understand. What an opportunity! Here is our Lord ready to hear us, to grant us our heart's desire, if it be according to His perfect Will. At this moment, we are speaking to the King of the Universe, to the Creator of all that is seen and unseen, and He is listening!

Our hearts beat a little faster! We are about to begin the Liturgy of the Eucharist.[50]

---

[50]Turn to the next chapter on The Liturgy of the Eucharist

The Liturgy of the Eucharist

The Offertory

In the Sermon on the Mount, His Sermon on the Beatitudes, which *"are at the Heart of Jesus' preaching,"*[1] Jesus fed the multitudes[2] with hope that the fulfillment of the promises made to the chosen people since Abraham, could be theirs, ordering them to no longer desire possession of things below, but those Above, the eternal Kingdom of God. Having fed them in the Word, telling them that true blessedness and happiness could only be achieved through total dependence on God, or *Anawim*,[3] He felt they were ready for the Bread of Life. They had followed Him to Capharnaum. There, He told them they could only have *eternal happiness and life* if they ate His Body and drank His Blood, the Eucharist. When they argued, *"'How can this man give us His flesh to eat?' Jesus said to them, 'Truly, truly, I say to you, unless you eat the Flesh of the Son of man and drink His Blood you have no life in you; he who eats My Flesh and drinks My Blood has eternal life, and I will raise him up on the last day.'"*[4] He also speaks of the unity that will come about when we

---

[1]Catechism of the Catholic Church - Page 426 - sec.1716
[2]over 5,000 men, not counting women and children
[3]Old Testament
[4]John 6:53

The Sermon on the Mount - Jesus fed the multitudes

receive the Eucharist: *"He who eats My Flesh and drinks My Blood abides in Me and I in him."*[5] We, at this time in the Mass, are preparing to eat His Body and drink His Blood, as He directed us to, so that *we* might have *life* in Him. Imagine, through our unity with Our Lord in the Eucharist, we will be *one in Him* as *He is in the Father*; He will abide in us and we will abide in Him. Do not tears come to your eyes, as you excitedly await this time when Jesus will come to dwell in your house, in the Tabernacle that you have prepared for Him, and as with Mother Mary, carrying Him under your heart?

Now, at the Mass, having heard the Word of hope, in the Liturgy of the Word, are we *now* like the little boy on the Mount who brought up his basket, filled with all he had, to Jesus? Will we offer now, all we have and allow Jesus to bless our gifts and multiply them, feeding others, as He did that day on the Mount overlooking the Sea of Galilee?

At this point in the Mass, we the Faithful, are chosen to bring up the gifts. [*Again, we see our Old Testament roots, our Jewish brothers and sisters as well as the Holy Family (during the Presentation of the Baby Jesus) bringing turtle doves and other*

---

[5]John 6:56

offerings to God.] It is stirring to see Altar servers process to the rear of the church, preceded by one of them carrying the Procession Cross, and then to see them lead those bearing gifts to the Altar. Our priest, after having received the gifts of wine and bread (in the form of hosts) and our gifts,[6] carries them up to the Altar of Sacrifice.

As the priest begins the prayers over the gifts, we feel an excitement building. We have learned about our Lord, through His Word. Now, Jesus is coming in His Eucharist! *We will become one with Him!* It will no longer be we who live but Jesus Who lives in us. We will be changed! We will not only become one with Him, but with our loved ones who have gone before us, in Heaven and in Purgatory; we become one with our whole Heavenly Family: Mother Mary, the Saints, the Martyrs and the Angels.

As the priest is offering up the Sacrifice, it is the Victim Himself, Our Lord Jesus Christ Who is presenting Himself to the Father. At this moment, as Our Lord is doing once again, as he did at the Last Supper, inviting us to eat and drink His Body and Blood, we should be offering our body and blood to Him, consecrating ourselves totally to Him, to the point of dying for Him, if need be. St. Augustine said: *"You know what this holy banquet is, and what nourishment is offered you at this table. Since Jesus Christ gives entirely His Body and His Blood, let no one approach without giving himself entirely to the Lord."* Do we come to the Altar, ready to receive Our Lord Jesus in the Eucharist, having given ourselves completely to Him, or are our minds off somewhere else? Are we here out of our Sunday obligation? Was Jesus obligated to die for us, for sinners?

We read that, when the priest mixes water with the wine, this represents the union which took place in the Incarnation of the Word when Divinity united with humanity. This also

---

[6]In the Early Church, the faithful would bring wheat, fruit and vegetables they had grown, or animals they had bred to the Altar, sharing, as in the Acts of the Apostles, all they had with the rest of the Body of Christ.

represents the intimate union that takes place between Jesus and ourselves, when we receive Holy Communion. [Whenever, a brother or sister in Christ (Protestant) asks us if Jesus is our personal Savior, we respond, He is our *intimate* Savior.] A drop of water is placed into the chalice of wine, indicating we will, by His Body and Blood, become less ourselves and more Him, being swallowed up in Him, as the water is absorbed into the wine. The Council of Trent commanded that priests do this during this time in the Mass, as it is believed that Jesus mixed the water with the wine at the Last Supper.

The priest washes his hands. When the priest washes his hands, he cleanses them, in respect to what is going to transpire on the Altar of Sacrifice. Those hands are about to touch the Lord Himself through His Sacrifice.

The Preface

After the priest has offered the gifts up to the Lord, we join him as he pleads with Our Lord to accept this sacrifice at his hands. The priest turns to us, asking the Lord to be with us. We respond that we pray that Our Lord is also with him.

Then he asks us to lift up our hearts. At this moment, if we see with the eyes of the heart, we see our Lord being raised up, on the Cross. Lord, we lift up our hearts to You. We love You. Again, we are called to give thanks. But are these only words? Do we realize *why* we are thanking Him? We agree it is right and just. Somehow, as we hear these words, they sound so inadequate. Lord, how do we give You thanks for what You are about to do for us, and for what You did for us? Are we at the Last Supper? Is Jesus telling us He is about to give His Life up for us?

Holy, Holy, Holy

For us, personally, there is sorrow mixed with joy, as we join our voices with the Angels in Heaven who are at the same time offering praise and glory to the Lord. Suddenly, we are transported to the Holy Land, to Jerusalem and the *Garden of Gethsemane.* Our eyes travel to the Golden Gates across from the rock where Jesus sweat Blood and Tears over the sins of the world. It was through those same gates that the people hailed Jesus as their king, when He entered triumphantly the Sunday before. Come with us into the Garden of Agony and listen to Jesus' thoughts. Was he thinking: *Just four days ago, they wanted to make Me King, and now they want to kill Me?* Are we part of those who had greeted Him on Palm Sunday with the words that we now repeat: *"Hosanna in the highest. Blessed is He Who comes in the name of the Lord?"* Did we want to make Him King and then desert Him in the Garden of Gethsemane when the going got rough? Do we go along with the crowd, not wanting to make waves, wanting to be one of the guys, accommodating the majority, just as many did, the night Our Lord suffered the Agony in the Garden? This is what we see during the Holy, Holy, Holy. What do you see?

The Eucharistic Prayer

You can feel an excitement building. Jesus is coming in His Eucharist. We will become one with Him! It will no longer be we who live but Jesus Who lives in us. We will be changed! Our Pope[7] calls the Sacrament of the Eucharist *"the Source and Summit of all life."* He states that in the Eucharist is *"contained the whole spiritual good of the Church, namely Christ Himself."*[8]

Through this ongoing Sacrifice, Jesus, in company with His priests, is offering Himself on this Altar on *earth* to His Father; and at the same time, in *Heaven*, on the Heavenly Altar, to His Father. If you could look beyond the veil between Heaven and earth, you might see Jesus offering Himself to the Father seated on the Throne, surrounded by the Angels and their Queen Mother Mary, the Saints and the Martyrs. You can hear the Angels singing their praises to Him. Kneeling before the Holy Trinity, are the Martyrs, their robes snow white, cleansed by the Blood of the Lamb and their blood. Mother Mary occupies the same place,

---

[7]Catechism of the Catholic Church
[8]Catechism of the Catholic Church

she had when He was on the Cross, beneath her Son. This whole Heavenly Family - Mother Mary and her Angels, and I'll bet St. Joseph, the Saints and the Martyrs are worshiping the Beatific Vision of God, as we will worship Him on the Altar momentarily. The priest places his hands[9] over the bread and wine and summons the Holy Spirit to descend upon the Altar and make the gifts (the bread and wine) holy, so that they may become the Body and Blood of Our Lord Jesus Christ, and through Him, the Perfect Sacrifice, acceptable to God the Father. The Angels who were created superior to man cannot call down the Holy Spirit. But the priest, through the Sacrament of Holy Orders, can and the Holy Spirit comes. St. John Chrysostom said that when the Holy Spirit descends upon the Altar, He is accompanied by thousands of Angels. [That's why we need such large Altars.] He would call out: *"Get away from the Altar; leave room for the Angels."*

St. Joseph Carfasso said: *"If the Angels could receive Communion only once, they would spend the rest of eternity thanking God for that privilege."*

In the Old Covenant when the priest, who sacrificed the lamb that was soon to lose its life to immolation, spread his hands over the victim, he was signifying by this action that he was offering his own life to God, as well. As our priest spreads his hands over the host and the chalice, it is with the same spirit of sacrifice that he is called to offer himself to God the Father.

The priest, in memory of the Passion of Jesus Christ, relates what the Lord did and said, on the night before He died on the Cross. In obedience to the Lord, the priest repeats the words of Consecration, the words uttered by Jesus Christ Himself at the Last Supper.[10] [It is imperative that the priest use Jesus' words and not his own for the consecration of the host and wine into the Body, Blood, Soul and Divinity of Jesus Christ.]

---

[9]*"When you see a priest celebrating Mass, imagine that his hands are the invisible Hands of Jesus raised to Heaven."* St. John Chrysostom

[10]St. Ambrose says that the priest does not use his own words, but those of Jesus Christ.

The day before He suffered
He took bread in His sacred Hands
and looking up to Heaven,
to You, His almighty Father,
He gave You thanks and praise.
He broke the bread,
gave it to his disciples, and said:

Take this, all of you, and eat it:
this is My Body which will be given up for you.

When the supper was ended,
He took the cup.
Again He gave You thanks and praise,
gave the cup to His disciples and said:

Take this, all of you, and drink from it:
this is the cup of My Blood,
the blood of the new and everlasting covenant.
It will be shed for you and for all,
so that sins may be forgiven.
Do this in memory of Me.[11]

This being completed, the priest elevates the Host and then the Chalice, and Jesus becomes present on the Altar. The host and the chalice of wine have turned into the Body, Blood, Soul and Divinity of Jesus Christ. When the priest repeats Jesus' words: *"This is the cup of My Blood, the Blood of the New and Everlasting Covenant,"* no longer is this a figure or symbol of Jesus Christ, as it was in the Old Covenant, but the real and true Blood of Jesus that we will now receive. At this moment, does the hymn *"Lift high the Cross"* come into your heart? Jesus said: *"and I, when I am lifted up from the earth, will draw all*

---

[11]Sunday Missal Service - Quincy, Illinois

men to Myself."[12] Our Lord has been lifted up on His Cross, and with the good thief, we will be with Him one day, in His Father's House.

At this point "*the power of the words and the action of Christ, and the power of the Holy Spirit, make sacramentally present under the appearances of bread and wine,*[13] *Christ's Body and Blood, His Sacrifice offered on the Cross once for all.*"[14] The bread and wine have changed into the Body, Blood, Soul and Divinity of Our Lord Jesus Christ; "*the Church calls to mind the Passion, Resurrection, and Glorious return of Christ Jesus; She presents to the Father the offering of His Son which reconciles us with Him.*"[15]

"If they only understood what the Eucharist is, souls would run to the Altar rail faster than the thirsting deer run to a fountain."[16]

Now, believing that Our Lord has died and has risen from the dead in this re-presentation *(making present)*[17] of the Sacrifice of the Cross, we proclaim the Mystery of Faith. We proclaim His death and Resurrection as we pray:

Christ has died,
Christ is risen,
Christ will come again.

---

[12] John 12:32

[13] The bread and wine cease to be. Only the appearance of bread and wine remain, for they have substantially changed into the Body, Blood, Soul and Divinity of Christ.

[14] Catechism of the Catholic Church-p.341 (1353)

[15] Catechism of the Catholic Church-p.341 (1354)

[16] Curé of Ars

[17] The Eucharist is thus a sacrifice because it re-presents (makes present) the Sacrifice of the Cross, because it is its *memorial* and because it *applies* its fruit. Catechism of the Catholic Church-p.344 (1366)

or
Dying You destroyed our death,
rising You restored our life.
Lord Jesus, come in glory.

or
When we eat this Bread and drink this cup,
we proclaim your death, Lord Jesus
until You come in glory.

or
Lord by Your death and resurrection
You have set us free.
You are the Savior of the world.

Have these become just words? Read them over and over again. At Mass, *listen* to the words, the priest says. These words are the Light at the end of the dark tunnel that life can be at times. This is our hope! We are saved. We will rise again. This is not all there is! We will see Jesus Face to face, one day.

The priest then prays **the second part of the Eucharistic prayer**, asking that the Father accept the sacrifice being offered by His Church, thus including us in the offering. He asks God that we might *"share in the inheritance of the Saints, with Mary, the Virgin Mother of God, the Apostles, the Martyrs, Saint* (he names the name of a Saint) *and all Your Saints, on whose constant intercession we rely for help."* He then prays *"for the world, for the Church on earth, our Pope, our bishop, and all the bishops along with the clergy and the entire people* (that's us) *that Your Son has gained for You."* He presents our prayers, pleading with the Father to unite all His children wherever they might be. He then asks the Father to welcome those who have died, into Heaven, that they might enjoy His Beatific Vision, along with Mother Mary, all the Saints and Angels. At this point, we pray for our dead and for all those in Purgatory who have no one to pray for them.

Do you mention those who have gone before you, praying that they might be in Heaven? Do you think that it has value?

Let us tell you briefly about St. Teresa of Avila.

"A young man came to St.Teresa and offered her a house, if she would start a Foundation in Valladolid. She gave him a reluctant yes. Two months later, the young man suddenly contracted an illness, and died. The Lord came to Teresa and said that He had mercy on him because of the house he had given to Teresa which would do honor to His Mother through the Carmelite Order. But the Lord said the young man would not leave Purgatory until the first Mass was celebrated in that house. Teresa was so conscious of the terrible sufferings of that soul, she plunged into the founding of a foundation in Valladolid.

"She left Malagón on the 19th of May, 1568, for Valladolid. The Lord came to Teresa in a dream, 'While I was praying one day, He told me to hurry: that the soul (of Don Bernardino) was suffering a lot. '[18]
*The house, Don Bernardino left them in Valladolid, was a disaster! Nuns could not possibly live here! Teresa hurriedly went about making the necessary adjustments for them to move in. The Lord was in a hurry, so who do you think just **happened** to visit them, but the Vicar General of the City. He issued the order for them to celebrate Mass immediately. It was the Feast of the Assumption. As Father Julian approached Teresa with Communion, she had a Vision of a young man beside the Priest. It was Don Bernardino; his face was illuminated, radiating joy. He thanked her for her "yes" that the Lord used to free him from Purgatory and welcome him into Heaven."[19]*

---

[18]Foundations, 10,3

[19]Read more about St.Teresa of Avila in Bob and Penny Lord's book: *"Saints and other Powerful Women in the Church"*

The Doxology of the Mass

Having asked for God's mercy, and believing it has been granted, the priest speaks of our *new* Home, and our eternal time with God the Father, Christ the Son and the Holy Spirit *"where we shall sing of His glory"*. Then our priest raises the Paten and the Chalice, no longer containing bread and wine but now the Body, Blood, Soul and Divinity, *high*, and we hear proclaimed our belief in the Triune God.[20] We began the Mass with the Holy Trinity, saying the *Lesser Doxology*; now having reached the Summit of the Mass, we encounter our God in the Holy Trinity, as the priest (*alone*)[21] proclaims the *Great Doxology*:

> *Through Him,*[22]
> *with Him,*[23]
> *in Him,*[24]
> *in the unity of the Holy Spirit,*
> *all glory and honor is Yours,*
> *almighty Father,*
> *for ever and ever.*

All the favors that we have asked, in the second part of the Eucharistic Prayer, were asked **through** the merits of our Lord Jesus, **with Him**, our Savior Jesus, and **in Him**, as He has been offering Himself to the Father for the redemption of the sins of the world, **in union with** *the Holy Spirit* Who descended from Heaven making holy the bread and wine, that it would become the Body, Blood, Soul and Divinity of Our Lord Jesus, the acceptable Sacrifice, *to God the Father Almighty*.

Acknowledging our agreement with the Sacrifice, we now exclaim the *Great Amen!, We believe!*

---

[20]Passed down to us, through the centuries, beginning with the Early Church Fathers. Attacks on The Holy Trinity began and were put down by Councils, from the Second Century on.

[21]Only the priest is allowed to say the Doxology. This is part of the Eucharistic Prayer and as such is reserved only for the priest.

[22]Jesus Christ

[23]Jesus Christ

[24]Jesus Christ

†

One of the arguments used against the Catholic Church, that sadly some of our priests contribute to, by not truly explaining the reason why not everyone may receive Holy Communion is: *Why, if the precious Blood of Jesus is sufficient to save all men, can we not receive?* The explanation given by St. Thomas Aquinas is that it saves only those who cooperate with grace.[25] And St. Paul says that anyone who receives unworthily suffers condemnation upon himself. This would include those who do not believe that Jesus is truly present in the Holy Eucharist *and* those in a state of sin. From the Host, Jesus, with infinite sadness, asks him who would commit sacrilege: *"Dost thou betray the Son of Man with a kiss?"*[26]

It is not sufficient to believe that Jesus is truly present to receive the Eucharist. We have to be in *communion* with the entire body of the Church, professing we believe and will follow *all* the Tenets[27] of the Roman Catholic Church, in obedience to the Chair of Peter His Holiness the Pope and the Magisterium.

The Lord's Prayer

What are we really saying when we pray the perfect prayer Our Lord Jesus taught us? Do we believe? Do we agree with the commitment we are making, as we intone these words that Christians, before us, have proclaimed for nearly 2000 years?

In our book *"We Came Back to Jesus,"* our first chapter is entitled *"The Day The World Stopped."* And that's what happened that dark day when the sun stopped shining for us and our family. October 23, 1971, our beloved son Richard died of an overdose of drugs. When I discovered the time he died, I remembered that was when I had been praying to our Lord, turning him over to Him.

---

[25] The Holy Eucharist by St. Alphonsus De Liguori-pg.44
[26]Luke 22:48
[27]beliefs, dogmas, doctrines

When we became aware that Richard was on drugs, we not only prayed night and day for our son, we pleaded with everyone we met to pray for him. I met a woman at a baby shower and she said:

"Every time he tries to make a decision, your worries stop him. From now on, when you start to worry, place the Face of Jesus over the face of your son, and say, 'He is Yours, Lord'.

"Oh, in the weeks ahead, I tried, how I tried, a thousand, two thousand, ten thousand times a day, I tried. I would see the Face of Jesus, and the face of Richard, but they were far apart, and I couldn't bring them together. I prayed over and over again,

"Oh, Jesus, he's Yours. You gave me the most precious son in the world. I don't know how to take care of him. I can't help him. You take care of him. Take him; he's Yours.

"It was five minutes after midnight, five minutes into a new day, October 23, 1971. My boy would be 20 years old in one month and seventeen days. The phone rang. It was Leo, our son-in-law. 'Richard just called,' he excitedly told my husband. 'He was crying. He said to tell you he was ready to come home. He gave me his address, and asked that you pick him up tomorrow. He also said to tell you he loves you Dad, Mama, his sister, the baby (our Grandson, Robby), and that he didn't take drugs because of you. It was something he was compelled to do. It was all his fault.'

"'What did he say,' I was almost shouting. 'Let's go and get him right now, tonight.' I was pleading, barely able to sit still, desperate.

"Bob replied, 'Come on, Penny. He's a young man. We have to stop treating him like a baby. He's ready to come home. He asked us to wait until tomorrow. If he wanted us to pick him up tonight, he'd have said so.

We have to respect his wishes.'

"I cannot explain the fear that overtook me. My heart was pounding in my chest. I felt like it was pumping out of my mouth. I was in a state of panic. I started to pray, as if my life depended on it, not knowing how much it did.

"As if he could hear my very thoughts, Bob said, 'I don't know what's wrong with you! You should be happy. Our son's coming home.'

"I couldn't put my fear into words, but it was there. It was so real! I saw the Face of Jesus, and the face of Richard. I must have been praying for at least an hour. It seemed like an eternity. I kept repeating, 'He's Yours, Lord. I've failed. You take care of him. He's Yours.'

"Slowly, the sad Face of our crucified Lord, His crown of thorns bleeding, His Face covered with sweat and wounds, came towards Richard's face, and covered my son's face, until all I saw was the Face of Jesus. My son was dead!"[28]

After three years of living hell, separated from Our Lord and His Church, He called us back home. But only Bob really returned. I held out until, through the tireless prodding and pushing of a loving, persistent couple, we went on a *Marriage Encounter* weekend. After a weekend of crying and laughing, Sunday night came and there was the final Mass of the weekend. Here is an excerpt from our book on what happened.

"....Sunday night came, and we renewed our Marriage Vows. We were asked to face each other, and say to one another, Our Lord's Perfect Prayer, the prayer I swore I would never say again, once I realized the ramifications of the prayer. 'Your Will be done...' Was I ready for that? After all, hadn't it been His Will that

---

[28]From chapter entitled "The Day the World Stopped" - Bob and Penny Lord's book *"We Came Back to Jesus"*

my son die! Would I give Him that much trust? I knew that what He wanted for me had always been best; but I still have a problem with that much surrender because I don't know how much I can handle. '....Give Us This Day our Daily Bread....' It's all up to you, give or take as You please. Was I asking the Lord for the gift to be secure enough in Him that I could be insecure in the world? '...and forgive us our trespasses as we forgive those...' Am I ready to forgive those who turned my son and the hundreds of thousands, no, millions of sons and daughters, on to drugs and death? We said to Him and to one another, this prayer of total surrender; and have been trying to live it ever since, falling seven times and getting up eight.

"There's a new world somewhere, they call the Promised Land...."[29]

What I didn't know that weekend was that there is a *new world called the Promised Land* here on earth in our Church, and through her, in the *New World*, the *Promised Land* of Eternal Life - Heaven. I thought I had given up control to Bob, but Jesus was the One Who took over in both our lives, making us one with Him, really proclaiming with these words the words He gave to Blessed Sister Faustina: *"Jesus, I trust in You."*

What do you think about, as you say the Perfect Prayer, The Lord's Prayer, that *"we dare to say because the Lord Jesus Himself commanded us"* to do so? Do you hold Our Father holy, above all the false gods who seduce us in our everyday lives? Do you desire with all your heart His Kingdom on earth as it is in Heaven? Are you giving Him permission to take over in your life as you say: *"Thy will be done"*? Do we agree to accept His forgiveness to the degree we forgive others? Jesus plainly is directing us to forgive one another, making it a condition, as He says:

---

[29]From chapter entitled "There's a new world somewhere" - Bob and Penny Lord's book *"We Came Back to Jesus"*

"For if you forgive men their trespasses, your heavenly Father also will forgive you; but if you do not forgive men their trespasses, neither will your Father forgive your trespasses." [30]

Sign of Peace

Our priest first asks Jesus not to look upon our sins, but to grant us the Peace that He promised to the Apostles when He said: *"Peace I leave with you; My Peace I give to you; not as the world gives do I give to you. Let not your hearts be troubled, neither let them be afraid."* [31] We join him in asking for Our Lord's Peace with our proclamation *Amen.*

St. Anthony in a Homily on Christ as our peace said: *"The Resurrection of Christ is the source of lasting peace. His place should always be in the center of our hearts.*

"Jesus came and stood in the middle of them. 'Peace be with you', He said. When He had said this, He showed them His Hands and His Side. At the sight of the Lord, the disciples rejoiced. 'Peace be with you', He said again." [32]

"In this Gospel passage, Jesus offers a threefold peace; first between God and man, by restoring man to friendship with God the Father through His Passion and death; second between man and the Angels, by assuming human nature and elevating it above the Angels; third, between man and man, by uniting them within Himself like a cornerstone.

"The Latin word for peace is 'Pax,' a three letter word which symbolizes the Triune and one God (the Holy Trinity). The first letter 'P' stands for Pater, the 'Father'; the 'a', the first letter of the alphabet stands for the first born, the Son of God; the 'x,' a consonant made up of two sounds 'k' and 's,' stands for the Holy

---

[30]Matt 6:14-15
[31]John 14:27
[32]John 20:19-21

Spirit, proceeding from both the Father and the Son."[33]

Early documents of the Church speak of the priest kissing the Altar before he exchanges peace with each and everyone of us, knowing that he can only offer the peace he receives from Jesus. Having received the peace that the priest in the Person of Christ has offered to us, and now free from the slavery that division brings about, we are able to offer him peace.

This having been completed, the priest asks us to exchange the Sign of Peace with our neighbor. Before we receive the Holy Eucharist, we need to be at peace with one another. The Lord tells us in Holy Scripture:

"....if you are offering your gift at the Altar , and there remember that your brother has something against you, leave your gift there before the Altar and go; first be reconciled to your brother and then come and offer your gift."[34]

With this in mind, when we offer Peace to our neighbor, at this time in the Mass, we in essence are forgiving not only our neighbor, but forgiving *anyone,* against whom we may have a grievance.

"If you do not forgive men, neither will your heavenly Father forgive you."[35]

Pope Pius XII spoke with deep concern over the state of the family, at that time. Dear Pope, I wonder what you would say about today? Would you cry, dear Pope Pius as our beloved Pope John Paul II does?

"In so many families, Jesus is scourged by quarrels and crucified by hatred."[36]

---

[33]St. Anthony's Sermons - *"Seek First His Kingdom"*
[34]Matt 5:23-24
[35]Matt. 6:14
[36]Pope Pius XII

The Breaking of the Bread

The priest breaks the consecrated Host in two halves and from one half breaks off a small Piece.[37] He then drops the Fragment[38] into the Chalice. This is a sign of Christ's unity with the Church, His Mystical body.[39] This Rite has been called by different titles. It is not only known as the Breaking of the Bread but has also been called the *Commingling* or *Commixture, Refraction rite.*[40]

In Rome, in the Early Church, the original function of the *Commingling* was to show *unity* between the Pope and his priests. When priests, from the churches in Rome, could not attend the Papal Mass, the Pope would send a Particle of the consecrated Host to them. Then the priests at their own parishes dropped the Particle into the Chalice, symbolizing their oneness with the Pope.

It would also appear that this part of the Rite was *originally* initiated to demonstrate graphically the *union* between the Body (under the appearance of bread) and the Blood (under the appearance of wine) of Our Lord Jesus Christ. Although the Host *appears* to represent solely the Body of Jesus, it has always been *completely* the *Body and Blood* of Our Lord Jesus, as has been the Blood in the Chalice been totally the Body and Blood of Our Lord Jesus. Therefore, when we receive the Host, we are receiving the complete Jesus, in His Body, Blood, Soul and Divinity, as when we receive solely from the Chalice, we are receiving the Body, Blood, Soul and Divinity of Our Lord Jesus Christ. At this point in the Mass, Mother Church is demonstrating *definitively*

---

[37]In the Tridentine Mass, the Priest would make the Sign of the Cross three times over the chalice, with the small portion of the Host, before dropping It into the Chalice. This was to indicate the three days that Jesus was in the tomb. But is not part of the *Novis Ordo.*

[38]St. Thomas Aquinas said that the smallest Particle of Host is the complete Body, Blood Soul and Divinity of Our Lord Jesus Christ. - *"Scandal of the Cross and Its Triumph"* by Bob and Penny Lord

[39]New Catholic Encyclopedia-Catholic University of America

[40]New Catholic Encyclopedia-Catholic University of America and *The Mass* by Father Guy Oury

this truth that has come down through the ages that when we receive under either one of the Holy Species, we are receiving *fully* the Lord in His Body, Blood, Soul and Divinity.

When the priest drops the Particle of the Host into the Chalice, it is in keeping with one explanation of what occurs during the *Commingling* of the Host and the Blood. The united *(Commingled)* Host and Blood in the Chalice symbolizes the *Resurrection*. When the host and the wine in the Chalice are consecrated separately, this represents the *death* of Our Lord Jesus, where His Body and Blood were separated. The uniting of the two Holy Species, the Host and the Blood in the Chalice, signify the return of life *in its bodily*[41] *Form* to Jesus at the moment of His Resurrection.

At this point in the Mass, the wait is over. The Sacrifice of the Cross is complete. Mary Magdalene, and Mary mother of James, and Salome[42] have been to the tomb and the Angel has told them that the Lord was not there; He has risen. He told them to go and announce to the disciples that He has risen. We have walked with Mother Mary, the other women and St. John, and stood beneath the Cross beside His Mother. We have gone to the tomb and Our Lord is not there; He has risen!

As the priest is breaking the Host, we all turn to the Lamb of God, Who takes away the sins of the world, through His Mercy. And then, knowing that He alone can grant us Peace, the only Peace that lasts, we ask Him for that Peace:

Lamb of God, You take away the sins of the world;
  have mercy on us.
Lamb of God, You take away the sins of the world;
  have mercy on us.
Lamb of God, You take away the sins of the world;
  grant us peace.

Suddenly we feel a wave of Serenity that words cannot describe. He is there! We are about to receive *Him*!

---

[41] *The Mass* by Father Guy Oury
[42] Mark 16:1

Holy Communion

Our priest prays silently, and invites us to do so.

What a time! Our Lord is present, and He is attentively awaiting our acknowledgement of His presence. He cares for us. He wants us to involve Him in our lives. *Mother Mary told St. Catherine Labouré that the Lord has many graces to pour through her hands, but no one asks for them.*[43] As we prepare to receive Him, why do we not bring up our petitions and lay them at His Feet? As we approach Him at the Altar, let us present our cares, our hopes and disappointments, our families, our loved ones to Our Lord the Healer Who has not stopped healing, to Our God of Mercy Who is still forgiving sins, to the Lamb of God Who is still interceding for us with His Father.

Our priest holds up the Lord in His Body, Blood, Soul and Divinity - the Eucharist:

This is the Lamb of God
Who takes away the sins of the world.
Happy are those who are called to His supper.

✝

"As He (Jesus) *entered Capernaum, a centurion came forward to Him, beseeching Him and saying, 'Lord, my servant is lying paralyzed at home, in terrible distress.' And He* (Jesus) *said 'I will come and heal him.' but the centurion said: 'Lord, I am not worthy to have you come under my roof; but only say the word and my servant will be healed.'"*[44]

Do we respond, as the centurion before us, believing? The centurion believed, and he did not have two thousand years of Saints and Martyrs who lived and died for that belief. What is in our heart and mind as we proclaim:

"Lord, I am not worthy to receive You,
but only say the word and I shall be healed?"

---

[43]an excerpt from the chapter: The Miraculous Medal - from the book "*Many Faces of Mary*" by Bob and Penny Lord
[44]Matt 8:8

One by one, the Faithful process up to the Altar to receive Our Lord. Some receive humbly on their tongues,[45] others form a royal throne to receive their King, their left hand on top and their right hand on the bottom, so that having received on the left hand, they can then place the Host reverently in their mouths with their right hand. And then, there are those who receive, as if they are receiving at best a piece of bread, and at worst a gum drop, as they irreverently pop Our Lord into their mouths. There are those who carry the Host away from the Altar. This is forbidden by the Church. You are to consume the Host at the Altar, not back at your pew. Do we believe, we are really receiving Jesus? If we don't believe, and we do receive, we invite condemnation upon ourselves.[46]

As you approach the priest at the Altar, what are you thinking? As he raises the Host and says to you: *"The Body of Christ,"* what does our priest see in your eyes? Remember, on the day of his ordination, our priest offered to the Father the gift, we have, of bringing new life into the world through offspring. But Our Lord will not be outdone in generosity. On the day of his ordination, as our priest was offering to the Father the gift of procreation,[47] God was by His power bestowing upon him the gift of passing on the Key to *our salvation.*[48] Through our priest's anointed hands, Jesus appears on the Altar; we through the reception of Holy Communion, at his hands, receive eternal life! *" ..he who eats My Flesh and drinks My Blood has eternal life, and I will raise him up on the last day. "*[49] Does our priest know

---

[45]Some of the faithful receive on the tongue for many reasons; as an act of humility, some believe as St. Thomas wrote that "only consecrated hands should touch the consecrated Host Who is Our Lord."

[46]1 Cor. 11:27-29

[47]siring children

[48] *"Ordination, the sacramental act which integrates a man into the order of bishops, presbyters, or deacons ...it confers a gift of the Holy Spirit that permits the exercise of a 'sacred power' which can come from Christ himself through His Church."* Catechism of the Catholic Church p.384 (1538)

[49]John 6:54 Revised Standard Version of the Catholic Bible

this, or have we, by our apathy, taken this from him? It is hard to hold on to your beliefs, when you are all alone. It is the Way of the Cross.

Prayer after Communion

The Hosts that have not been received, are placed in the Tabernacle. We all sit, as our priest sits, and pray silently. Our Lord is in us. We are one with Him. His grace is ours for the taking. He holds out His grace. We can take it or leave it. He asks us only to participate in openness to His Love. St. Augustine said that we do not consume the Lord; He consumes us. Through the reception of the Eucharist, we have become one with the Lord. As St. Paul said we no longer live but Jesus lives in us.[50] Change has come about. We are a new creation! It is time to give thanks. We have been forgiven; we have received the King of the world; it is a new day for us. We now have that which we can take with us, His Love! All else is passing away.

Concluding Rite

We all stand, as our priest says: *"The Lord be with you."* We respond, as we did earlier in the Mass: *"And also with you."*

And then, our priest, who has been given authority to bless us in His Name, blesses us, making the Sign of the Cross. And as we join him, and make the Sign of the Cross, do we now know what just happened? Do we understand what this sign means; the cost to our Lord, and through Him, the gift to us?

---

[50]Gal 2:20

The Dismissal

Our priest closes with either:

"Go in the Peace of Christ." or

"The Mass is ended, go in peace." or

"Go in Peace to love and serve the Lord."

Well, brothers and sisters in Christ, we have learned more about Our Lord, through His Word; we have entered into relationship with Him in a truly personal way, through His Eucharist. He has given us Himself. Do we love Him? If so, we can do no less than serve Him! How? Do we believe that Jesus is truly present in His Word and in His Eucharist, and that we become one with Him, at Mass? Do you believe that Jesus is alive and He is in our Church? When was the last time you invited someone to come to your church, saying: *"Jesus will be in my church. Would you like to meet Him?"*

Do we believe? If we do, then we have an obligation to share the best kept secret in the world with all our brothers and sisters. Are we afraid of persecution, of losing our friends and maybe our families? Jesus, before us at Capernaum, lost most of His followers when He made that statement of truth that was to lead Him to the Way of the Cross. He knew the consequences of His words, but He did not back down. He knew they would leave. He even asked the twelve who remained, if they would leave Him, too. He would not compromise, even though it meant losing all whom He had been teaching and healing, all He had come to save. Being God, He could not lie. He had to tell them the whole truth, even to death on that Cross.

Do we believe? Do we cry out, with the Mexican Martyrs, who held up a cross and a rosary and proclaimed: *"Long Live Christ the King?"* They died because they believed. Jesus died that we might believe. Do we believe?

Epilogue
The Age of the Eucharist

Do you think it possible that Our Lord Jesus was giving us a preview of the Age of the Eucharist over ***thirty years ago***? Penny had an image appear before her eyes. She shot up from the couch. She hadn't been sleeping, or we would have thought she were dreaming. It was so distinct; she could make out the details. She couldn't stop talking about it.

"You will never believe what I just saw! I saw Jesus on top of a mountain. His arms were outstretched; He was hovering over the earth, as if protecting it; The sky was dark blue, almost black, but where He stood, there was a light, an aura emanating from Him; He was bleeding and the blood was flowing from His Head and Hands, spilling down the mountain, nourishing the ground, changing it from dry dead earth to rich green land with roses covering most of the mountainside." I started to make fun of Penny. I made that eerie sound from the *"Twilight Zone"* music playfully, but I could see that something had really touched her.

Now at this time, we were Sunday go-to-church Catholics. Penny knew very little about the Faith. Her knowledge was based on a once-a-week CCD preparation, for *one* year, to receive First Holy Communion and Confirmation, and that was it. She was in love with Jesus, and I didn't want her to get too heady and lose the innocent love and trust she had for Jesus. What she lacked in *head knowledge,* she more than made up for it with *heart knowledge.*

The next day, Penny had a hard time trying to get the picture out of her mind. At dinner, she shared with our two children what she had seen. Our son Richard said, *"Let's go, Mama, and buy a canvas and some paints."* The store owner soon knew Penny had no training because as he would bring out canvases, she would say, *"no....big - no....bigger than that."* The owner of the store asked if she had any idea how she intended to fill the canvas. She knew exactly what she was going to put into the painting. And so they ordered canvas and some tubes of red, yellow, etc. etc., and only one brush! That night, she stayed up until after midnight, sketching the entire picture, calling out *"Oh, there's His Knee; there's His Chest and Its collapsed; He's looking over the earth."* It was as if she were not sketching the canvas; it was unfolding before her, and she were an observer. It went on and on like that, until the entire sketch came to life on the huge canvas. The painting took more than a year to complete. All that time, Penny would not allow anyone to see it, but us.

One day, near completion, our young Jewish neighbor Bruce, our son's friend, knocked on the door. *"Mrs. Lord,"* he asked, *"may I see the painting?"* We lived in an all Jewish neighborhood, and somehow it had gotten out about the painting. You can just imagine the speculation and curiosity that was circulating around the neighborhood. Penny let Bruce in. Now, not even Penny had any idea what the Lord was saying through the painting. Bruce stared deeply at the painting for a long time. *"Why did they kill Jesus? I think the painting is saying that Jesus had to die, so that Love would spread over all the earth."*

Penny had seen the entire picture in her mind, except the bottom; it was hazy. She turned to us, her intimate family and asked, if we believed Jesus' Love had spread over all the earth. At that time, not even suspecting the hell we would be experiencing and the path of destruction and culture of death, the world would enter into, our family decided *"No, His Love has not reached the four corners of the earth. That dry brown crusty part of the painting is the section where the earth is parched."*

Now this happened over thirty years ago, and the painting has remained in a prominent place on our wall from that time till now, even through our period away from Jesus and his Church. We would look at it whenever someone came into the house to ask about the unsigned painting. We would at that time, tell them what Bruce had said.

The painting has become part of our family; but we haven't paid much attention to it for the past year or so. We had been speculating, the last few days, what to write in this epilog, what the Lord may want you to remember. This morning, on the way to Church, the painting flashed before Penny again. Penny received a word: *This is what the painting means! It is the foretelling of the coming Age, The Age of the Eucharist! The Blood that is pouring from My Hands and Head is My Body and Blood in the Eucharist.*

"And He took bread, and when He had given thanks He broke it and gave it to them, saying, 'This is My Body which is given for you. Do this in remembrance of me.' And likewise

the cup after supper, saying, 'This cup which is poured out for you is the new Covenant in My Blood." (Luke 22:19)

We felt as if Our Lord Jesus was saying to us, *Thirty years ago, I gave you the message, and although you didn't understand, you said yes. Then when tragedy struck, you left Me and My Church. But when I called you back, three years later, I revealed My Presence on the Altar to you, and you fell in love with Me. This painting reveals that there will be one flock with one shepherd in the Third Millennium, and I, through the Eucharist, will unite all My children, so that the splinters of the Cross will be no more.*

"The blessing cup that we bless is a Communion with the Blood of Christ, and the bread that we break is a Communion with the Body of Christ." *(1 Cor 10:15-18)*   The fact there is only one loaf means that, though there are many of us, we form a single body because we share in this one loaf. He was saying, we will be one body, one Church with Him, in Him, and through Him! The tower of Babel that has existed will be no more. It will be the Age of the ongoing Sacrifice of the Cross, the Sacrifice of the Mass, our beloved Jesus offering Himself as Victim to the Father, as He did on the Cross for us! Suddenly, we understood why the brutal war is being waged against our beloved Church. Satan knows that the Lord is ushering in a new time, a truly new age. Not only will we know Him truly Present to us on the Altar, in the Monstrance and in the Tabernacle, the world will know Him! *"Then, the wolf will be the guest of the lamb, and the leopard shall lie down with the kid. The calf and young lion shall browse together, with a little child to guide them."* (Isaiah 11:6) **Peace will reign over all the world.**

See and believe! Your God comes to you, during the Mass!

Bibliography

Broderick, Robert, - *The Catholic Encyclopedia*
   Thomas A. Nelson, New York 1976
Butler, Thurston & Atwater - *Lives of the Saints*
   Complete edition in 4 volumes Christian Classics
   Westminster, Maryland, 1980
Catechism of the Catholic Church - Libreria Editrice Vaticana 1994
Collected Letters of St. Thérèse of Lisieux
   Sheed & Ward - London 1949
De Cesaris - *Il Miracolo Eucaristico di Alatri,* Alatri 1927
Dempsey, Martin Fr.- *Champion of the Blessed Sacrament*
   Eymard League, New York 1963
Giannini, Antonio OFM - *L'Italia dei Prodigi Eucaristici*
   Il Tesoro Eucaristico di Siena 1992
Ladame Jean & Duvin Richard - *Prodiges Eucharistiques*
   Editions France Empire - Paris - 1981
Laurenti P. - *Le Meraviglie del SS. Sacramento* 1898
Liguori, Alphonsus St. - *The Holy Eucharist*
   Redemptorist Fathers, Brooklyn 1934
Lord, Bob & Penny
   This Is My Body, This Is My Blood, Miracles of the Eucharist 1986
   Saints and Other Powerful Women in the Church 1989
   Scandal of the Cross and Its Triumph 1992
   Martyrs, They Died for Christ 1993
Martin, Thérèse St. - *Autobiography of a Soul*
   William Collins & Sons - Glasgow 1958
Missionari del Preziosissimo Sangue -
   Guida della Basilica di S. Maria in Vado, Ferrara 1971
New Catholic Encyclopedia
   Catholic University - Washington DC 1967
O'Carroll, Michael - *Corpus Christi*
   Michael Glazier, Wilmington DE 1988
Piccini U. - *Il Tesoro Eucaristico* - Siena 1978
Santuario Eucaristico Diocesano (a cura)
   Il Miracolo Eucaristico di S. Pietro a Patierno - Naples 1974
Spaccucci F - Curgi G. - *La Storia del 'Ostia Miracolosa di Trani*
   Laurenziana, Naples 1989
Sutto F. - *La Sacra Tovaglia da Valvasone*
   Il Tesoro Eucaristico - Siena 1979

Index

Journeys of Faith®

To Order: 1-800-633-2484

Books

Bob and Penny Lord are authors of best sellers:

This Is My Body, This Is My Blood;
  Miracles of the Eucharist Book I $8.95 Paperback only
This Is My Body, This Is My Blood;
  Miracles of the Eucharist Book II $12.95 Paperback only
The Many Faces Of Mary, A Love Story $8.95 Paperback $12.95 Hardcover
  We Came Back To Jesus $8.95 Paperback $12.95 Hardcover
Saints and Other Powerful Women in the Church $12.95 Paperback only
Saints and Other Powerful Men in the Church $14.95 Paperback only
Heavenly Army of Angels $12.95 Paperback only
Scandal of the Cross and Its Triumph $12.95 Paperback only
The Rosary - The Life of Jesus and Mary $12.95 Hardcover only
Martyrs - They Died for Christ $12.95 Paperback only
Visionaries, Mystics, and Stigmatists $12.95 Paperback only

Please add $3.00 S&H for first book: $1.00 each add'l book

Videos and On-site Documentaries

Bob and Penny's Video Series based on their books:
A 13 part series on the Miracles of the Eucharist - filmed on-site
A 9 part Eucharistic Retreat series with Father Harold Cohen
A 15 part series on The Many Faces of Mary - filmed on-site
A 20 part series on Martyrs - They Died for Christ - filmed on-site
A 10 part series on Saints and Other Powerful Women in the Church
A 12 part series on Saints and Other Powerful Men in the Church
A 14 part series on Visionaries, Mystics and Stigmatists
Many other on-site Documentaries based on Miracles of the Eucharist, Mother Mary's Apparitions, and the Heavenly Army of Angels. Request our list.

Our books and videos are available in Spanish also

Pilgrimages

Bob and Penny Lord's ministry take out Pilgrimages to the Shrines of Europe, the Holy Land, and the Shrines of Mexico every year. Come and join them on one of these special Retreat Pilgrimages. Call for more information, and ask for the latest pilgrimage brochure.

Lecture Series

Bob and Penny travel to all parts of the world to spread the Good News. They speak on what they have written about in their books. If you would like to have them come to your area, call for information on a lecture series in your area.

Good Newsletter

We are publishers of the Good Newsletter, which is published four times a year. This newsletter will provide timely articles on our Faith, plus keep you informed with the activities of our community. Call 1-800-633-2484 for information.